TERRACE LEGENDS

CASS PENNANT AND MARTIN KING

TERRACE LEGENDS

JOHN BLAKE

Published by John Blake Publishing Ltd,
3, Bramber Court, 2 Bramber Road,
London W14 9PB, England

First published in hardback in 2003

ISBN 1 904034 95 0

British Library Cataloguing-in-Publication Data:

A catalogue record for this book is available from the British Library.

Design by ENVY

Printed in Great Britain by Creative Print and Design (Wales)

3 5 7 9 10 8 6 4

Papers used by John Blake Publishing are natural, recyclable
products made from wood grown in sustainable forests.
The manufacturing processes conform to the environmental
regulations of the country of origin.

Dubbed 'the General' by the press, he was 50 years old when he was caught up in the infamous cross-channel ferry battle between supporters of West Ham and Manchester United. He would be a prime candidate for this book, unfortunately he has passed away and will be sorely missed by Hammers fans who knew him as good old Joe Harris.

Three other prime candidates are legendary amongst football fans: Chelsea Shed legend Mick Greenaway, Sheffield United main man Lister Divers and Arsenal's Johnny Hoy. Terrace Legends.
R.I.P.

Cass

To Susan – wife of Dave Kinchett (Potters Bar Dave) – who has sadly lost her three-year battle with cancer. She was as tough and hard a fighter as any in this book and will be sadly missed, all our thoughts are with Dave and their children, Daniel and Harry. God bless you, Sue – a light has gone out in our lives. You will be missed by all.

Martin

CONTENTS

Introduction 1

BILL
GARDNER
*West Ham
United*.......... 7

JERREL
Feyenoord.... 47

FRANK
HARPER
Millwall....... 13

DANNY
Feyenoord.... 57

STEVE,
'HICKEY'
HICKMOTT
Chelsea........ 21

DIRK
*Fortuna
Dusseldorf*.... 65

ANDY
NICHOLLS
Everton........ 29

MARK
'JASPER'
CHESTER
Stoke City..... 71

STEVE
COWENS
*Sheffield
United*......... 37

RICHARD
GREY
*Derby
County*.......... 81

GILROY
'GILLY' SHAW
*Wolverhampton
Wanderers.........
.... 103*

MAC
*Cardiff City.........
.... 145*

JOHN
WESTWOOD
*Portsmouth......
.... 113*

NEIL
Wrexham..... 155

TREVOR 'T'
TANNER
*Tottenham
Hotspur...... 121*

MR B
Barnsley....... 163

ANGUS
NUTT
*Bristol City......
.... 129*

LEE 'OATHEAD'
OWENS
*Middlesbrough...
.... 171*

ANDY 'THE
BEAR' PHILLIPS
*Bristol Rovers...
.... 137*

DAVID
'SKEENY'
SKEEN
*Nottingham
Forest........... 179*

 GARY JOHNSON *Wolverhampton Wanderers....* 189

 ALAN 'MONTY' MONTGOMERY *Newcastle United........* 231

 STEVE 'WING NUT' LYONS *Charlton Athletic........* 195

 GARY 'SUNDERLAND A.F.C.' LAMB *Sunderland A.F.C. ....* 241

 GINGER HOWARD *Portsmouth......... .... 203*

 PAT 'FAT PAT' DOLAN *Chelsea......* 251

 TERRY 'TESS' MANN *Newcastle United..........* 211

 IRVINE WELSH *Hibernian........ ....265*

 FRANK WHEATLEY *Sunderland A.F.C. ....* 221

Conclusion 275

ACKNOWLEDGEMENTS

CASS

The production of this book is down to various people who will know who they are as they helped in the tracking down and introduction of many of the respected characters we've featured here. Our appreciation of help given also goes to those who for various reasons we were unable to feature. We also gratefully acknowledge the respect and hospitality shown by the one-time rival firms and their friends that we have met throughout the many interviews we conducted in various corners of the earth including Leeds, which may be another story, another chapter someday. And hey chaps that play-off weekend in Bristol involving three chapters could have been another storm but we rode that one out.

Moving closer to home it wouldn't be right not to say a special thanks to Wendy Sanford, Julia Rowley, Mick Dandy, Shaun Colling, all at Blake Publishing and finally my family, Elaine, Marcus and Georgina plus my close friends and sponsors that support whatever I do.

MARTIN

Martin King would like to thank Martin Knight and John King, Tony Rivers and especially Pat Dolan for all their help in getting this book together; my wife Mandy and children Kortney and Rory

-Ben for their love and support and for putting up with me disappearing for hours on end on my computer, and being uptight and permanently grumpy; also to all the fellas featured in these pages for having the bottle to appear and tell it how it really was: cheers, lads.

INTRODUCTION

Youths, and sometimes grown men, misbehaving at a football match is nothing new; it's been around and reported in the media for nearly a hundred years. West Ham fans were fighting with Millwall supporters well before the Second World War. Author Irvine Welsh wrote about a battle between Greenock Morton and Port Glasgow Athletic that happened well over a century ago. So what's new? Well, nothing actually. Violence and hooliganism have been part and parcel of football since the advent of the game, but it wasn't sensationalised until the press decided to jump on the bandwagon and report trouble at matches.

Back to the early '60s. The Second World War was over, the Suez crisis was yesterday's story and Teddy boys razoring cinema seats, and one another, was old hat. Enter the mods and rockers. Fighting at Margate and Brighton on a Bank Holiday was headline news for a while, but how many punch-ups and pictures of greasers being pulled by the hair by arresting police officers would keep the general public's attention?

Enter the skinheads. With their shaven heads, trousers held up by a pair of braces that could have been worn by their dads or grandads, and a big pair of working, sometimes steel-toe-capped, boots, they cut an imposing figure. They became the new phenomenon on the front pages of the press. And what added fuel to the fire of bullshit reporting was the fact that this 'mindless minority' loved nothing better than dividing themselves into rival gangs and slogging it out on the terraces of football grounds. Shock, horror. 'Mindless minority'? My arse! During the '60s and '70s if there was a 40,000 gate, well over half would be up for a fight – the rest were there to watch. Even the players were known to take their eyes off the ball and cast an interested eye at the terrace rumblings.

The culture grew and grew, and many a young man became involved. It was easy to join in and even easier to step down. Certain clubs and certain faces within the scene became legendary in what had become a national pastime. 'THUGS ON RAMPAGE', 'TERRACE TERROR', 'HOOLIGANS' screamed the headlines. Even 'hooligan', the name given to people getting into rucks at football matches, was a joke. Supposedly it is derived from the surname of a south-east London family named the 'Houlihans'. They were a troublesome Irish clan that loved to fight, and caused untold grief to anyone within a left hook of them. To me, a hooligan is someone that smashes up a train or a phone box, sprays graffiti on a wall or kicks the mirrors off a parked car – not someone that fights at a football match.

Let's not forget there isn't trouble at every match that's played. But there are certain fixtures where there's a history between two clubs – be it a defeat in a semi-final, a cup final or a just a local derby – and you're never going to stop it. It's in the blood – in the genes.

Like the mods and rudeboys before them, the first skinheads were bonded by their working-class roots, their passion for music and their love of dress code. Black and white skinheads alike weren't interested in politics or racism, only in camaraderie, beer-drinking, music gigs and raising a ruckus on football terraces.

Into the '70s the skinhead look began to change slightly. The close-cropped hair was still in, except it was topped off with a razored parting, and Harrington jackets became the all the rage. Made famous by Rodney Harrington, a character from the TV series *Peyton Place*, the Harrington was a sort of casual, golf-type jacket that had a tartan lining and was available in a multitude of colours. It had slanted, side-buttoned pockets, a turned-up collar, an elasticated waist and a zigzag line across the lower shoulders. Ben Sherman, Brutus, Jaytex and Fred Perry were the chosen shirts, usually worn with Levi's Sta-Prest trousers, which came in all colours. The most popular ones were mint green, sky blue and white, with navy blue or black being worn as school trousers by the younger skin. Mohair and two-tone tonic suits, in red and blue or green and gold, were the in thing, as were Crombie overcoats and blue-beat pork-pie hats balanced on one side of the head. The hats were favoured by the West Indian skins, of which there were many. After all, skinheads in the late '60s and early '70s were far from right wing – the whole movement was based on the reggae, ska and blue-beat sounds of the Caribbean.

Commando steel-toe-capped boots were replaced by Doctor Martens or monkey boots. The Dr Marten had the revolutionary AirWair sole, in oxblood or brown, which was connected to the upper part with yellow stitching. The monkey boot was its cheaper relative and for a while was favoured by skin girls. For nights out at the local youth club disco or Meccano club, boots were replaced with wet-look Gibson shoes, brogues or 'smooths' (brogues without the pattern), but the most popular were the tasselled loafers with or without a fringe and buckle.

Football, fashion, fanny and music went hand in hand, and nights chasing birds were spent dancing around a record player listening to the sounds of the *Tighten Up* albums on the Trojan label.

After the skinhead craze the casual look was born: Mexican cardigans, as favoured by TV cops Starsky and Hutch, high-waistband trousers, platform soles, patchwork jean jackets with brushed denim jeans, South Sea bubble jumpers and cheesecloth shirts. Tamla Motown and soul replaced the reggae sounds, while chart acts like T-Rex, David Bowie, Roxy Music and Slade were also popular. Punk and Johnny Rotten came and went, and the casual look went upmarket. Designer labels such as Burberry, Aquascutum, Hugo Boss and Armani could be found on the terraces as well as on the dance floors as jazz funk made an appearance in discos and clubs up and down the country.

The '40s and '50s look, connected with the big-band sounds of Glen Miller and the like, could also be found on the terraces and in nightclubs such as The Goldmine, Canvey Island, in Essex, and Scamps in Sutton. Army shirts with badges on the sleeves, peg-leg trousers and brown-and-white spats shoes were in vogue. But it didn't last, as football fans in the early '80s turned to the sporty tennis style of Bjorn Borg and John McEnroe. Ellesse, Tacchini, Fila and Lacoste were trendy labels and, like other fashions before them, found their way on to the terraces.

The early '80s was also the beginning of the 'dawn raids' period, where police carried out their well-publicised and silly code-named sport of kicking in the front doors of known and unknown faces. 'Operation Own Goal' and other undercover police operations were always carried out with a film crew in tow – how convenient for them to be there just as the person's door is kicked off its hinges. Most hardware stores enjoyed increased sales for front doors and Yale locks during this period.

The usual array of weapons were rolled out and displayed for hungry news hounds, eager to show the gullible general public that this scourge sweeping the country was now under control by our honest, hard-working policemen, which in fact turned out to be utter bollocks. Many of these showcase trials collapsed. The Chelsea Headhunters trial at the Old Bailey ended with convictions and ten-year sentences handed out. The Old Bill were, to say the least, over the moon and after the trial they stood outside grinning for the gathered press, happy in the knowledge that these hard-nosed hooligans and criminals were, at long last, behind bars.

Maggie Thatcher's promised drive on hooligans was paying dividends – or a least that's what the public were being led to believe. Two and a half years after they were sentenced, all the Chelsea boys' convictions were quashed. Later, a huge sum of money was paid out in compensation and we were back to square one – the hooligans were still in our midst.

Next they called in the 'experts'. Boffins from universities around the country were all too quick to jump on the hooligan bandwagon and, with their years of experience, give their professional thoughts and analysis on why the problem exists and how it could be eradicated. Don't make us laugh; they didn't have a clue and still don't. The only thing they achieved was to publish nonsensical myths about football behaviour. It is a never-ending cycle of bullshit. After all those years of in-depth studies they're no nearer to ending soccer violence than I am, or Cass is. What a waste of taxpayers' money. 'Money for old rope' springs to mind. But just where does the funding come from? The national lottery? The Football Association? The taxpayer? Or is it supplied by the government because if it is there's some serious money being shelled out here.

Also the press were still up to their old tricks. They ran a story in a Sunday paper about a railway clerk who they claimed was a racist thug. He was a fanatical fan of the club he loved dearly – he was just a cheerleader. But that didn't stop him getting the sack and having his life ruined. He died recently and the effect of this episode on his life was there to see by all who knew him And the club he supported through thick and thin later named a bar inside their ground in his memory. Some hooligan.

The '90s saw the start of the rave scene and acid house, peace and love, and all that old bollocks. Some people even went so far as to say that the rave scene killed the hooligan scene. Again, what shit. Known faces and foot soldiers alike within the hooligan gangs saw a chance to earn a pound and make a killing. Given the chance to earn a few quid or have a ruck at a football match, the choice was easy. There were vast hordes of brain-dead, E-fuelled youths driving around the M25 in cloak-and-dagger, cat-and-mouse games with the

Old Bill, searching out the next rave. The money was piss easy and security was a cinch. Just employ a few of the football boys for a bit of muscle and you killed two birds with one stone.

But when the rave scene came to an end, the football violence would still be there. It was never going away. And now it had a hard-core element. The mobs were smaller but they were even more determined to have a row. The firms were now a minority. Gone were the days of thousand-strong mobs – Hillsborough and Heysel had seen to that. And, with the introduction of all-seater stadiums, the chances of away firms congregating in the same part of the ground and having a ruck were long gone. All-ticket games made that impossible, and nowadays most games are sold out to season ticket holders only, so the hard-core troublemakers have had to take the action well away from the stadiums and out on to the streets, sometimes miles away from where the game's being played. Mobile phones were good for arranging offs.

Then came the 'keyboard warriors' living at home with their mum and operating from their bedrooms. They surfaced and spread the word, albeit mostly bullshit. 'We run you', 'Where were you?', 'Meet you here', 'Meet you there'. These people posting messages on websites were, and are, pretty sad and some of the names they give themselves are laughable.

Even worse are certain non-scene people who have never been involved and yet set themselves up as so-called experts, claiming to offer a grim, blow-by-blow insight into the world of the football thug. 'We can stop the disgusting violence,' they say and in the next breath they're asking for your stories about when so and so played, and had it with so and so. Total bollocks. How can you call yourself an expert when you've never been involved? I've been going to football for over forty years and around the boys for nearly thirty of them – but me an expert? No, never. I wouldn't have a clue how to stop the violence and I don't profess to know how to stop it, nor would I be vain enough to even think I had the grey matter or the answers to do such a thing. I don't go to the media making such claims, but certain people do. They seem to like the sound of their own voices. I've got no time for the pricks. What's the old saying? 'You want to run with the fox and hunt with the hounds.' The name 'leeches' springs to mind. I jokingly once said that the only way to stop football violence was to ban all males aged 15 to 75. 'Ban alcohol and you'll stop a lot of the problems,' so-called experts have said. So why is there trouble at twelve o'clock kick-offs when the pubs aren't even open? We'll throw that theory out the window, eh? Football is a highly charged spectator sport, where feelings run high and for some people it's more important than life and death.

The '90s saw a return of football hooliganism. An avalanche of 'hoolie' books appeared on the shelves of bookstores – some good, some bad and some total bollocks – and next came the films. *The Football Factory*, based on John King's top book, has just been made and Tony Rivers and Dave Jones's *Soul Crew* looks like being next. Also to follow shortly will be the film of Cass's *Congratulations, You Have Just Met the I.C.F.* Anyway, good luck to these films.

The ugly scenes that marred England's Euro 2004 qualifier win over Turkey has again brought hooliganism back into the public eye, but, to us in the know, it had never gone away. The firms and mobs are growing rapidly with a youth element interested in the culture, joining up with the existing dinosaurs that never died. In this book we let the real people, not just from Britain but from around Europe, describe their own lives and their own experiences. They tell stories never heard by anyone outside their circles. Some people might say we are glorifying soccer violence by writing a book like this; read it and draw your own conclusions.

As I said earlier, some of the mob members had hero status across the nation, with their names heard not only across the terraces but also in nearly every pub, club, youth club and school playground the length and breadth of the UK. Some of these people were legendary; they were, and still are, terrace legends. Some were famed for their fighting skills, some for the way they organised others (both in combat and travel), and others for the ability to make people laugh and were fun to have around. A couple were famed for taking their fanatical support of their chosen club to another level, and on their own admission never getting involved or being interested in the violent side of things. They are not hooligans, nor do they profess to be.

In their day the people in this book were bigger than some TV personalities, pop stars and film stars, and even the players themselves, and were the born leaders of a majority of fans at that time. After meeting, talking and interviewing all of them one thing comes across. They are true football fans, despite how the media likes to portray them. To me the only mindless minority were the so-called journalists that over the last forty years are no nearer the truth. Read and learn. Enjoy the book.

Cheers,
Martin King

CASS PENNANT MEETS

BILL GARDNER
CLUB: WEST HAM UNITED

BILL GARDNER

THE MEET

There's been plenty said and written about Bill. And Bill's never been one to talk himself up. He was even very modest when he spoke about himself in the *Congratulations ...* book. To me he is a gentleman and I class him as a real good family friend. I first came across him up at Middlesbrough in 1975 and what an eventful day that was! One thing was for sure, in the '70s and '80s you'd always find Bill at the front of the West Ham mob. So, besides the keyboard warriors of today, every football fan and face in the know would have heard of Bill's name. He really needs no introduction. He's an Upton Park legend and has been for a long, long time. Here are Bill's experiences about his days following the Hammers.

BACKGROUND

I first started watching West Ham in 1958. My mum was from Poplar and my dad was from Bethnal Green in the East End of London. After leaving school I worked in a factory, then I became a stonemason – the job I still do to this day.

WHAT'S YOUR FAVOURITE TERRACE FASHION?

An orange boiler suit I wore in the early '70s, and yer old Dr Martens. I had quite a few pairs of them over the years.

WHAT'S THE WORST FASHION YOU'VE EVER SEEN ON THE TERRACES?

That's got to be them stripy tank tops.

DESCRIBE YOUR WORST FEELING AT A GAME.

I was coming home from Chelsea away in the early '70s. We pulled in at Whitechapel train station and some Millwall were on the platform. The doors opened and they jumped on and started slapping a few young West Ham fans about. I steamed into them thinking that the rest of our boys on the train would back me up, but no, I ended up steaming into them on my own.

Plus losing a game – being relegated has to be the worst feeling of all. If you follow my team then these things happen. But the spineless way we went down in the 2002/3 season and taking into account the squad of players we had, well ...

HAVE YOU EVER INCURRED ANY SERIOUS INJURIES OR BEEN BADLY BEATEN UP AT A MATCH?

I've never been injured or beaten up at football.

HAS YOUR OWN SIDE EVER BEEN INVOLVED IN A FULL-SCALE RIOT?

The Harry Cripps testimonial over at Millwall in '72. I've never seen anything like that – it was unbelievable. Definitely the worst I've seen in all my years of going.

DESCRIBE THE BEST TAKING OF AN END YOU'VE EVER WITNESSED.

The North Bank at Wolves. We went in there that day and someone sang 'Bubbles' and the whole end just cleared. You couldn't see their arses for dust. I mean, in them days there was a lot of end taking but this one stands out.

WHICH WAS YOUR OWN TEAM'S POPULAR END?

The North Bank.

WHERE DID YOU STAND OR SIT IN THE GROUND?

The Chicken Run. It was a good crack in there and a good laugh.

CAN YOU RECALL A BATTLE YOU HAVE BEEN INVOLVED IN, EITHER INSIDE OR OUTSIDE A GROUND?

There's far too many to really mention but Man. United in '75 springs to mind. And the games we've had with Millwall – they've always been a lively encounter.

CAN YOU RECALL THE BEST EVER MOB YOUR TEAM HAS PUT TOGETHER?

Man. United away in 2003 in the FA Cup. We had a firm of about 300 hundred top faces. Now that mob would take some beating.

WHO'S THE BEST RIVAL FIRM YOU'VE EVER SEEN?

Never seen one. No man from another firm has ever faced me one to one.

WHO ARE YOUR BIGGEST RIVALS TEAM-WISE?

Manchester United.

WHO ARE YOUR BIGGEST RIVALS FAN-WISE?

Millwall, Man. United – in that order.

HAVE YOU EVER JOINED UP WITH ANOTHER TEAM'S FIRM?

No, never. But I've got a lot of friends at QPR.

DID YOU EVER FOLLOW ENGLAND AND WOULD YOU PUT ENGLAND BEFORE YOUR CLUB?

I've been to a few England games. I went to the World Cup in '82 and Norway the same year in the qualifiers. And I've been to Wembley a few times. But West Ham comes first. I don't go to England games now because too many people get pissed and silly, and that isn't for me.

WHICH WAS THE BEST ENGLAND ROW?

None. I've not been involved in any of the England troubles.

HAVE YOU EVER SUPPORTED OR LOOKED OUT FOR ANOTHER TEAM'S RESULTS?

No. I've followed my son James's results when he played for Wycombe Wanderers and Woking and Burnham. But no, never supported another team.

NAME YOUR TOP FIVE FIRMS, IN ANY ORDER.

Two bob, the lot of them.

WHICH IS THE WORST GROUND YOU'VE EVER BEEN TO AND WHY?

Liverpool and Man. United. They pack too many fans in and it's so tight for room because there's too many seats. They charge £30 to £40 and you're crammed in. It's more about making money. They don't put the fans first, do they?

WHICH IS THE BEST STADIUM YOU'VE BEEN TO?

Don't be surprised – Blackburn Rovers have got a nice stadium. The top seats or the lower tier both give you a good view, there's plenty of legroom, and the facilities are good. Also Spurs have got good seats with good views for watching football.

WHO ARE THE FAIREST COPPERS YOU'VE COME ACROSS AT A MATCH?

West Ham Old Bill are fair.

AND THE WORST OLD BILL?

Manchester are a bit heavy-handed. Remember us up there in the Cup in the 2002/3 season. There was more of them than us and they were all dressed like Robocop. It's a shame they couldn't get their act together when there was real trouble about. They've left it a bit too late. In the old days they couldn't catch a cold.

WHAT WOULD HAVE STOPPED YOU GETTING INVOLVED WITH THE BOYS AT MATCHES?

If I'd have been a coward, maybe that would have stopped me getting involved.

DESCRIBE SOME OF THE METHODS AND TACTICS USED BY THE POLICE AND AUTHORITIES TO STOP FOOTBALL VIOLENCE, AND DO YOU THINK THEY WORK?

The retirement of the faces involved helped stop it. And CCTV cameras, and the use of police spotters have helped stop it spreading further.

HAVE YOU EVER BEEN SICKENED BY SOMETHING YOU'VE WITNESSED AT A GAME?

Every violent scene I saw or came across made me sick. I'm not a violent person – I just stood my ground.

WHAT'S YOUR FAVOURITE FOOTBALL SONG OR CHANT AND WHICH IS THE WORST YOU CAN RECALL HEARING FROM ANOTHER TEAM?

I can't sing! Ha, ha! No, 'Bubbles' is the best. I know 'Bubbles' is our song but it's a bit of a defeatist song. I also like 'You'll Never Walk Alone' – it's a great rousing football song. I don't go a lot on songs about Munich '58 and Aberfan. I don't like Man. United but these type of songs are in bad taste. I wouldn't like to hear songs bad-mouthing Bobby Moore.

WHAT WAS YOUR FAVOURITE BAND/RECORD DURING YOUR FOOTBALL DAYS?

Elton John's 'Saturday Night's Alright (For Fighting)' was a football fan's favourite in the '70s. Carl Douglas and 'Kung Fu Fighting' was another you'd hear in them days.

WHO WAS YOUR ALL-TIME FAVOURITE PLAYER?

Paulo De Canio is the most skilful player I've ever seen in a West Ham shirt. But my favourite all-time player was the legendary Bobby Moore. To me, he typified what West Ham's all about and he was an East End boy done good. Also Alex Young of Everton and George Eastham of Stoke City were two players I admired.

WHERE DO YOU THINK THE NEW ENGLISH NATIONAL STADIUM SHOULD BE BUILT AND WHAT ARE YOUR THOUGHTS REGARDING THE WEMBLEY FIASCO?

I think the national stadium should stay at Wembley. They should have rebuilt and modernised the new stadium around the existing twin towers and brought the ground up to a better standard. But as usual the real fans don't get a look in. It's all about pound notes and ripping the arse out of the fans. The worse thing to happen was they got a German firm in to knock it down – now that's really taking the piss.

MARTIN KING MEETS

FRANK HARPER
CLUB: MILLWALL

FRANK HARPER

THE MEET

I met Frank just after he'd finished filming one of the main characters in *The Football Factory*. Most people remember Frank for his part in Guy Ritchie's film *Lock, Stock and Two Smoking Barrels*, but I was surprised to learn that he'd also appeared in films alongside stars such as Michael Caine (*Shiner*), Bob Hoskins (*24-7*), Daniel Day Lewis and Emma Thompson (*In The Name of the Father*), and hosts of other top actors. He told me the drama school he went to was SMADA, which spells the Smithfield Market Academy of Dramatic Arts. One thing about Frank is he doesn't look like an actor. For a start, he's a big fucker, but he's nice with it. We met down on the coast in Eastbourne in East Sussex, where he'd gone to see his mum and dad. And over a few beers and a spot of lunch he told me about the days of his dad being a pro at Millwall, his acting career, and everything and anything. So, lights, camera, action.

BACKGROUND

I grew up on the Downham Estate, which is between Catford and Bromley, in south-east London. It's a hotbed of Millwall support and most people from that area follow Millwall. I grew up following Millwall as my dad played for the club between 1957 and 1965, and won the Fourth Division Championship while he was there. He later moved on to Ipswich. Harry Cripps and Alex Stepney were there at Millwall with Dad, and there was a lot of real characters at the club. I dreamed about following in Dad's footsteps and becoming a pro footballer, but on leaving school I ended up working at Smithfield Market. One day a mate of mine took me down to a youth theatre at the Albany Empire in Deptford and from then on I had the bug. Did I get some shit from the boys at the market! I was insulted by experts for ten years – acting became a hobby. As a kid there's probably three jobs you dream of – pro footballer, Grand Prix driver or actor. I took the latter road. I'm 40 now and my younger brother runs all the kids' football for Lewisham Council, and Mum and Dad have retired down in Eastbourne, East Sussex.

WHAT'S YOUR FAVOURITE TERRACE FASHION?

Back to the early '80s and I'd say Burberry fly-front macs. I think I went through about three of them. Football's such a big fashion statement.

WHAT'S THE WORST FASHION YOU'VE EVER SEEN ON THE TERRACES?

Dodgy flared trousers still being worn by northerners in the '80s.

DESCRIBE YOUR WORST FEELING AT A GAME.

Me and four mates got caught by Charlton fans after a night game at the Valley. We were thirteen or fourteen years of age and a mob of geezers flocked on us and ambushed us. Millwall had taken the piss over there all night and we came close to getting a good hiding.

HAVE YOU EVER INCURRED ANY SERIOUS INJURIES OR BEEN BADLY BEATEN UP AT A MATCH?

One of my most frightening experiences at football was when Millwall played Ipswich at the Den in the '70s. Somehow a mob of Ipswich came into the Cold Blow Lane End of the ground. Everyone pushed down the terraces towards them, and I was being carried and shoved by one mass of angry bodies. My head was heading towards a metal barrier and I just ducked underneath it, but my mate hit his head and I had to drag him up because he was nearly out cold.

HAS YOUR OWN SIDE EVER BEEN INVOLVED IN A FULL-SCALE RIOT?

There's been more than a few with Millwall but the one that sticks in my mind is Luton away in the Cup. I think the main reason behind the troubles there was that the game wasn't made all-ticket. Fans from lots of other clubs turned up that night, many packed like sardines behind the goal with the bulk of Millwall fans. I remember my mate commenting that there'd be people injured because of the packed crowd swelling around the terraces. It was a sea of bodies and the only escape for some was the safety of the pitch. A few spilled over and for a moment it looked like people were going to get seriously hurt. Later the seats were ripped out as a mob of Millwall had it with the Old Bill. It was a mental night and the pictures of it say it all.

DESCRIBE THE BEST TAKING OF AN END YOU'VE EVER WITNESSED.

Chelsea away. Millwall came into the Shed in about four different mobs and it was going off all over the place. It ended with the bulk of the Millwall firm standing on the dog track behind the goal.

WHICH WAS YOUR OWN TEAM'S POPULAR END?

Cold Blow Lane. But in the '70s and '80s Millwall's gates were that small you could walk around the ground. I've seen people sunbathing on the terraces on a sunny day, stretched out with one eye on the game.

WHERE DID YOU STAND OR SIT IN THE GROUND?

Cold Blow Lane. It was always a giggle.

CAN YOU RECALL A BATTLE YOU HAVE BEEN INVOLVED IN, EITHER INSIDE OR OUTSIDE A GROUND?

Leeds at home in the league. I was in a pub and suddenly it emptied. The ones that couldn't get out the door were climbing out the toilet windows to get out on to the street. Thousands of Millwall came out of nowhere as bottles and glasses rained down on the Leeds lot. The Old Bill pulled a transit van across the pub doorway to try to stem the flow of Millwall fans. That day Leeds were dead lucky to reach the ground.

CAN YOU RECALL THE BEST EVER MOB YOUR TEAM HAS PUT TOGETHER?

A couple of seasons ago, when the Wackers went up to Maine Road to play Man. City. We took an unbelievable firm up there that day. The Wackers have now become an urban myth. That's why I think no top face has written a serious book about Millwall's exploits over the years.

WHO'S THE BEST RIVAL FIRM YOU'VE EVER SEEN?

West Ham has always had a serious firm and a lot of my good pals are ICF. And, besides the hatred between Millwall and West Ham, I think there's a mutual respect between the two. Both teams come from tough areas, and tough areas breed tough people.

WHO ARE YOUR BIGGEST RIVALS TEAM-WISE?

The main one has to be West Ham, but I like to get one over Crystal Palace. My dad used to have The Clifton Arms pub right near the ground so it was nice when we beat them and took a few quid off them, having won a bet.

WHO ARE YOUR BIGGEST RIVALS FAN-WISE?

Cardiff, because they're Welsh.

HAVE YOU EVER JOINED UP WITH ANOTHER TEAM'S FIRM?

Yeah, I've got a couple of really good pals who follow Chelsea, so sometimes it's nice to watch Premiership football. I remember when Millwall were in the top flight and we played Forest, and Brian Clough came out the tunnel and got a standing ovation. We can be fair at Millwall and appreciate good football and characters.

DID YOU EVER FOLLOW ENGLAND AND WOULD YOU PUT ENGLAND BEFORE YOUR CLUB?

I've been abroad a few times watching England but, as an Englishman, I'm used to being hugely disappointed when a major tournament comes around. As for club or country, it would be nice if Millwall had three or four English internationals on our side. But I don't suppose we're ever going to be in a position like Man. United or Chelsea and worry about our players going off for internationals.

WHICH WAS THE BEST ENGLAND ROW?

There've been one or two, but just general stand-offs with the Old Bill really. Me and some mates nearly came unstuck out in Italia '90. A few experienced campaigners advised us off going down a certain street, a load of idiots did, and got well bashed by the Italians lying in wait.

HAVE YOU EVER SUPPORTED OR LOOKED OUT FOR ANOTHER TEAM'S RESULTS?

I always look out for Leyton Orient's results, simply because my dad played there for a while.

NAME YOUR TOP FIVE FIRMS, IN ANY ORDER.

West Ham, Chelsea, Pompey, Leeds and Cardiff – in no order.

WHICH IS THE WORST GROUND YOU'VE EVER BEEN TO AND WHY?

Grimsby. You can smell fish twenty miles outside the town. It's a shithole. I hear they call themselves the Millwall of the North. Dream on! Let them think that if it makes them happy.

WHICH IS THE BEST STADIUM YOU'VE BEEN TO?

I've not been to any of the Premiership grounds since they've been done up, but I think Wembley had to be one of the best stadiums to go to. I went and watched Millwall play Wigan there. We sold nearly fifty thousand tickets. It was surreal walking up Wembley Way before the game.

WHO ARE THE FAIREST COPPERS YOU'VE COME ACROSS AT A MATCH?

Barnsley. They just wanted to get rid of us without any problems.

AND THE WORST OLD BILL?

Portsmouth. In the '80s a big mob of us were surrounded by Old Bill and they didn't know what to do with us, so we all sat down in the road and blocked all the traffic for a few hours.

WHAT WOULD HAVE STOPPED YOU GETTING INVOLVED WITH THE BOYS AT MATCHES?

My dad being a pro and seeing the game from the other side was one factor, but to a lot of people hooliganism is all part and parcel of the game and what happens on the Old Kent Road any night of the week has nothing to do with football. It's a social thing, it's society's problem, and it just so happens it visits football some weekends. The British are a tribal race. You can get blokes from Bermondsey fighting blokes from Catford on a Friday night, but come Saturday they'd be standing shoulder to shoulder having it at football.

DESCRIBE SOME OF THE METHODS AND TACTICS USED BY THE POLICE AND AUTHORITIES TO STOP FOOTBALL VIOLENCE, AND DO YOU THINK THEY WORK?

Cameras have stopped a hell of a lot of people from going to football. I had a copper chasing me around the pub at the first game of the season after the Millwall v Birmingham riots, and it wasn't for my autograph. He had a photo board with all the suspects from that game on. He kept looking at me, looking at his boards, and all my mates made matters worse by telling him to arrest me and that I was scum and one of the ringleaders. He came right up close to me. I turned away and went to the toilet but he followed me in and tried to nick me. A sergeant turned up and led the young copper away. As he got to the door I could see the sergeant talking to him and the young copper looked back and smiled. He now knew where he'd seen my face.

HAVE YOU EVER BEEN SICKENED BY SOMETHING YOU'VE WITNESSED AT A GAME?

I think on numerous occasions fans have gone well over the top. At the end of the day, if like-minded people want to fight one another, then that's fine. If a phone call's made and two mobs fight in a field or on waste ground and kick shit out of one another, then who are they hurting? However, if innocent people get caught up, then that's wrong.

WHAT'S YOUR FAVOURITE FOOTBALL SONG OR CHANT AND WHICH IS THE WORST YOU CAN RECALL HEARING FROM ANOTHER TEAM?

'No one likes us, we don't care' is one of my all-time favourite songs as it sums Millwall up.

As for worst, when we played Leeds our lot started singing, 'Did the Ripper fuck ya mum?' That's the worst, along with the song about Bobby Moore. That's the line that shouldn't be crossed. Few players transcend club rivalry, but Bobby Moore's one of them. He's the only England skipper to ever lift the World Cup, and how he died so young – it was tragic. The way the football authorities treated him was nothing short of scandalous. He should have at least been taken on with the England coaching staff.

My dad tells a great story about Bobby Moore. Ipswich were playing West Ham in the Cup, and Bill McGary, the Ipswich manager, had told the speedy Ipswich winger to hassle Moore every time he had the ball. 'Don't give him time and he's just any other normal player,' McGary said in his pre-match talk to his team. The pitch was a mudbath and West Ham won 4–0. All the players trooped off at the end, cold, wet and covered from head to foot in mud and dirt – all bar one. That was Bobby Moore, my dad said, who was immaculate – not a hair out of place and not a speck of mud on him. He looked just how he had looked when he had run on to the pitch at the start of the game, ninety minutes earlier. He was one cool customer.

WHAT WAS YOUR FAVOURITE BAND/RECORD DURING YOUR FOOTBALL DAYS?
I was into The Jam, The Clash, The Sex Pistols and The Specials.

WHO WAS YOUR ALL-TIME FAVOURITE PLAYER?
It has to be George Best, but in recent years I loved watching Eric Cantona play. I've never seen someone that big have such a good touch on the ball. He was so skilful, plus he didn't give a fuck. He had a great attitude. Keith Weller and [Derek] Posse of Millwall, along with Teddy Sherringham, have been fantastic at Millwall over the years, but my favourite Millwall player has to be Tony Hurlock. He was one tough bastard who got stuck in and was hard as nails.

WHERE DO YOU THINK THE NEW ENGLISH NATIONAL STADIUM SHOULD BE BUILT AND WHAT ARE YOUR THOUGHTS REGARDING THE WEMBLEY FIASCO?
Wembley was special. The facilities were crap and it was overpriced, but the place was just full of football history. Every great player in the world has played there – Eusebio, Pele, Maradona, George Best, Bobby Moore, Puskas. They should have refurbished it and left it where it was. How the hell did the FA get away with knocking it down? The twin towers were art deco and things just don't add up. Surely it was a listed building? Going to Wembley was a special day out for everyone – even going up the steps to get the trophy was special. No money should have been spared having it modernised and saving the history that went with the place. Let's not forget we won the World Cup there. In a few years time the truth will come out and I bet some cunt's been lining his pockets again at the expense of football fans.

MARTIN KING MEETS

STEVE 'HICKEY' HICKMOTT

CLUB: CHELSEA

STEVE 'HICKEY' HICKMOTT

THE MEET

I've known Hickey for years and was well pleased when he agreed to do his bit in the book because he's a real character, and he can have you in stitches with some of his tales. I met him in Brighton when he was on one of his brief visits to the UK to play a cameo part in the new *Football Factory* film. Take it away, Steve.

BACKGROUND

My first game was Chelsea v West Ham in the 1965/6 season and it ended in a 5–5 draw. I was eleven years old and I went with some mates from Tunbridge Wells. I'd always followed Chelsea, just like a lot of kids from around my area. A few years later I began to notice the main faces in the Shed End, like Eccles, Jesus and Premo. From then on I wanted to be just like them – they were heroes. I left school at fifteen and went into engineering and I'm now retired and live in South-East Asia.

WHAT'S YOUR FAVOURITE TERRACE FASHION?

From 1969 to 1972 I wore Sta-Prest Levi's, boots, braces, Crombies and Harringtons. This was, and still is, my favourite fashion. I've never been without a pair of Dr Martens. I've only ever worn trainers once to football and I broke my foot after kicking a geezer out in Copenhagen – I never wore them again.

WHAT'S THE WORST FASHION YOU'VE EVER SEEN ON THE TERRACES?

The worst has got to be budgie jackets and high-waistband trousers with side pockets, with stack-heel shoes. Our lot had this gear on in 1973 at Derby away, and the Derby lot were still skinheads. I've still got the pictures and it's fucking embarrassing.

DESCRIBE YOUR WORST FEELING AT A GAME.

My worst feeling has to be coming out of Millwall's ground in 1976. There was none of our mob left at the end of the game. I'd been in the ground once and came out, and went back into the CBL (Cold Blow Lane) with another Chelsea firm. I was stood on my own halfway through the second half and just kept my trap shut. I was surrounded by Millwall. Outside a bloke pulled a huge diver's knife out and was shouting, 'Where's all these Chelsea cunts?' I just carried on walking with my head down.

HAVE YOU EVER INCURRED ANY SERIOUS INJURIES OR BEEN BADLY BEATEN UP AT A MATCH?

I was injured at Bristol City. We'd just come out of a pub and four or five geezers walked towards us carrying a sports bag. They hit me over the head and I was taken to hospital to have my head stitched up.

HAS YOUR OWN SIDE EVER BEEN INVOLVED IN A FULL-SCALE RIOT?

Derby v Chelsea in 1973 when there must have been 3,000 fans fighting on the pitch. Newspaper reports said there were twelve policemen on duty inside the ground and they were unable to contain the trouble – it was hand-to-hand combat.

DESCRIBE THE BEST TAKING OF AN END YOU'VE EVER WITNESSED.

Villa in the late '70s. I ran two coaches and Colin Daniels (a child actor who became a Chelsea face) ran a couple. We came in from the north of Birmingham to avoid the Old Bill. The first pub we came to was The Tennis Court. We smashed everyone in there and moved on to The Crown and Cushion, which was Villa's main boozer, and we had a huge row before going into the Holt End, which is where all Villa's boys stood. We came in from one side and Villa scattered everywhere, and, like a pincer movement, another mob of Chelsea came in from the other side, and we murdered them. Plus I've had good days out at Stoke in '73 and Sheffield United. Rumour had it they'd joined up with Leeds but we still took their end. The thing was, with Chelsea in them days we had a big following from up north. We had lads with us from Wolverhampton and loads from Leeds. Some games we'd have more fans from up north than had travelled up from London.

WHICH WAS YOUR OWN TEAM'S POPULAR END?

I enjoyed standing at the North Bank at Arsenal after we'd cleared it.

WHERE DID YOU STAND OR SIT IN THE GROUND?

I stood at the Shed End up until about '76 and then I moved up the other end to the North Stand, simply because there was more action.

CAN YOU RECALL THE BEST EVER MOB YOUR TEAM HAS PUT TOGETHER?

Boxing Day, when we took the Arsenal North Bank and the '76 game over at Millwall.

WHO'S THE BEST RIVAL FIRM YOU'VE EVER SEEN?

West Ham at Upton Park. We'd gone into the South Bank armed with baseball bats and we got properly ironed out – we were well and truly murdered. That's where the song 'Hit them over the head with a baseball bat' came from.

WHO ARE YOUR BIGGEST RIVALS TEAM-WISE?

Tottenham. I get more pleasure from them losing than I ever could Chelsea winning. I fucking hate them.

WHO ARE YOUR BIGGEST RIVALS FAN-WISE?

Tottenham. I despise them.

HAVE YOU EVER JOINED UP WITH ANOTHER TEAM'S FIRM?

I used to run the EFK Gothenburg's mob out in Sweden. I was working there selling T-shirts and tickets, and there was loads of good birds out there. The EFK boys were regularly getting turned over by the Black Army mob from Stockholm. That all changed when myself, Danny from West Ham, Nobby and Tom, and a couple of Yugoslavian geezers joined up with about eighty of the locals and smashed the Stockholm firm everywhere. That was a first for their boys and they've not looked back since. I also used to follow my local team, Tunbridge, who in the '70s had some right battles with near neighbours Maidstone. We even had a right row with Millwall once in a pre-season friendly.

DID YOU EVER FOLLOW ENGLAND AND WOULD YOU PUT ENGLAND BEFORE YOUR CLUB?

Yes, I've always followed England but I wouldn't put them before Chelsea.

WHICH WAS THE BEST ENGLAND ROW?

Hungary, when Trevor Brooking scored two goals in an England victory. I think it was '83 and we won 3–1. There was trouble in the ground and a big street battle after the game, and on the trains the Old Bill fired gas inside and we jumped off and steamed into them, running them everywhere. It went on for an hour and a half. Another time was at an Under-21s game in Greece, when we were taken from the ground and put on armoured buses for our own protection. We were attacked with bricks and bottles, and surrounded by the hostile locals. The buses drove us from the stadium to the port in Piraeus and left us there. A mob of Greeks a couple of hundred strong attacked us again and we had to fight for our lives.

HAVE YOU EVER SUPPORTED OR LOOKED OUT FOR ANOTHER TEAM'S RESULTS?

Gothenburg and Glasgow Rangers. Rangers because I once went to watch Celtic play Chelsea, which was part of the deal that took Scottish international David Hay to Stamford Bridge, and I've never received so much abuse in my life. They fucking hated us. But when I watch Rangers it's a different story. They love us and make us more than welcome.

NAME YOUR TOP FIVE FIRMS, IN ANY ORDER.

Millwall, West Ham, Man. City in the early '70s, Everton in the '70s and Newcastle.

WHICH IS THE WORST GROUND YOU'VE EVER BEEN TO AND WHY?

Man City, Maine Road – it's a terrifying place to go. One hundred and twenty of us travelled up only to see the game called off with just ten minutes to go to kick-off. My mate had been stabbed and had his sheepskin coat nicked off him. I was saved by Kojak, a big black Chelsea lad who sadly is no longer with us. We were chased all the way back to the station and on to the train. The fighting was still going on as the Chelsea team boarded the train for the journey back to London.

WHICH IS THE BEST STADIUM YOU'VE BEEN TO?

Charlton because they sold Stella Artois.

WHO ARE THE FAIREST COPPERS YOU'VE COME ACROSS AT A MATCH?

Plymouth Old Bill were very fair. If they caught you fighting they'd tell you to fuck off and kick you up the arse. Even though I was bit on the arse by a police dog, I'd say they're one of the best set of coppers I've come across.

AND THE WORST OLD BILL?

The Scousers. They were horrible cunts, especially their sergeants with them canes they carried.

WHAT WOULD HAVE STOPPED YOU GETTING INVOLVED WITH THE BOYS AT MATCHES?

Nothing, I liked it. I looked forward all week to going to football – it was a laugh. It was the best days of my life. My reputation exceeded me and that's why not many people ever had a fight with me. I could walk into a ground, stand in front of a mob of rival fans, not say a word, and they would flee in absolute terror. I loved it. The only time it never worked was at my court case when I received ten years from the Right Honourable Sir George Schindler.

DESCRIBE SOME OF THE METHODS AND TACTICS USED BY THE POLICE AND AUTHORITIES TO STOP FOOTBALL VIOLENCE, AND DO YOU THINK THEY WORK?

CCTV. You can get caught on camera doing something and a week or six months later you can be arrested.

HAVE YOU EVER BEEN SICKENED BY SOMETHING YOU'VE WITNESSED AT A GAME?

I don't know about sickened, but I was a bit pissed off when someone threw themselves on the tracks and committed suicide on the Circle Line [London Underground] and I missed the beginning of a match. I was sickened by that.

WHAT'S YOUR FAVOURITE FOOTBALL SONG OR CHANT AND WHICH IS THE WORST YOU CAN RECALL HEARING FROM ANOTHER TEAM?

My favourite is 'You're going to get your fucking heads kicked in' and the worst has got to be 'One man went to mow'.

WHAT WAS YOUR FAVOURITE BAND/RECORD DURING YOUR FOOTBALL DAYS?

'Ballroom Blitz' by The Sweet, Elton John's 'Saturday Night's Alright (For Fighting)' and Gary Glitter's 'I'm the Leader of the Gang' (Come on, Come on …). I remember in 1974 Jimmy Hill saying, 'and they're still fighting as they sing the new Gary Glitter song "Come on, Come on" and they're all on the pitch'. That was a piece of classic *Match of the Day* broadcasting.

WHO WAS YOUR ALL-TIME FAVOURITE PLAYER?

Peter Osgood – he was fantastic. I loved him and still do. I've met him and he's a gentleman.

WHERE DO YOU THINK THE NEW ENGLISH NATIONAL STADIUM SHOULD BE BUILT AND WHAT ARE YOUR THOUGHTS REGARDING THE WEMBLEY FIASCO?

It should be at Wembley and should just have been revamped and modernised. We should have our national stadium in the capital city, which everyone knows is London.

MARTIN KING MEETS

ANDY NICHOLLS
CLUB: EVERTON

© Jayne Walsh

ANDY NICHOLLS

THE MEET
Cass and I both met Andy up in Liverpool when we were doing a bit for the 2002 Writing on the Wall literary festival, and he came over and introduced himself to us. He told us he was in the process of writing a book himself. Since then the book, called *Scally: Confessions of a Category C Football Hooligan*, has been released and caused quite a stir up in Merseyside. Here's what Andy had to say.

BACKGROUND
I'm currently banned from Goodison Park for life and have been arrested nineteen times for football-related incidents. I served a jail sentence for an attack on Arsenal fans on Blackstock Road at Highbury in 1989, was banned from every ground in the country for two years following the Arsenal stretch, and have been deported from Belgium, Sweden and Iceland for football-related offences.

WHAT'S YOUR FAVOURITE TERRACE FASHION?
Lacoste tracksuits. That's a joke, by the way. All the sports gear in the late '70s and early '80s was top-notch as very few wore it or could afford it.

WHAT'S THE WORST FASHION YOU'VE EVER SEEN ON THE TERRACES?
The Burberry hats and Stone Island clobber that the plastic hooligans wear today makes me sick.

DESCRIBE YOUR WORST FEELING AT A GAME.
I'd go for any of the following: 1–0 down against the Red Shite and the Kop blurting out their fucking anthem; getting nicked at Wembley five minutes before the kick-off at the Cup Final; ten of us going in Man. City's end and getting sussed before the other 200 Everton boys had got in.

HAVE YOU EVER INCURRED ANY SERIOUS INJURIES OR BEEN BADLY BEATEN UP AT A MATCH?
I got slashed on the arm at Southampton once, which was bad, and I've taken a few bottles to my head over the years. My worst injury was when I fucked my back up slinging a concrete slab at a few Yids who were ready to cut me up. I had to sleep on a board for six

months the pain was that bad. Although not at the match, I got in a fight with some Bristol City fans when I was working there, and one hit me with an iron rod and nearly took my head off. In hospital the doctor said an inch lower and I would have died.

HAS YOUR OWN SIDE EVER BEEN INVOLVED IN A FULL-SCALE RIOT?

In the mid-80s there were too many to mention but they were never on the scale of some of the footage I've seen of the likes of Leeds and Millwall. Pre-season 2001/2, though, we had it in Brussels with Anderlecht and after the game hundreds of Everton had the Belgium bizzies on the run and took the place. It was as good as you could get – unbelievable, really, in this day and age. I wish we had those numbers every week, but those days are long gone in this country. I was also at Heysel but that's best left alone.

DESCRIBE THE BEST TAKING OF AN END YOU'VE EVER WITNESSED.

England v Wales in 1980. Five hundred Scousers went on the Wales end, took it and spent the rest of the match fighting to keep it – not from the Welsh but from the Mancs, who came on and took the other half ten minutes after us. It was the last home international between the two countries and I'm not fucking surprised – it was bedlam.

WHICH WAS YOUR OWN TEAM'S POPULAR END?

Behind either goal in the '70s. The Gwladys Street was the main home end, where seven Millwall were stabbed in 1973 when they had a go but failed to take it. No one else ever got close to taking it. The Park End was my favourite. It was mixed up until about 1980 and was a fucking evil place unless you had serious numbers.

WHERE DID YOU STAND OR SIT IN THE GROUND?

The old Park End until it got fashionable to go in the seats, then we all just went in the Stand above the terrace.

CAN YOU RECALL A BATTLE YOU HAVE BEEN INVOLVED IN, EITHER INSIDE OR OUTSIDE A GROUND?

Too many to mention, but we have had some top battles with both the Manc sides and the main Cockney mobs. Aberdeen was good in 1995. We had a top mob out and they gave it a go but weren't good enough on the day, and they are the first to admit it. Inside the ground, one of the best I ever got involved in was against Southampton at Highbury in the '84 FA Cup semi-final. Running battles on the pitch, horses, dogs loose biting every fucker, over 100 arrested and eighty in hospital – it was the norm then. Today, it would be made into a film.

CAN YOU RECALL THE BEST EVER MOB YOUR TEAM HAS PUT TOGETHER?

I missed the mob we took to Millwall in about 1989 as I was on the ban, but I was at Chelsea in '85 on a Friday night and we had 400 of the tastiest lads you could hope to have on your side. Years earlier, Everton had been battered at Kenny High Street and this was our first time back there, as they had been relegated ever since. It was payback and we pulled it off big time.

WHO'S THE BEST RIVAL FIRM YOU'VE EVER SEEN?

We went to Boro a few years ago after doing them at ours, got off the bus and walked into about 400 of the bastards. They mullered us – end of. At Everton, United have brought some tasty mobs over the years but it has been numbers rather than quality, whereas West Ham never had the numbers but always the quality.

WHO ARE YOUR BIGGEST RIVALS TEAM-WISE?

The Red Shite. Total cunts. Horrible, horrible smug bastards. Some of their lads are sound but the majority of the fans, players and staff make me vomit.

WHO ARE YOUR BIGGEST RIVALS FAN-WISE?

It has eased off for a couple of seasons but I think Boro will always be number one on our list. It went on from the '70s to the late '90s and there were some bad casualties on both sides – pure hatred at times.

HAVE YOU EVER JOINED UP WITH ANOTHER TEAM'S FIRM?

Bristol Rovers when I was working down there. They had a small mob but didn't give a flying fuck for anybody. I always thought City were the main mob down there but, the year I went, it was Rovers who ran the show – they were fucking crackers. They were pissheads but loved a fight.

DID YOU EVER FOLLOW ENGLAND AND WOULD YOU PUT ENGLAND BEFORE YOUR CLUB?

I went to Euro '88 and Italia '90 and to loads of games abroad, but it was for the crack. Not many Everton or Liverpool lads give a fuck about the national side. I cannot believe anybody would rather watch any country before their own club side. I can't cheer when someone like Heskey or Gerrard scores for England because they are Red Shites. Owen is okay as I know him, but I'd rather not cheer any of the twats.

WHICH WAS THE BEST ENGLAND ROW?

Luxembourg, early '80s. They took the place and had the army on their toes, looted the place, then kicked off on each other. Someone could write a book about that trip alone.

HAVE YOU EVER SUPPORTED OR LOOKED OUT FOR ANOTHER TEAM'S RESULTS?

Not supported, but I have a soft spot for Bristol Rovers – top 'kiddies' as they call each other. I always look out for the Red Shites' result and pray they've been fucking hammered!

NAME YOUR TOP FIVE FIRMS, IN ANY ORDER.

It is hard to leave out the likes of Stoke, Birmingham and Millwall, but for one reason or another – mainly that they had shite sides and were always in lower divisions – we never met them much when it mattered. Loads of the Burberry brigade reading this will be saying, 'Who the fuck are Everton?' but anyone in the know will admit we took it to the best when it mattered.

A top five is hard, as on their day anybody can get a result against the so-called main firms, but for home and away combined, over a period of 25 years, I'd go for: 1. West Ham. We never had a major result there and they always looked for it away when it mattered; 2. Boro. They got better as the years went by and had a close-knit firm a bit like Everton. I respect them 100 per cent. Game as fuck and fair; 3. Chelsea. The Man. United of London but over the years they've had some unbelievable turnouts; 4. Man. United. Purely because of their numbers and the time they have been at it. Like them or not, you have to respect them for it; 5. Spurs. Always showed away and, unlike many Cockney mobs, always came looking for it at Euston.

WHICH IS THE WORST GROUND YOU'VE EVER BEEN TO AND WHY?

Exeter City. There was a wasps' nest at the back of the terrace behind the goal and they went mad. In the Premiership, Anfield by a mile – the place is a cesspool. Most grounds, including ours, need knocking down and rebuilding. They're the pits compared with the new ones you go to.

WHICH IS THE BEST STADIUM YOU'VE BEEN TO?

Juventus's Stadium delle Alpie. For Brazil v Argentina in Italia '90 it had just been built and was pure class at the time.

WHO ARE THE FAIREST COPPERS YOU'VE COME ACROSS AT A MATCH?

Boro. They only nick you if they 100 per cent have to and seem to be as mad as the Boro lads.

AND THE WORST OLD BILL?

Since my book came out, the Scouse bizzies have been a nightmare and try and nick me for fuck all, as they got a bit of stick in *Scally*. Over the years the twats in Birmingham are pure snides. They must have been on courses on 'How to be a total cunt'.

WHAT WOULD HAVE STOPPED YOU GETTING INVOLVED WITH THE BOYS AT MATCHES?

A marriage offer from Julia Roberts! Fuck all, really. I have had good kickings, fines and jail, and still went back for more. If it's in you, you're hooked. It's worse than a drug – there's no rush like it. Someone was quoted as saying, 'Scoring a goal is better than sex.' Well, I'll tell you, a full-scale off at the match is better than scoring a hat-trick in the Cup Final then shagging Kylie in the showers after!

DESCRIBE SOME OF THE METHODS AND TACTICS USED BY THE POLICE AND AUTHORITIES TO STOP FOOTBALL VIOLENCE, AND DO YOU THINK THEY WORK?

Banning orders, and stuff like that, are bollocks and will never stop it, as it's so easy to travel today. The spotters are a good idea but, with new lads coming through all the time, you would need a lot more of them. CCTV is the one. When you see those cameras everywhere, you think twice about it. They are the main deterrent.

HAVE YOU EVER BEEN SICKENED BY SOMETHING YOU'VE WITNESSED AT A GAME?

Heysel was bad, believe me. It was very, very bad. I still think of it now and think, fuck me – that was horrible. At home I have seen a few lads slashed, including plenty of Everton, and it is never a pretty sight. A few of the refs today sicken me, as well as the Red Shite!

WHAT'S YOUR FAVOURITE FOOTBALL SONG OR CHANT AND WHICH IS THE WORST YOU CAN RECALL HEARING FROM ANOTHER TEAM?

Everton always run out on to the pitch to the old TV *Z Cars* tune and that always gives me a tingle down my spine. As for a song, we don't have one! The chant 'You're gonna get your fucking heads kicked in' in the '70s was boss when it was sung at you during an away game.

The Red Shites' anthem is bad, and when them and Celtic sang it together during the 2002/3 season, I was cringing for the silly cunts and spewed up before turning the telly over.

WHAT WAS YOUR FAVOURITE BAND/RECORD DURING YOUR FOOTBALL DAYS?

The Jam – pure quality. Some of the gigs saw worse violence than the footy. It was a mental time. 'Tube Station' is still my all-time classic. Even today kids love The Jam. In my book, they will never be bettered. Pity they were Cockneys, really!

WHO WAS YOUR ALL-TIME FAVOURITE PLAYER?

Bob Latchford, Everton's record signing in 1974, was my boyhood hero. I met him at a do last year and he looked ten years younger than me. I was gutted! Latchford came to Everton and Howard Kendall went to Birmingham in exchange, and he is my next best. He's our most successful ever manager and a top bloke. He has done a few after-dinner speeches for me and even now I look at him and think, you are a fucking god! Embarrassing, really, at forty!

WHERE DO YOU THINK THE NEW ENGLISH NATIONAL STADIUM SHOULD BE BUILT AND WHAT ARE YOUR THOUGHTS REGARDING THE WEMBLEY FIASCO?

I prefer it to be in London, as the whole day out down there for us lot is a buzz. The fiasco is nothing new, as the tits who run the show are pure gobshites. If they were answerable to anybody bar themselves, they would have been fucked off long ago. Fucking disgrace one and all! It is catching, though, as Everton's top men have made a bigger mess of our ground move, and we're fucked big time. Same problem – ten-bob businessmen trying to run what is now a multimillion-pound industry. Pricks. I'll get my coat!

CASS PENNANT MEETS

STEVE COWENS
CLUB: SHEFFIELD UNITED

STEVE COWENS

THE MEET

I'd been on the trail of a Sheffield United face for nearly a year. After many meets, driving many miles, and going up more cul-de-sacs than a milkman, I finally found who I was looking for.

I'd been to see Sheffield United play Liverpool and missed Steve. Then I thought I might have bumped into him at a benefit night for big local face Lester Divers, who was tragically murdered, but yet again we managed to miss one another. Finally it was my mate, Shaun, a Rotherham Blade, who made the connection, and at last I got to meet Steve Cowens, author of the *Blades Business Crew*.

The meet with Steve was in a picture-postcard country setting – not somewhere you'd expect someone involved in the hoolie scene to live. Steve turned out to be very sincere and was very passionate about his team. He and a couple of his mates were great company. Steve has another book coming out later in 2003, called *Business as Usual*, which he wrote in fond memory of the late Lester Divers: 'The finest boy ever to grace Bramall Lane. Gone but not forgotten.' God bless ya, mate. Here Steve tells me about his life with the BBC.

BACKGROUND

I was born in June 1964. In the early '80s firms up and down the country started to give themselves a name. Around twelve of us had a meeting on London Road to discuss what name we should give ourselves. Blades Firm Force, Bulldog Blades and H-Block Hooligans were all ideas, but then a lad from Anston came up with Blades Business Crew – BBC for short. The name had a good ring to it and was adopted. Calling cards were made with 'Congratulations, you have just been tuned in by the BBC' on them. At the time I was a salesman for a timber merchant. I currently hold a job as a supervisor at a tool company in Sheffield, my hometown.

WHAT'S YOUR FAVOURITE TERRACE FASHION?

In the early '80s when everyone was Pringled or Lyle 'n' Scotted up to fuck, I used to love Cerruti 1881 because not many geezers were into it. I used to travel to Lilywhites in London and buy a few 1881 trackies 'n' jumpers. Knick-naks in Soho was also a good shop at the time and was the first with Armani and Hugo Boss. I used to love the Boss training tops that we wore at the time – later Sly Stallone wore them in the *Rocky* films.

Currently I wear a lot of Paul & Shark. I've been into it for around nine years now and think it's quality clobber. I also like Osaki

Etienne and Evisu, but Evisu tops are made for the water drinkers not the beer heads like myself. What I'm saying is, I'm a fat cunt who can't get in the fuckers.

WHAT'S THE WORST FASHION YOU'VE EVER SEEN ON THE TERRACES?

The worst fashion has to be the patchwork leathers of the early '80s (Chelsea leathers, I think they were called) – they were fuckin' minging. All the Cockney crews wore them and a few of our lot got into 'em. I also hated the shitty cycle tops that casuals started wearing around '84. On a personal front, my own fashion disasters include leg warmers. But what about this beauty – in 1985 I went to the Burberry shop in London and bought a Burberry blanket! I had it made into a poncho and went to Leeds in it. I thought I was the bollocks with my beige Lois cords on, but all the lads were calling me twit Eastwood and giving me the 'Ewy ewy ew' from the spaghetti westerns. Looking back, what a cock!

DESCRIBE YOUR WORST FEELING AT A GAME.

Going to Wembley to see England v Scotland in 1983/4. The Jocks used to take over Wembley, so me and two mates went down to defend England's pride. On the way to the ground all the Jocks were singing 'Spot the looney' at me as I walked up Wembley Way in my (this time we'll get it right) England shirt. One took a slug at me when I told him to fuck off. I couldn't do fuck all as the sweaties [sweaty sock, ie Jock] were all over the gaff. I thought we were going to get mullered, but once in the ground we were pleasantly surprised to be mixed in with a load of Chelsea and West Ham that were on one. We were at the Tunnel End and it kicked off, the Jocks got battered and it was the beginning of the end for the skirt-wearing ginger nuts. To be fair to the sweaties, on the way home I had a flat tyre and, like a cunt, I had no car jack. I limped my Morris Marina into the services and a van full of Jocks lifted the car up and changed the wheel for me, bless 'em.

HAVE YOU EVER INCURRED ANY SERIOUS INJURIES OR BEEN BADLY BEATEN UP AT A MATCH?

I was nearly blinded at Blackburn, of all places. Some snidey cunt smashed half a brick in my face from the side. I lost a tooth, broke my nose, and had a detached retina in my right eye. I was also slashed at Hull by some cunt from the Stanley family.

HAS YOUR OWN SIDE EVER BEEN INVOLVED IN A FULL-SCALE RIOT?

At the end of the season United fans always acted up at the last home game. It was the usual stuff – running on to the pitch, attacking away fans, going at it with the Old Bill and so on. At the end of the 1983/4 season we'd just lost to Wimbledon at home and it had dented our promotion hopes. It was the height of the miners' strike and tensions between the working class and Maggie Thatcher's militia were at fever pitch. Sheffield and its surrounding towns had a lot of people who worked down the pit. Anyhow, as the plod tried to clear a large crowd of around a thousand lads away from the bottom of Bramall Lane, the lot went up.

Police were chased, which led to a mounted police charge. Around twelve officers on horseback galloped into the crowds, only to be greeted by a hail of bricks. Two bizzies were pulled from their mounts and shovelled in, and the others turned and galloped back from whence they came. A huge roar went up and United hooligans chased the plod right up Bramall Lane. Police vehicles were turned over and 'full-scale riot' is the only way to describe it. Bolton and Bristol City away were two games in the late '80s where the lot went up as well.

DESCRIBE THE BEST TAKING OF AN END YOU'VE EVER WITNESSED.

I was sort of at the end of the era when taking Kops was fashionable, but sixty of us took West Brom's Kop and we had a beano on Barnsley's once. The best taking of an end has surely got to be Lorraine Bobbit's effort!

WHICH WAS YOUR OWN TEAM'S POPULAR END?

Sheffield United's Spion Kop, the Shoreham End. I have preferred to sit in the South Stand since 1974 but the Shoreham saw some proper running battles – with Leeds, Arsenal and West Ham all coming on.

WHERE DID YOU STAND OR SIT IN THE GROUND?

At Bramall Lane, I've always liked the South Stand.

CAN YOU RECALL A BATTLE YOU HAVE BEEN INVOLVED IN, EITHER INSIDE OR OUTSIDE A GROUND?

Inside was Bristol City away, two years running, in the late '80s. Outside was Leeds at home around 1985. The Bristol sessions were both end of season and had everybody going down, lagered up, and what have you. Proper beano, like. At one of them, I was wearing '70s flares and platform boots. The day was mental.

CAN YOU RECALL THE BEST EVER MOB YOUR TEAM HAS PUT TOGETHER?

We turned a massive 600 out for a Leeds visit in 1983. The two clubs hadn't played each other for years and leaflets had been distributed to urge United's lads to turn out in numbers and give it to Leeds. We also took 600 to the FA Cup semi-final at Wembley against Sheffy Wendy. That was an absolutely awesome firm too.

WHO'S THE BEST RIVAL FIRM YOU'VE EVER SEEN?

Pompey in '84 when the 6.57 brought around 300 lads who were well up for it, and they splattered us all over that day. Leeds also brought around 300 in '85. The plod couldn't keep things under wraps that day and it was mayhem. Leeds were well up for it.

WHO ARE YOUR BIGGEST RIVALS TEAM-WISE?

Sheffield Wendy.

WHO ARE YOUR BIGGEST RIVALS FAN-WISE?

Leeds United, although Wolves have, of late, become a hated mob because they attacked shirters at Molineux the season, 2002/3. Plus the Turks from Galatasaray, as an Englishman.

HAVE YOU EVER JOINED UP WITH ANOTHER TEAM'S FIRM?

No, but I've been out with Everton a few times and I'm very good pals with a few of their lads.

DID YOU EVER FOLLOW ENGLAND AND WOULD YOU PUT ENGLAND BEFORE YOUR CLUB?

I've travelled away with England, most notably to France '98 for the World Cup, but England wouldn't come before my club.

WHICH WAS THE BEST ENGLAND ROW?

Hampden Park in 1985. England took a massive firm up to Scotland and we took it to the Jocks who were shocked by the sheer size of the numbers we had out. We chased the sweats all over the place from the start of the day to the end. The Old Bill escort to the ground contained 1,000 to 1,200 proper boys – it was the cream of English firms up 'n' down our green and pastured lands.

HAVE YOU EVER SUPPORTED OR LOOKED OUT FOR ANOTHER TEAM'S RESULTS?

I'm a Glasgow Rangers fan. It started at school. At the time I liked Celtic out of the two of them. On United's Shoreham Kop I shouted 'Celtic!' when our fans went into the Rangers – Celtic chant. Soon after I saw Rangers on TV in Europe, and all their fans had the Union Jacks out and I realised they were British, and proud of it. My allegiance changed and I support them and buy my son, Jack, their kits. I'm not really into all the political aspect of it, but the Union Jacks did it for me.

NAME YOUR TOP FIVE FIRMS, IN ANY ORDER.

In any order, Pompey's 6.57 from the '80s and likewise West Ham's ICF of that era. Another good firm from the early '80s were Man. City's Cool Cats/Mayneline firm. Then two mobs who have been good for two decades, Boro and Millwall. Respect goes out to the following, though: Chelsea, Leeds, Lincoln, Birmingham and, of course, the Soul Crew.

WHICH IS THE WORST GROUND YOU'VE EVER BEEN TO AND WHY?

Without doubt that's Millwall's old Cold Blow Lane. Everything about the place was intimidating, – the flats and surrounding areas, the clueless Old Bill, and every man and his granny wanted to rip your 'norven' head off. I went down there five times and they were at it, every one of them. So it's Millwall by a country mile.

WHICH IS THE BEST STADIUM YOU'VE BEEN TO?

The Olympic Stadium in Rome. I was lucky enough to be invited over there by my good pal Paul Heaton. He's an expert on Italian football and is an avid Inter fan. Channel Four had invited him over to commentate with James Richardson, the expert.

Lazio were playing Inter and the atmosphere was brilliant. The

game itself was a great 2–2 draw and we went for a meal after with ex-Chelsea skipper Paul Elliot, who is a boss geezer, by the way, but one greedy cunt. He can eat two potatoes more than a pig. Cheers, Mr Heaton. On the English front, Old Trafford is a brilliant ground to visit.

WHO ARE THE FAIREST COPPERS YOU'VE COME ACROSS AT A MATCH?

It's got to be the Met in London. In the early days they didn't have a fuckin' clue. No wonder the London firms built up good firms with them in tow.

AND THE WORST OLD BILL?

I used to think South Yorkshire Police were pretty fair. You fucked them about and they fucked you, but now my opinion has changed. Lately our plod are no more than legalised thugs themselves. They have hidden agendas and take great delight in mullering anything that moves, guilty or not. The mufty squad [riot police] take off their ID numbers so they can't be identified before they dish out their treatment. As football lads know, that's the gamble, but when innocent fans are getting twatted by the Old Bill then there's something seriously wrong.

WHAT WOULD HAVE STOPPED YOU GETTING INVOLVED WITH THE BOYS AT MATCHES?

Apart from a 12-inch cock, I think the only thing that would have stopped me is if I had received a jail term after the birth of my first child. I think that when you have a youngster your priorities change and you start to think, what if I go down? Will my little 'un be okay? Fatherhood definitely changed me as a person and it probably came at the right time.

DESCRIBE SOME OF THE METHODS AND TACTICS USED BY THE POLICE AND AUTHORITIES TO STOP FOOTBALL VIOLENCE, AND DO YOU THINK THEY WORK?

I think this new Section 60 law is total bollocks. [Section 60 of the Crime, Justice and Public Order Act, 1994, introduced by Tory Home Secretary Michael Howard to tackle noisy ravers and football hooligans]. How can the bizzies stop you on the strength that they think you're going to do something? Lads should read up on the facts of Section 60 because the plod are breaking the rules of it with regularity. They don't have the rights that you think they have. The best, but most alarming police tactic, use is football grasses. They get lads on a bad charge, offer them a deal, then pay large amounts of cash for information about where a firm's meeting and who's doing/done what, but all the time the informers are usually up to things twenty times worse than proper football lads. They use the plod like they are being used; you can get involved in all sorts of shit but don't get lifted because you are on their payroll. Football grasses are vermin of the highest order.

HAVE YOU EVER BEEN SICKENED BY SOMETHING YOU'VE WITNESSED AT A GAME?

Without doubt the scenes from the Heysel Stadium disaster were sickening. The two Leeds lads murdered in Istanbul got to me as well. On a personal front, in 1982 two Barnsley lads were slashed at Bramall Lane, which sickened me big time. I went home thinking that's not what it's all about for me. Two geezers had their backs opened up for the sake of football – it's not my cup of tea. We can all take a beating but to me Muppets carrying blades is the lowest of the low.

WHAT'S YOUR FAVOURITE FOOTBALL SONG OR CHANT AND WHICH IS THE WORST YOU CAN RECALL HEARING FROM ANOTHER TEAM?

Football songs now are shite. I much prefer the '70s/'80s songs. They had character and a meaning rather than this shit people sing nowadays. A '70s United lad (Mr Sharpe) had a CD out called *Walking Down Shoreham Street Swinging a Chain* – 24 great terrace battle hymns. It's class. So my favourite has to come from that album.

WHAT WAS YOUR FAVOURITE BAND/RECORD DURING YOUR FOOTBALL DAYS?

I think most football lads from the '80s will agree that the Stone Roses were like a breath of fresh air to the music scene. It coincided with the football hooligans' love in during the rave and ecstasy years, so my favourite is 'Waterfall' by the Roses. 'If the Kids are United' by Sham 69 is also a favourite of mine for obvious reasons.

WHO WAS YOUR ALL-TIME FAVOURITE PLAYER?

Tony Currie, a legend and a god down at beautiful downtown Bramall Lane. He used to run out to 'You can do magic', which he certainly could. I remember crying when Leeds bought him in 1975. On the England scene my favourite player was Stuart Pearce. He epitomised what I see as being an Englishman – pride, courage and aggression. It makes me puke that the players who play for England now can't be arsed to sing the national anthem. They all think they're too hip 'n' trendy to be seen singing. They just want to get back into their Prada suits and drive off in one of many top-of-the-range vehicles. Cunts, the lot of 'em. I know if old Psycho was still in the

England set-up he'd make the twats show some pride in their country and shirt. Rant over.

WHERE DO YOU THINK THE NEW ENGLISH NATIONAL STADIUM SHOULD BE BUILT AND WHAT ARE YOUR THOUGHTS REGARDING THE WEMBLEY FIASCO?

Wembley has, and always should be, the home of English football. It fucks me off big time that a few twats sat up in ivory towers can stall and fuck around with the project of rebuilding Wembley. They can spend millions on the white elephant that constitutes the London Dome, but our national football stage and the heritage that goes with it can be overlooked. Cocks, the lot of 'em. I wish they could have somehow kept the twin towers.

MARTIN KING MEETS

JERREL
CLUB: FEYENOORD

JERREL

THE MEET

I'd heard about Jerrel from my Dutch mate, Robbie. Although a Feyenoord fan, he can often be found at Stamford Bridge cheering on the Blues. I made arrangements to fly out to Holland and meet up with the boys, and take in their home game with PSV. I wasn't disappointed. It was like going back 30 years; the atmosphere was just like an English ground was in the '70s. My hosts treated me with the greatest respect, even though they did get me stoned before, during and after the game. Afterwards we met up at Robbie's home and had a nice meal, and more beer. The evening was one to remember and the stories flowed as everyone relaxed, if you get my drift. Jerrel's a big man with an even bigger heart and he spoke a lot of sense. It's a good job I had my tape recorder running because, come the end of the evening, I couldn't remember a lot. Cheers, boys, nice one!

BACKGROUND

I was born in Holland in 1970 and my parents were originally from Surinam. My first game was a tournament at Rotterdam Stadium. I was aged seven and Everton from England were one of the teams playing. I will never forget that day. I went with my father and I was sitting in the top tier of the stadium eating an apple and taking everything in. It made a big impact on my life. When I was fifteen years old my friends asked me to go to a game with them but I said, 'Why go to today's game when tonight it will be shown on television?' They laughed and explained it was different. They told me about the atmosphere at a live game, and the fun, and the singing and the noise. I ran home and asked my mum if I could go with them. After I left school I got a job in a factory, and I now work as a driver. My nickname is 'Riot Negro Number One'.

WHAT'S YOUR FAVOURITE TERRACE FASHION?

Just casual or a Feyenoord shirt, like the one I wore for our game against Real Madrid in the Super Cup in the 2001/2 season.

WHAT'S THE WORST FASHION YOU'VE EVER SEEN ON THE TERRACES?

When most Dutch supporters had long hair, like hippies.

DESCRIBE YOUR WORST FEELING AT A GAME.

I went with a few mates to Eindhoven on a Saturday night. We were playing PSV the next day and we decided to have a night out before the game. There was trouble and some got arrested. I ended up sleeping in a squat. The next day a train with Feyenoord fans arrived and I managed to slip in with them as the police escorted the 2,000 fans along the two-mile walk to the stadium. They were singing and chanting, and it felt good to be among my own fans. I looked around for any familiar faces, but I didn't recognise anyone. I noticed three skinheads behind me, but I carried on walking. Then I heard them say, 'Nigger, nigger, nigger, out, out, out.' I took no notice and carried on walking, not thinking it was directed at me. 'Nigger, nigger, nigger, out, out, out' came the chant again. I didn't look back but then I knew the chants were for me. 'Nigger, nigger, nigger, out, out, out.' I just kept walking. I was a skinny seventeen-year-old black kid minding my own business but I must admit I was scared.

HAVE YOU EVER INCURRED ANY SERIOUS INJURIES OR BEEN BADLY BEATEN UP AT A MATCH?

I was once hit by a police baton in Amsterdam. I was standing outside the ground three hours before kick-off and a man came round and gave me a bundle of 'Kick out racism from football' leaflets. 'Can you pass these leaflets around the Feyenoord fans?' he asked. I said a few words to him, and then from behind a policeman hit me with his baton. I nearly passed out. The power of the blow and the shock of getting hit made my brains scramble and my head spin. I threw the leaflets at him and asked him what the fuck he was playing at. I could tell by his eyes that he was shocked I hadn't gone down. He mumbled something about being too close to the stadium gates, but later that evening I felt the full effect of that blow. He didn't open up my skull but it hurt like hell.

HAS YOUR OWN SIDE EVER BEEN INVOLVED IN A FULL-SCALE RIOT?

Yes, at Beverwyk. The fight happened because of something that had taken place six weeks previously. Feyenoord had clashed with Ajax fans and we'd yet again got the better of them, and they were forced to run away. They complained there were too many of us and we were out of order because we had such huge numbers. The fight at Beverwyk came about as we travelled in a convoy to an away game, which took us through an area of Amsterdam. As we drove along the motorway we could see a large group of men gathered in a field – there must have been about 250 of them. We pulled over and stepped from our vehicles. I didn't think we'd stumbled across them by chance as I had a hunch that they'd be looking for revenge for what had happened a few weeks previously.

They slowly walked towards us as we stood at the metal barrier, which ran along the side of the road. A few of our boys were tooled up and were banging their weapons on the barrier. I looked along our lines and could see all our top faces were ready. Without a word we stepped over the metal barrier and walked towards the Ajax firm, which were a couple of hundred yards in front of us. I had a bottle of beer in my hand, took a swig and clutched it. This time I hoped that Ajax would not run because, if they were up for it, it was going to be one hell of a fight. I could see in the distance a police car with its light flashing, but I knew they were too far away to stop it. Perhaps that was their whole intention – that we kill and maim one another. The hatred between Ajax and us has been around for years, and this was the day that would sort out the men from the boys. There was only going to be one winner.

As they came closer I could see them slowing down and fanning out. It didn't look together and I could see some of them had doubt in their minds. They were splitting into two groups with the larger of the two lagging behind. We were standing on top of a small hill and for a split second we stopped and then charged. It was toe to toe, with both sides hitting out at each other with every weapon imaginable. The fighting went on for a couple of minutes but the bulk of their mob froze to the spot. There was only about forty of their lot actually fighting. I saw one of them felled by a blow from a baseball bat and that was it. We just overpowered them and they were forced to run.

One of their main boys became bogged down in the mud and didn't have the legs to get away. He dropped to his knees as kicks and blows rained down on him. Certain people in our firm were pleased he was there and even happier he'd been caught. A few years earlier he'd stabbed one of our boys at a game and now it was payback time. Three of his mates stayed and fought but slowly they too were overpowered. Because of the savage beating they were getting, they had to leave him and run. As I passed him I stopped a couple of our boys from hitting him. 'Leave him, he's had enough,' I said, and I could see him trying to get up on to his knees. I knew he was badly injured as he collapsed into a heap. We left him and walked back to where our cars were parked.

We pulled away and we heard on the car radio that there had been clashes between Ajax and Feyenoord supporters. We all cheered and the news reporter went on to say that it was believed a man had died. Silence fell on the minibus we were travelling in. I couldn't believe it. I went through every possible emotion in moments. I was scared, fucked up. This wasn't meant to be – how could this happen? Shit, shit, shit. I felt guilty even though I never touched him, but I was there. The victim wasn't innocent – he came to fight and he was one of Ajax's main men. Some would say he was a nutter. On the day he died he'd told his wife he was going to go out to buy a loaf of bread.

I was arrested with many others following this incident and spent time in jail on remand but was never charged for the man's murder. There's been lots written, both in the Dutch press and by so-called experts in England, and all of them are way off the mark and are far away from the truth. There was no posting of a meet on the Internet, nor was the fight arranged by phone. If it had been, then where were the police? I'm saddened that a man has lost his life but there's a saying: 'Those that live by the sword die by the sword.' I'll leave it at that.

DESCRIBE THE BEST TAKING OF AN END YOU'VE EVER WITNESSED.
It's not a custom in Holland, but six hours before the game in Eindhoven we took over their favourite bar – 500 of us took the piss.

WHICH WAS YOUR OWN TEAM'S POPULAR END?
Vak S.

WHERE DID YOU STAND OR SIT IN THE GROUND?
I stood in Vak S for a couple of games, then in Vak R for a few games, and then me and my brother and a few mates stood next to the away fans in Vak JJ.

CAN YOU RECALL A BATTLE YOU HAVE BEEN INVOLVED IN, EITHER INSIDE OR OUTSIDE A GROUND?
Beverwyk.

CAN YOU RECALL THE BEST EVER MOB YOUR TEAM HAS PUT TOGETHER?
Werder Bremen for the game in Germany. There were 500 top boys out for that trip and it seemed half of Germany would be out to meet us. There had been calls on the Internet for the German clubs to unite against us. We were arrested on arrival by the German Police, and as I was led away by a policeman either side of me I couldn't feel the floor below me as there was every weapon imaginable discarded, and they'd begun to pile up.

WHO'S THE BEST RIVAL FIRM YOU'VE EVER SEEN?
Holland v Germany in 1989. I saw the German mob at Rotterdam Central Station and it was unbelievable. I've never seen a firm like it. Total Germans.

WHO ARE YOUR BIGGEST RIVALS TEAM-WISE?
Ajax. When you learn to love Feyenoord, at the same time you learn to hate Ajax.

WHO ARE YOUR BIGGEST RIVALS FAN-WISE?
The same, Ajax. Maybe because of their history. They've had more success than us – more European cups anyway. I hate them – 365 days of the year I hate them.

HAVE YOU EVER JOINED UP WITH ANOTHER TEAM'S FIRM?
No, but I went to watch FC Twente play Munich with a mate of mine, who seemed very pleased to have me in his company.

DID YOU EVER FOLLOW HOLLAND AND WOULD YOU PUT HOLLAND BEFORE YOUR CLUB?
I've watched Holland v England and Holland v Belgium. We didn't go to fight the Belgians, we went to fight other Dutch mobs, but it never happened.

WHICH WAS THE BEST HOLLAND ROW?
I can't remember one. If a team are playing Holland in Rotterdam, then only the Feyenoord boys will turn out. The national team has no real mob.

HAVE YOU EVER SUPPORTED OR LOOKED OUT FOR ANOTHER TEAM'S RESULTS?
I've followed Everton since I was a little kid – maybe because my first game was watching them in a tournament in Rotterdam Stadium. My brother followed Aston Villa and we used to play Everton v Villa in the street. I used to catch up with their results on teletext.

NAME YOUR TOP FIVE FIRMS, IN ANY ORDER.
Germany and England, and in Holland, Den Haag and Ajax. Other than that I'm still looking.

WHICH IS THE WORST GROUND YOU'VE EVER BEEN TO AND WHY?
FC Twenter. It's a big, boring stadium with no atmosphere, and with an athletic track running around the pitch that makes it seem that you're miles away from the action.

WHICH IS THE BEST STADIUM YOU'VE BEEN TO?
Tottenham. It was my first time in England and I loved the stadium. It seemed like it was an indoor arena and I loved the singing and the atmosphere. We won 1–0 in the first leg and got the most beautiful

0–0 draw I've ever seen in the return leg. 'Come on you Spurs,' sang the Tottenham fans and we sang back, 'We fucked you Spurs!'

WHO ARE THE FAIREST COPPERS YOU'VE COME ACROSS AT A MATCH?
None.

AND THE WORST OLD BILL?
Amsterdam. They don't like football fans and history has proved that.

WHAT WOULD HAVE STOPPED YOU GETTING INVOLVED WITH THE BOYS AT MATCHES?
Nothing would have stopped me. I've been banned for four years and I'm back, so it proves nothing will stop me. But not being able to see my team hurts.

DESCRIBE SOME OF THE METHODS AND TACTICS USED BY THE POLICE AND AUTHORITIES TO STOP FOOTBALL VIOLENCE, AND DO YOU THINK THEY WORK?
Being banned from the ground, as I say, hurts.

HAVE YOU EVER BEEN SICKENED BY SOMETHING YOU'VE WITNESSED AT A GAME?
The story Danny told about the Down's syndrome boy in Belgium [see page 62]. I've heard it so many times from different people. I think it's disgusting.

WHAT'S YOUR FAVOURITE FOOTBALL SONG OR CHANT AND WHICH IS THE WORST YOU CAN RECALL HEARING FROM ANOTHER TEAM?
My favourite is 'We fucked you Spurs' and the worst song we ever sang was to the Ajax coach, Louis Van Gaal, during a cup match in Amsterdam. His wife had just died a week before the game. The ball went out of play and the crowd was silent as we sang:

'Louis didn't let his wife have radiation treatment, He didn't care at all. Then she got cancer, And now she's dead, The Jewish whore.' Four thousand sang that as it echoed around the stadium. Later, when asked if he'd heard what we were singing, he replied, 'Yes.' And, if it were the other way round, the Ajax fans would do the same to the Feyenoord coach.

Another song we sang at a game was aimed at a PSV player's wife, who was in the media after being accused of being a hooker. Someone noticed her in the crowd and we sang to her about her life as a prostitute. Even the PSV players were finding it hard not to laugh.

WHAT WAS YOUR FAVOURITE BAND/RECORD DURING YOUR FOOTBALL DAYS?

We once hired a boat from Rotterdam to Amsterdam leaving at 1.30 a.m. and arriving at 10 a.m. It had never been done before. There were 500 of us on board, and many staggered off the boat drunk and stoned. Speedy J's 'Pullover' song was played as the trip turned into a rave party. We were met on the quayside by the police and taken straight to the ground. Afterwards we travelled back to Rotterdam by train.

WHO WAS YOUR ALL-TIME FAVOURITE PLAYER?

It has to be Maradona, who I saw play in the flesh, and also Pele, who I only saw on TV.

WHERE DO YOU THINK THE NEW ENGLISH NATIONAL STADIUM SHOULD BE BUILT AND WOULD YOU BE PREPARED TO SHARE YOUR NATIONAL STADIUM WITH THE ENGLISH?

It's a pity I never did get to Wembley and I wish I had gone, what with all the history of the place, but I would be more than happy to share our Rotterdam stadium with the English. We're the same type of people and I think we'd get along fine.

MARTIN KING MEETS

DANNY
CLUB: FEYENOORD

DANNY

THE MEET

I met up with Danny along with his good mate, Jerrel, over at my mate Robbie's place in Rotterdam. He's a great bloke with a gruff voice and the looks of Axle Rose from Guns 'n' Roses. There isn't a stroke he hasn't pulled and some of his stories are top-drawer. He's a great bloke and fantastic company.

BACKGROUND

I was born in Schiedam, just outside Rotterdam, and the first game I went to was in 1970 when I was six years old. I went to watch Feyenoord with my father and we won 2–0 against AC Milan in the European Cup. After I left school I went to work in the construction industry.

I used to go to football regularly with the boys that lived in my street. I remember standing with my father when we played Tottenham and a couple of their firm were stabbed and chased from the terraces. That was in 1974 and I still remember it well. During the bad periods, around 1989, the crowds were down but our firm got bigger. Originally our main firm only came from Rotterdam but now they come from all over Holland. My nickname at the club is 'the Voice' due to my gruff tone.

WHAT'S YOUR FAVOURITE TERRACE FASHION?

Just casual. We did have a period when body warmers were the thing, due to Conan The Barbarian. Everyone wanted to be like him.

WHAT'S THE WORST FASHION YOU'VE EVER SEEN ON THE TERRACES?

When everyone wears orange-coloured clothing and clogs to support the national team.

DESCRIBE YOUR WORST FEELING AT A GAME.

When I hit a policeman in Belgium and they battered me with truncheons. I went home and my aunt phoned my parents, who were on holiday. She was shocked. I was black and blue and covered in cuts and bruises. I was only trying to rescue my friend who was taking a beating from the police.

HAVE YOU EVER INCURRED ANY SERIOUS INJURIES OR BEEN BADLY BEATEN UP AT A MATCH?

I once had my head split open with a rock thrown by a Den Haag fan.

HAS YOUR OWN SIDE EVER BEEN INVOLVED IN A FULL-SCALE RIOT?

Beverwyk, in 1997, when an Ajax fan was killed after we clashed with their firm on some waste ground on our way to a game near Amsterdam.

DESCRIBE THE BEST TAKING OF AN END YOU'VE EVER WITNESSED.

Trying to get into Ajax's F side at a night game. We were nearly in there but at the last second the police saw what we were trying to do and beat us back with their batons.

WHICH WAS YOUR OWN TEAM'S POPULAR END?

Vak S.

WHERE DID YOU STAND OR SIT IN THE GROUND?

Vak S and Vak R.

CAN YOU RECALL A BATTLE YOU HAVE BEEN INVOLVED IN, EITHER INSIDE OR OUTSIDE A GROUND?

Spurs in 1983. They were in the G section and were chased everywhere by our boys. A lot of our boys were arrested after the clashes were shown on TV. One of the Spurs lads was stabbed in revenge after one of our boys had a knife pulled on him after the game at Tottenham.

CAN YOU RECALL THE BEST EVER MOB YOUR TEAM HAS PUT TOGETHER?

Werder Bremen in Germany. The police were waiting for us and arrested all 500 of us. We were surrounded by 1,500 cops, many in riot gear, and taken to a military camp. We were kept there until the game started, put into handcuffs, driven back to the railway station and taken to Holland. It was the craziest night – I've never seen so many policemen in one place.

WHO'S THE BEST RIVAL FIRM YOU'VE EVER SEEN?

The craziest mob I've ever seen was out in Greece in 1984. We were playing Panathinaikos and I've never heard so much noise in a football stadium. There were 80,000 Greeks inside and, from the age of eight to eighty, they just wanted to get their hands on you and kill you. There were 150 Feyenoord supporters, surrounded by the same amount of police. Among us was a man we call 'the White One' because of his hair. A Greek fan came into our section from the corporate seats and attacked him. Before we could do anything, the police arrested 'the White One' and allowed his Greek attacker to escape. Outside we were loaded into buses and driven away from the stadium. It wasn't long before the windows were smashed by the Greeks throwing stones and I was surprised we arrived at the airport in one piece.

WHO ARE YOUR BIGGEST RIVALS TEAM-WISE?
Ajax.

WHO ARE YOUR BIGGEST RIVALS FAN-WISE?
Ajax because they're so fucking arrogant.

HAVE YOU EVER JOINED UP WITH ANOTHER TEAM'S FIRM?
Never, I'm Feyenoord and that's it.

DID YOU EVER FOLLOW HOLLAND AND WOULD YOU PUT HOLLAND BEFORE YOUR CLUB?
I've followed the Dutch national team to Italy and Germany selling T-shirts, scarves and flags.

WHICH WAS THE BEST HOLLAND ROW?
I was selling my merchandise outside Feyenoord Stadium in 1989 when Holland were playing Germany. I was making money, and not trouble, and then the Germans turned up on to the forecourt with a mob nearly a thousand strong. The Dutch had about 250, but the Germans were too strong and too well organised, and strolled around taking the piss.

HAVE YOU EVER SUPPORTED OR LOOKED OUT FOR ANOTHER TEAM'S RESULTS?
I like watching European football on TV and I don't mind Manchester United.

NAME YOUR TOP FIVE FIRMS, IN ANY ORDER.
The English national team, the Germans, and in Holland, Den Haag – just those three teams. I can't recall meeting any other real strong firms.

WHICH IS THE WORST GROUND YOU'VE EVER BEEN TO AND WHY?
Panathinaikos because of the intimidating atmosphere. And even our own ground. Before its renovation, it used to smell like piss – the toilets were always overflowing.

WHICH IS THE BEST STADIUM YOU'VE BEEN TO?
San Siro because of Feyenoord's history in that stadium. We won the European Cup there in 1970.

WHO ARE THE FAIREST COPPERS YOU'VE COME ACROSS AT A MATCH?

None. If they can stab you in the back, they will.

AND THE WORST OLD BILL?

Arnham, Rotterdam and Eindoven. If you step from the kerb into the road they will arrest you; look at them the wrong way and you will be taken away. Amsterdam Police are always looking for trouble. Last year 35 people were injured, including many women and children. There's currently a lawsuit being taken out against the police in Amsterdam after these fans were crushed on the stairs after police allegedly used their batons.

WHAT WOULD HAVE STOPPED YOU GETTING INVOLVED WITH THE BOYS AT MATCHES?

Getting banned from the stadium. I love my club and I love watching my club play football. In Holland if you get caught doing anything, no matter how small, it's an automatic 1,000 euro (£600) fine. A fan was recently caught pissing in a field after leaving a bar and the police spotted him, arrested him and he received a six-month ban from watching football.

DESCRIBE SOME OF THE METHODS AND TACTICS USED BY THE POLICE AND AUTHORITIES TO STOP FOOTBALL VIOLENCE, AND DO YOU THINK THEY WORK?

The square just outside Feyenoord Stadium was where trouble would always begin. The police decided that after each game whoever stood around waiting for trouble would be moved on, so their tactic was to batter with their batons anyone who was slow to move on. It worked. It was the best tactic I've ever seen.

HAVE YOU EVER BEEN SICKENED BY SOMETHING YOU'VE WITNESSED AT A GAME?

We were playing in Belgium and there was a local kid in our section of the terrace who had Down's syndrome. As he started kicking a ball around with the Feyenoord supporters a bloke came from our fans and headbutted the fourteen-year-old in the face. Then police came in and arrested the drunken bully. I couldn't believe it as the boy was taken away by medics. He was just a simple lad enjoying himself and having some fun. Even if he had worn an Ajax shirt and was hurling abuse at us, he didn't deserve what he got.

WHAT'S YOUR FAVOURITE FOOTBALL SONG OR CHANT AND WHICH IS THE WORST YOU CAN RECALL HEARING FROM ANOTHER TEAM?

'Hamas Hamas' and 'Gas Gas Gas', all aimed at the Ajax fans who we call the Yids, and 'Hand in Hand', the Feyenoord song, are my favourites. 'O-lay, O-lay, O-lay, O-lay' has got to be the worst.

WHAT WAS YOUR FAVOURITE BAND/RECORD DURING YOUR FOOTBALL DAYS?

The Rolling Stones are my favourite band, along with the Beatles. I've loved their music since I was a little kid.

WHO WAS YOUR ALL-TIME FAVOURITE PLAYER?

Diego Maradona and van der Donk.

WHERE DO YOU THINK THE NEW ENGLISH NATIONAL STADIUM SHOULD BE BUILT AND WOULD YOU BE PREPARED TO SHARE YOUR NATIONAL STADIUM WITH THE ENGLISH?

Why not? It's all money for me – I'd sell more scarves and T-shirts! I think it's a great idea. I've seen European Cup Finals played in Rotterdam and there've been no problems. We have a five-star stadium. I'm proud of it.

MARTIN KING MEETS

DIRK

CLUB: FORTUNA DUSSELDORF

DIRK

THE MEET

I was introduced to Dirk by my good mate Pat Dolan, from Chelsea, who had met him through the England scene. I phoned Dirk and explained that I was putting together this book. Here are his responses, sent by e-mail.

BACKGROUND

My name is Dirk and my nickname is MFC Dusseldorf, I'm 40 years old and married with a little son aged one and a half. I run a fashion agency for children's wear and also work independently for different children's wear producers.

I first went to watch Fortuna play in 1972, when I was nine years old, along with a few friends and one of their dads. We were playing Wupperfal, which was and still is a local derby. In recent years Fortuna have been relegated from the Bundesleague and through the lower divisions, and we now play in one of the German regional leagues. I've supported Fortuna Dusseldorf for a long time and they are an old established club with a long and colourful history.

WHAT'S YOUR FAVOURITE TERRACE FASHION?

Timberland and Stone Island.

WHAT'S THE WORST FASHION YOU'VE EVER SEEN ON THE TERRACES?

Anything worn by the fans of FC Pauli Hamburg. They're all scruffy bastards with long hair.

DESCRIBE YOUR WORST FEELING AT A GAME.

That has to be watching Champions League football on TV just after the terrible events of 11 September.

HAVE YOU EVER INCURRED ANY SERIOUS INJURIES OR BEEN BADLY BEATEN UP AT A MATCH?

Yes, I have. I've been punched on the nose a couple of times.

HAS YOUR OWN SIDE EVER BEEN INVOLVED IN A FULL-SCALE RIOT?

Yes. Some weeks it's been a regular event.

DESCRIBE THE BEST TAKING OF AN END YOU'VE EVER WITNESSED.

It was at the Bayern Munich Stadium in the late '80s when we tried to take their end with a big firm. There was trouble everywhere inside the ground, but the Old Bill just managed to push us back as we reached their home terrace.

WHICH WAS YOUR OWN TEAM'S POPULAR END?
Block 36 at the old Rhine Stadium in Dusseldorf.

WHERE DID YOU STAND OR SIT IN THE GROUND?
We either stood in Block 36 or we would sit somewhere close to it.

CAN YOU RECALL A BATTLE YOU HAVE BEEN INVOLVED IN, EITHER INSIDE OR OUTSIDE A GROUND?
Yes, the World Cup in '98 at Marseilles when England played Tunisia and the fighting between the fans went on the night before, and the day of the match.

CAN YOU RECALL THE BEST EVER MOB YOUR TEAM HAS PUT TOGETHER?
It was away to Schalke in '88 – there was trouble all day. Also at the 1979 Cup Winners Cup Final in Basel when we lost to Barcelona.

WHO'S THE BEST RIVAL FIRM YOU'VE EVER SEEN?
Schalke 04. They're well organised and one of their top boys is an English lad.

WHO ARE YOUR BIGGEST RIVALS TEAM-WISE?
Cologne FC. There's a long-standing rivalry between the two cities – we're only about twenty miles apart.

WHO ARE YOUR BIGGEST RIVALS FAN-WISE?
Cologne FC.

HAVE YOU EVER JOINED UP WITH ANOTHER TEAM'S FIRM?
Yes, Millwall. The reason I also follow Millwall is we are very similar in lots of ways. No one likes them in England and likewise over here rival teams hate us. Plus our fans are from working-class backgrounds and the areas around both stadiums are very similar, and inside the grounds the atmosphere is the same.

DID YOU EVER FOLLOW GERMANY AND WOULD YOU PUT GERMANY BEFORE YOUR CLUB?
I did for a long time, but not at the present.

WHICH WAS THE BEST GERMANY ROW?
The World Cup '90 in Italy. It was before the German v Yugoslavia

game and it kicked off in Milan city centre with the Italian Old Bill and the locals.

HAVE YOU EVER SUPPORTED OR LOOKED OUT FOR ANOTHER TEAM'S RESULTS?
Yes, Millwall.

NAME YOUR TOP FIVE FIRMS, IN ANY ORDER.
BFC Dynamo Berlin, Schalke, Cologne, Munich, and my own team. In the past we could pull a 500-strong mob at some games.

WHICH IS THE WORST GROUND YOU'VE EVER BEEN TO AND WHY?
Bayer Uerdingen FC. It's a real shithole with no crowds and no atmosphere.

WHICH IS THE BEST STADIUM YOU'VE BEEN TO?
Borussia Dortmund. It's just like an English stadium – it's got everything.

WHO ARE THE FAIREST COPPERS YOU'VE COME ACROSS AT A MATCH?
I have never met such a thing.

AND THE WORST OLD BILL?
Munich. They can arrest you and hold you under Bavarian law for two days without any charge.

WHAT WOULD HAVE STOPPED YOU GETTING INVOLVED WITH THE BOYS AT MATCHES?
Weapons.

DESCRIBE SOME OF THE METHODS AND TACTICS USED BY THE POLICE AND AUTHORITIES TO STOP FOOTBALL VIOLENCE, AND DO YOU THINK THEY WORK?
CCTV cameras seem to work and for now it's stopped the violence at most German games.

HAVE YOU EVER BEEN SICKENED BY SOMETHING YOU'VE WITNESSED AT A GAME?
No, never.

WHAT'S YOUR FAVOURITE FOOTBALL SONG OR CHANT AND WHICH IS THE WORST YOU CAN RECALL HEARING FROM ANOTHER TEAM?
'In der Sudkurve viertel vor vier', which in English means 'We've got

your mascot hanging by the neck', and it would be sung to the Cologne fans. The worst I've heard is 'Bobby Moore, Bobby Moore running from the den' sung to the tune of 'Robin Hood'.

WHAT WAS YOUR FAVOURITE BAND/RECORD DURING YOUR FOOTBALL DAYS?

'Football's Coming Home' by The Lightning Seeds, with Frank Skinner and David Baddiel.

WHO WAS YOUR ALL-TIME FAVOURITE PLAYER?

The Dutchman Johann Cruyff. He was technically brilliant.

AFTER THE WEMBLEY FIASCO, DO YOU THINK IT WOULD BE A GOOD IDEA TO LET THE ENGLISH NATIONAL TEAM SHARE WITH THE GERMANS UNTIL WE BUILD OUR OWN STADIUM?

No, I don't think that would be a good idea. It could possibly start World War III.

CASS PENNANT MEETS

MARK 'JASPER' CHESTER

CLUB: STOKE CITY

MARK 'JASPER' CHESTER

THE MEET

I hadn't been to the Potteries since the '70s and '80s. Stoke City the team fell from grace many a year ago but that wasn't to say their fans couldn't pull a decent firm – just ask the likes of Cardiff or Forest about Stoke's firm in the '90s as they were going around the lower leagues doing the business. But, being an unfashionable team and not really deemed as newsworthy, the media left them alone. Stoke have always been known in football circles as well game. My link to their main man came surprisingly via my Portsmouth connection. As with a lot of these things, it can be unexpected – maybe a meeting on holiday or an association through the rave scene. Many of these one-time sworn enemies are now pals. The one thing I remember about Stoke was that they had a big end and always came at you near the graveyard on the walk back to the station. They have a brand new ground now, called the Britannia Stadium.

I met Jasper, their top man, in the pub opposite the graveyard – and all those past memories started to flood back. Here's what he had to say in advance of the launch of his new book, *Naughty*.

BACKGROUND

I was born in 1964. I was an unwanted child raised by my grandmother in Alsager, a nice little village just north of Stoke, in rural surroundings. I got my nickname Jasper playing football as a ten-year-old when the other team thought my mates were calling me Jasper, instead of Chester, and the name just stuck. I was taken to my first Stoke City game at the Victoria Ground when I was eight. I went with an older lad from school and saw us play Derby County. I left school at fifteen and joined the army. Later on I went with Stoke's Naughty Forty – we got the name after forty of us travelled down in three vans to Portsmouth. Being from a military background, I currently work in personal security.

WHAT'S YOUR FAVOURITE TERRACE FASHION?

For me it was about 1979 to 1981 when everyone was wearing box cords and Stan Smiths and had wedge haircuts – the early casual scene if you like.

WHAT'S THE WORST FASHION YOU'VE EVER SEEN ON THE TERRACES?

In my opinion the worst was around 1987 to 1990 when everyone was taking too much gear and getting a bit hippyish – you know, peace and love and all that shit. Too many paisley flowered shirts and baggy jeans, and the clobber that went with the rave scene. All that long hair – it was terrible.

DESCRIBE YOUR WORST FEELING AT A GAME.

I'd say the worst feeling for me was watching our lads in action in someone else's end or seats, and you're watching it come on top for them, with me being at the other end of the ground unable to help them. It's happened a few times at places like Derby, Pompey and Wrexham. Stoke always made the effort to take the fight to the opposition, so these things happen to us.

HAVE YOU EVER INCURRED ANY SERIOUS INJURIES OR BEEN BADLY BEATEN UP AT A MATCH?

The worst time we ever became unstuck was on a night out in Blackpool in about '84/'85 in the Beer Keller. There was about thirty or forty of us in there and you could tell the doormen didn't particularly want us there so they made up a story that some of our lads were getting battered by a load of Man. City outside. Half our firm ran out and the other half stayed. The ones left inside were battered by the bouncers who'd called in two van loads of reinforcements from other clubs. They battered us badly – we were well fucked. It's a trick they've used on more than one occasion. But my worst injury has to be having my bollocks kicked into my stomach in '87 by Man. City fans. Of all the injuries I've ever had in my life, that's the one that still makes me feel sick. It was the Boxing Day game. They brought thousands and came in fancy dress. We were fighting Bongo and Popeye and people like that.

HAS YOUR OWN SIDE EVER BEEN INVOLVED IN A FULL-SCALE RIOT?

Birmingham away in '92. We scored a last-minute equaliser and the Zulus came on to the pitch and tried to storm our end. We were on top of the fences defending our end, holding on with one hand and fighting with the other – it was mental. Also Cardiff at home when it was a Sunday kick-off. It went mad that day and Cardiff came up here and brought it right to us.

DESCRIBE THE BEST TAKING OF AN END YOU'VE EVER WITNESSED.

I was thirteen years old, it was 1977 and I travelled to watch us play Preston. It was only my third or fourth away game and our boys were in the Preston end. The sun was shining, and from where I was stood you could see that the lads were having a great time. They were enjoying it – fantastic. It just went on and on. From that day on I knew I wanted to be one of the chaps when I grew up.

WHICH WAS YOUR OWN TEAM'S POPULAR END?
The Bootham End at the old Victoria Ground.

WHERE DID YOU STAND OR SIT IN THE GROUND?
The Bootham Paddock.

CAN YOU RECALL A BATTLE YOU HAVE BEEN INVOLVED IN, EITHER INSIDE OR OUTSIDE A GROUND?
Grimsby because Grimsby are game as fuck and we've got 100 per cent respect for them lads down here. We had about 400 lads out. We took a double-decker up on that one and, as always, Grimsby were just picking you off, cos Stoke were arriving at different times. They were saying, 'Are you Towners? Are you Towners?' and we said, 'No, we're fucking Stoke', and it just went nuts from then on. At twenty to two we headed to the ground in a big number. Grimsby came to us again. Some of our lads were getting it with garden shears and anything they could lay their hands on. Inside the ground they were still trying to get at us and, as soon as the final whistle went, Grimsby came on to the pitch. It was 1991/2 so you were fenced in, but they were throwing coins, stones – whatever they could – over at us. The police were holding us back until the lads kicked the gates in that led on to the open terrace, where we could get on to the pitch. Thereon it just went full board, toe to toe, for about twenty minutes with the fighting carrying on out into the streets. The Old Bill just couldn't control it. It was a bad atmosphere, and is every time we've been to Grimsby, but they'd never ever come to Stoke.

CAN YOU RECALL THE BEST EVER MOB YOUR TEAM HAS PUT TOGETHER?
Bolton and Wigan. We took about 600 to Bolton in '91 for a league game and about 700 to Wigan just after Stanley Matthews died. Nice tight firms, where everyone was together.

WHO'S THE BEST RIVAL FIRM YOU'VE EVER SEEN?
That must be Birmingham as every time they've come to Stoke they've always looked impressive. I think they look at us as an easy day out.

WHO ARE YOUR BIGGEST RIVALS TEAM-WISE?
I don't really hate anyone that much but I do enjoy seeing Man. City lose.

WHO ARE YOUR BIGGEST RIVALS FAN-WISE?

Again, I don't hate anybody but I do dislike Leeds. Them and the scabs from Sherwood Forest. It all stems from the miners' strike – the fucking scum are a disgrace.

HAVE YOU EVER JOINED UP WITH ANOTHER TEAM'S FIRM?

I don't go for joining up with other teams' firms.

DID YOU EVER FOLLOW ENGLAND AND WOULD YOU PUT ENGLAND BEFORE YOUR CLUB?

I have followed England but my club comes first.

WHICH WAS THE BEST ENGLAND ROW?

Poland away in '91. It was a European Championship qualifier. Before the game we had a row with about forty East German skinheads in black flight jackets on a garage forecourt. Some local Poles that looked like miners with shit on their shoes – real scruffs – joined in and it was said some undercover police were getting stuck in. We were coming off slightly worse when a mob of Lincoln Transit elite pulled up and joined in. This swayed the balance and we got the result. There were a few injuries on both sides that day.

HAVE YOU EVER SUPPORTED OR LOOKED OUT FOR ANOTHER TEAM'S RESULTS?

No, Stoke City's my team.

NAME YOUR TOP FIVE FIRMS, IN ANY ORDER.

Middlesbrough, Tottenham, Birmingham, Cardiff and Pompey. I recently saw Boro on the move at the England v Turkey game at Sunderland, and they had some good lads out. They must have had 200 to 300 boys there, all pretty much in the mid-30s age group.

WHICH IS THE WORST GROUND YOU'VE EVER BEEN TO AND WHY?

The worst ground, or the most frightening experience I've had at a ground, was when I was fifteen and we played Arsenal at Highbury. We were at the old Clock End and Arsenal were terrifying the life out of us. I don't think a punch had been thrown, they were just taking the piss out of us, but through the eyes of a child Arsenal were very daunting.

WHICH IS THE BEST STADIUM YOU'VE BEEN TO?

My favourite ground is Maine Road as it's always a great day out for us. The game always seems to flow. You come off at Piccadilly and it's down one long road to the ground, and you always get a good row there. I enjoyed my days out at Maine Road.

WHO ARE THE FAIREST COPPERS YOU'VE COME ACROSS AT A MATCH?

Hampshire Police are fairly decent. We were playing Pompey just before Christmas and left Stafford at six o'clock in the morning. We pulled in at Reading and the transport police came on board and told us their colleagues would be waiting for us at Fratton Station, and were going to escort us straight into the ground. So when we reached Havant we all got off and got the cabs into Portsmouth. However, at Portsmouth the Old Bill were sound with us and were very fair. They were chatting with us and, because of the way they were treating us, they got respect back. They didn't Section 60 us and all that shit.

AND THE WORST OLD BILL?

That's easy – fucking West Midlands. It doesn't matter if you're playing West Brom or Villa, the West Midlands Police are the worst I've ever come across.

WHAT WOULD HAVE STOPPED YOU GETTING INVOLVED WITH THE BOYS AT MATCHES?

Incapacity. But seriously, my girlfriend's been great for me so I don't want to bring trouble too close to home.

DESCRIBE SOME OF THE METHODS AND TACTICS USED BY THE POLICE AND AUTHORITIES TO STOP FOOTBALL VIOLENCE, AND DO YOU THINK THEY WORK?

The latest tactic at Stoke is ID cards, similar to what Leeds had in the '80s, and it's crippled the lads from getting into the games. This new membership scheme not only stops supporters with convictions for football violence, it stops the normal fan with convictions of the everyday kind, so if you've been in a pub fight or not paid your TV licence, you ain't getting in. Millwall have brought in a similar scheme and their gates have suffered. Plus you can only buy a ticket for an away game if you provide your ID card and travel on the club bus, and at the other end you're put straight in the ground.

HAVE YOU EVER BEEN SICKENED BY SOMETHING YOU'VE WITNESSED AT A GAME?

Yeah, down here against Newcastle United in a Cup match. It was a night game, and from ten in the morning the Geordies were coming in vans all day. We were out by eleven and by two o'clock we was coming through when we heard a van load of Geordies had a fight in a pub and a little girl had been glassed, which we didn't believe until we got the local radio reports. Then everybody just came out for revenge. People were coming straight from work without having a wash. They'd heard the reports in their cars and the place just went berserk. I mean 90 per cent of Stoke fans would never hit a shirt fan, but this day all of Stoke, including our own shirters, turned on anything that wasn't either child, female or too elderly to fight. Anything that looked game Stoke attacked that night. Some of it was horrendous.

WHAT'S YOUR FAVOURITE FOOTBALL SONG OR CHANT AND WHICH IS THE WORST YOU CAN RECALL HEARING FROM ANOTHER TEAM?

My favourite football song is 'We are the Potters, the Midlands we rule'. It's from the '70s and reminds me of being a kid. The daftest song has to be 'Blue Moon', sung by the Man. City fans. It's not offensive, but what the fuck is that all about?

WHAT WAS YOUR FAVOURITE BAND/RECORD DURING YOUR FOOTBALL DAYS?

My favourite band is the Eagles, but my favourite song from football is the UK Subs and 'Stranglehold'.

WHO WAS YOUR ALL-TIME FAVOURITE PLAYER?

Mickey Thomas – he's a legend.

WHERE DO YOU THINK THE NEW ENGLISH NATIONAL STADIUM SHOULD BE BUILT AND WHAT ARE YOUR THOUGHTS REGARDING THE WEMBLEY FIASCO?

As far as I'm concerned Wembley's the home of English football, but the only drawback is the price of beer in London.

MARTIN KING MEETS

RICHARD GREY
CLUB: DERBY COUNTY

RICHARD GREY

THE MEET

I'd heard about Richard through my mate John King (author of *The Football Factory*) during their days of going to England games together. I spoke to Richard a few times on the phone and one time when he was watching Derby's reserves with a group of school kids he'd taken along to the game. He's an interesting bloke, to say the least. Go on, Richard, get it off your chest. Tell us all about your days as a young hooligan.

BACKGROUND

I was born in Wandsworth, south London, in May 1961. We moved to Derby in 1970 when I was nine years old. This was in the heyday of the Brian Clough era and Derby County had just finished fourth in the old First Division in their first season back in the top flight. Having been brought up with Rugby Union in Cornwall for the previous four years, I was consumed by the football fervour that was sweeping Derby at the time. I soon decided that I wanted to go to a football match. My mother then got interested and started taking me. We became season-ticket holders and went on to win the League Championship in 1971/2. I relinquished my ticket when joining the Merchant Navy in 1977.

I travelled round the world three times in the couple of years I was in the Navy before getting into trouble and leaving in time for the 1979/80 relegation season. I then spent ten years going through a variety of jobs, many of which I did not stick at for more than six months at a time. I became a semi-professional horse-racing punter by the mid '80s and gave up full-time work to go full-time on the race course for a year. I made enough money to retrain and embark on a new career in the health and sports industries. I largely gave up football and this led to the first meaningful job of my life as I spent eight happy years as a therapist at a private health clinic in Suffolk.

The relaxed lifestyle allowed me to pursue a successful career as a marathon runner, which took me all over Europe. I then made the monumental decision to advance my career further by going into higher education to study Sports Science at Loughborough. This brought me back to Derby and postgraduate studies kept me at university for five years. I supported myself by freelancing in health and sport. I now take care of a caseload of difficult children in Educational Welfare and Behavioural Management.

As far as I know, Derby has had a firm of potential hooligans since the 1960s. It was certainly small then, numbering about a dozen really hard cases that were capable of pretty well anything. They were still around throughout the 1970s and, with the explosion in widespread football hooliganism, numbers involved reached an all-time peak.

Derby did not have a name for their firm until 1980. Those youngsters brought up with the violence of the '70s were now instigating their own acts of hooliganism and got together after Derby's relegation season of 1979/80 to organise vans to away matches. On one such van to Chelsea in 1980/1 the occupants, myself included, came up with the name of the Derby Lunatic Fringe (better known by all as the DLF). The name was a bit of a joke at the time and I spent more time with an older crew. They decided to call themselves the Pot-Bellied Lunatic Army (PBLA) and in no time at all both crews had their own song and business cards were printed.

WHAT'S YOUR FAVOURITE TERRACE FASHION?

I was never one for football fashions. I started off wearing a donkey jacket because they did not get damaged in fights. West Ham wore the same at the time and then green bomber jackets from Flip's in London caught on, but not with me. I used to wear a sheepskin a lot in the winter, but they are damned difficult to fight in and I've ripped off so many sleeves when fists have been flying. I was into the new wave and futurist scene that followed the punk era, and I became anti-fashion when everybody was chasing designer labels.

WHAT'S THE WORST FASHION YOU'VE EVER SEEN ON THE TERRACES?

The earliest football fashion I can remember was the *Clockwork Orange* influence on Leeds fans in the early 1970s. They used to paint their faces like Alice Cooper, wear white overalls and paint their Docs silver – moon boots they were called. I have had so many coats, trousers, even shoes, wrecked in fights over the years that I tend to dress so as not to draw attention to myself. The Burberry Brigade, as I call them, seem to have been around for so long as to be dated. I think they look like Muppets and the latest young followers might as well have 'Learner Thug' tattooed across their foreheads. Even the police hone in on these idiots.

DESCRIBE YOUR WORST FEELING AT A GAME.

When returning from Chelsea v Derby. I walked into 200 Cockney Reds at Charing Cross station as they were returning from QPR v Man. United. I got caught in the middle of fifty Millwall taking on 9,000 Tottenham behind the goal at Charlton v Tottenham and on another day 500 Crystal Palace spent all afternoon fighting Tottenham behind one of the goals at Selhurst Park in a crowd of 40,000.

But the worst feeling for me was standing on my own in the Clock End at Arsenal and watching Derby win 3–1 in 1977. Derby didn't take many to London in those days and the hundreds they had were in the seats down one side. I had 200 Arsenal behind me and couldn't celebrate for fear of a hiding. It was so cold my arms went numb and I could do nothing about it. I had the satisfaction of returning the following season while my ship was docked in Tilbury and joining a crowd of 52,000. I saw Arsenal beat the new champions, Nottingham Forest, and give their following of only 200 a hiding in the Clock End. There was very little crowd segregation at London grounds in those days, and certainly Arsenal, Charlton, Tottenham and West Ham had none.

HAVE YOU EVER INCURRED ANY SERIOUS INJURIES OR BEEN BADLY BEATEN UP AT A MATCH?

I've been quite lucky in and around football grounds, but my worst injury followed the FA Cup Fourth Round match at Coventry in January 1998. The DLF took about sisty good lads to Coventry and the whole town turned out for us. Coventry isn't usually that good, but they made an effort and got at least 200 to meet us on the main road near the ground after the match. A free-for-all followed and we were doing great, except their numbers were growing all the time. To be honest, I don't think we could have held our ground much longer. I had already been hit by a flying bottle before the police arrived to break up the fight. That was the end of that particular fight and we returned to Derby.

I had been drinking late and needed to call at a cashpoint in Derby on the way home. It was 12.30 a.m. and I was just getting some money out when I was hit by another bottle. That was enough for me! I turned to see four geezers walking away from me, so I pursued and confronted them. I asked if they had thrown a bottle at me, which they didn't like, and a fight ensued. I had knocked two of them out and was toying with the other two when I was kicked in the back of the leg. I went down on one knee and took a punch in the face. I got up and found another four behind me. There had been eight in all and I remember getting dropped again and somebody having hold of my arm. I could not defend myself properly and could clearly see the boot coming towards my face that was to knock me out. I remember saying, 'Not in the face!' at the time, but then everything went blank. I woke up in hospital an hour and a half later unable to open my eyes and with tubes coming out of practically every orifice. I was told I'd been in an accident and was asked if I could remember what had happened. I said there was a fight, but apparently I'd been found by a taxi driver who had reported finding 'a man's body lying in a pool of blood in the middle of the road'. It was another day and a half before I could open my eyes and I was detained in hospital for five nights.

I had suffered a fractured optical socket, fractured cheekbone, broken nose, dislocated jaw, three broken teeth, retinal damage and haemorrhaging to both eyes, and somehow managed to fracture both my thumbs in the melee. I'd lost a sleeve off my sheepskin, which was soaked in blood along with everything else but my socks. Even my pants were soaked in blood and I was checked for stab wounds before the police removed all my clothes for forensic examination.

I later needed root-canal surgery and crowns at the dentist, and remained an out-patient at the maxillofacial clinic for head injuries for three months and at the eye clinic for eight months. I had an aversion to artificial light while in hospital and had to be kept in a darkened ward on my own. For up to six months my eyes couldn't track movement, which was frightening when crossing the road. I could not tell if the cars were parked or coming towards me. At university I remember playing basketball and the ball just froze suspended in mid-air. It took a long time to get my confidence back.

HAS YOUR OWN SIDE EVER BEEN INVOLVED IN A FULL-SCALE RIOT?

I think the biggest riots Derby fans have been involved in were at England matches. The DLF were represented at all the recent large-scale riots, such as Marseilles in 1998 and Charleroi in 2000. The biggest riot for me was in Copenhagen against Denmark in September 1982. It was a European Championship qualifier and the first match after the World Cup finals in Spain. Derby took a game mob of 23 mainly PBLA types. We went to the Under-21 international the night before and one of my mates, nicknamed Animal, got nicked for robbing the hotdog stall. He missed all the fun that followed the next day at the full international. England took about 2,000, and bars and jewellers were being smashed up all day.

My fun really got under way inside the ground. Most of the England fans were sitting in the lower-tier seats down one side, but there were large numbers standing in both ends. I was among them and just before half-time another England fan told me that some Danish wanker was trying to set fire to the red ensign I had draped across my back. I followed this geezer down the back of the stand at half-time and waited for my moment. He was already picking a fight with a couple of England fans, who didn't really want to get involved. I moved in and smacked the fucker a few times until the police baton-charged me to the ground. I did not mind! It was only to be expected, but I then felt myself being dragged away, face down, by the feet. I'd been dragged into the toilets by Danish fans. Much to my surprise they then picked me up, brushed me down and let me go without so much as a fight. Fair play or what! The best was yet to follow outside the ground after the match. Large England mobs met at each end of the ground. Derby's 23 was one of the bigger crews and led their particular England mob. We did the business on anyone prepared to stand and those we put down were finished off by West Ham's Under-5s (teenagers supposed to be under 5 feet tall) following on behind.

I was having one particularly good exchange with one geezer, got the better of him and was finishing him off with classic boxing precision as he slowly collapsed over the ropes (a fence). In the seconds before he went, I could see another bloke running across the road towards me, waving a windmill of a punch in my direction. I knew it was coming my way, but wanted to finish what I was doing first. Just as I completed my mission and turned to face my pursuer, I was met by a haymaker of a right hand that popped my left eyebrow wide open. I actually saw a jet of my blood squirt straight into his face. As I continued turning, I was in the perfect position to follow through with a right hook. My fist landed right in his mouth and he immediately sank to the floor in a heap.

My knuckles were ripped open and I'm sure he must have lost some teeth, but didn't wait to find out as the Under-5s finished off the remains like a shark-feeding frenzy. There were only two punches thrown, but two of the best I've encountered in such a brief exchange.

DESCRIBE THE BEST TAKING OF AN END YOU'VE EVER WITNESSED.

This was the ultimate test of a firm in the days before segregation and could be done on a large scale in the '60s and '70s. It became increasingly more difficult to get large numbers unnoticed by the police through the turnstiles in the '80s. Derby attempted quite a few small-scale covert operations during the '80s, but the police always got you out before it was conclusive one way or the other.

When Derby were first promoted to the top-flight First Division in 1969 they were taking silly numbers everywhere. Brian Clough had gripped Derby with football fever and I've heard stories of 15,000 going to Sheffield Wednesday and over 10,000 going to Newcastle. They may not all have got in the same end, but, when I went to Coventry for my first away match in the FA Cup Fourth Round in January 1974, Derby took 17,000 in a crowd of 40,000. We filled the old open Kop End and had two-thirds of the terrace at the other end. Coventry were trapped in between two very large groups of Derby either side of them and it could be called a pretty comprehensive double-end taking.

WHICH WAS YOUR OWN TEAM'S POPULAR END?

At the Baseball Ground Derby used to frequent the Vulcan End of the Pop Side – this was the side terrace of the Ley Stand, built in 1970. Visitors had the other half, called the Colombo End. A large number of Derby fans preferred being behind the goal. It gave you the opportunity of clashing with the away fans in the corner and meeting them outside as they only had one exit right next to that used by the Ossie Enders. When old enough I joined the Ossie End and most of the real thugs were found in there. About 4,000 combatant lads occupied the Pop Side and about 3,000 were in the Ossie End.

WHERE DID YOU STAND OR SIT IN THE GROUND?

Having departed the Baseball Ground I do have fond memories of everywhere I stood or sat in that ground. I suppose the Ossie End must be my favourite end just for the nostalgic memories. The ground is due to be sold and demolished for development of the site quite soon and I recently attended what will go down in history as the last ever couple of matches to take place at the old ground. The fact wasn't made too public because of crowd-safety fears if thousands turned up. I took groups of children and some school-age students on foreign exchanges to see Derby Under-19s beat first Leeds 4–0 and then Newcastle 6–0 in the last two matches at the Baseball Ground. I'm sure some stars of the future will come out of those matches.

CAN YOU RECALL A BATTLE YOU HAVE BEEN INVOLVED IN, EITHER INSIDE OR OUTSIDE A GROUND?

In the early '70s practically every other home match was concluded with a pitch invasion. The biggest were against Chelsea in 1973 and Man. United in 1976, both spilling on to the streets outside. They were the closest Derby ever came to being taken on their own ground. I was too young to play a major role, but remember them well. Fans were even fighting in the players' tunnel against Chelsea and after Man. United the *Sunday Express* back-page headline suggested that 'Derby may fence them in'. The worst thing about it was that the coppers lined the front of the Pop Side to prevent them from getting on to the pitch, only to allow the full weight of Man. United's enclosure (7,000) to meet all the Ossie End (3,000) head-on. The Ossie Enders were fighting on the back foot until the police line broke and the Pop Siders could also get on to the pitch.

Derby County had experimented with their crowd control by

giving away fans the Ossie End terrace, which didn't go down well with the locals. The first match it was returned to Derby fans was against Leeds and the club made the unprecedented error of giving Leeds the Ossie middle- and upper-tier seats. It was great having the Ossie End back, but we were bombarded by seats being ripped out and thrown from the middle and upper tiers behind. We were ducking seats for most of what was an exciting 3–3 draw. A mob of Leeds got done by our Rowditch pub crew in the Ley Stand seats before the excitement on the pitch spread to those on the Ossie End terrace. The Rowditch were older than the DLF who were on the Ossie End terrace with me.

Towards the end of the match the DLF and myself climbed into the front of the middle-tier seats and started fighting with anyone that wanted it. Leeds soon started to back off as more climbed into the stand and we all steamed in. I remember one Leeds fan throwing a seat at Crossy, of DLF fame, and myself as we approached down a row of seats. Crossy caught the seat, walked up to the bloke who threw it and smashed him over the head with it. After that the whole lot of them ran out of the back of the stand with the match still in progress. I counted sixteen major fights that day and I was fortunate to have been involved in thirteen of them.

In the 1983 FA Cup home teams were obliged by the FA to give a third of their ground capacity to their visitors, and Chelsea were given the whole of the Ossie End. In typical copycat fashion Chelsea felt duty-bound to outdo Leeds and also had a go at ripping out the seats. Not content with that, they also ripped out the plumbing in the toilets after the match. The real trouble started after the match. There must have been a police cock-up as Chelsea were allowed to turn left out of their end of the ground, which meant they walked straight into Derby's mob assembling in Shaftesbury Street. The sheer weight of numbers involved meant that those at the front couldn't go backwards or forwards. There were two police horses trying to keep the mobs apart, but everyone around them was just piling in. You were plain unlucky if a horse got in your way. The Rowditch crew were trapped inside the ground and were fighting Chelsea off with the wooden barriers that lock the main exits shut. You needed to be fit to keep on fighting because it went on for ages with no other way through the crowd.

Eventually I decided a clever ploy would be to double-back from the front line, take the first right-hand turning, then the next right on to Reeves Road and then right again to attack Chelsea from behind. Having taken no more than twenty with me, I found at least as many Chelsea with the same idea coming the other way towards us on Reeves Road. The dark backstreets around the Baseball Ground must have been intimidating to visitors, but on this occasion I felt very nervous myself about whether or not we were going to get through this scrap in one piece. There were no police on Reeves Road and the fight became as inconclusive as the main fight, as more numbers came running round the corner to see what all the noise was about.

As the fighting fragmented on the way into the city centre we clearly got the upper hand. We chased one vanload from the Home Counties on foot all the way to their van. I dropped one of them on the way and he feigned unconsciousness in the hope we would go straight on and leave him. Normally I would have done, but I wasn't happy about the vandalism to our seats again. He was face down so I stood over him and paused until he lifted his head. This isn't really my style, but I took a big swing and booted him straight in the face saying, 'Don't you ever come to Derby and rip our seats out again.' We went on after the van, found it and giving them no time to board they had no alternative but to run straight past it. We chased them right across the city centre, arming ourselves with broomsticks snatched from outside a hardware store as we passed. By now the police were on to us and they managed to split us up. Reduced to small groups of roughly threes left us ineffective and Chelsea were able to regroup and get back to their van. We were then on the run from the Old Bill for the rest of the proceedings. We were so knackered from our exertions that night that some of the Rowditch didn't make our piss-up to celebrate our Cup victory and good fight.

CAN YOU RECALL THE BEST EVER MOB YOUR TEAM HAS PUT TOGETHER?

Undoubtedly the DLF were in their heyday throughout the '80s. There were older crews and harder individuals in the early days, but the DLF had the numbers when it mattered most. They often took on the bigger firms when the odds were stacked against them. They were game and looked for trouble everywhere over the years.

To my mind the best single firm Derby ever got together was for the England v Holland friendly at Wembley in 1988. We'd heard that the Dutch were coming to do the business and every club firm in England was, or should have been, represented in London. We heard that West Ham even went to Harwich to meet the Dutch, but they didn't come. Very few of our Derby firm even bothered to get tickets for the match. That wasn't what we were there for and I didn't bother myself. I think the Dutch brought about 5,000 on coaches and planes in the end and just watched the match. They completely bottled it.

The day had the makings of becoming a complete non-event, but I took the view that this was an opportunity too good to be missed.

Every firm in the country was in London at the same time and what were we going to do about it? Fuck Holland, we weren't going to get an opportunity for domestic violence on this scale, and all at one time, again!

Derby had about 200 of their best lads from all their crews. The regular England mob were joined by the DLF England's representatives and the Rowditch came for the day out. I cannot think of a better man-for-man big Derby mob assembled outside Derby. I would have pitched them against anybody. We spent ages drinking in the Chandos on Trafalgar Square and nobody else would come anywhere near the pub. I know Millwall and West Ham were across the Square, but they wouldn't come over and did not like our mob-handed numbers. Inevitably, as the beer flowed, the fights started.

On the road towards Charing Cross station about fifteen lads approached me and asked who we were. I said, 'Derby. Who are you?' They said, 'Leicester!' I said, 'I fucking hate Leicester' and steamed in. I remember Crossy calling over, 'Rich, what you doing?!' I didn't answer. I was enjoying myself.

Sporting a black eye, I went off with a couple of mates down Villiers Street and then back up to Trafalgar Square, St Martin's Lane and then Soho looking for the crack. We had skirmishes with small groups of West Ham and then Forest at the bottom of St Martin's Lane, and then with Hull in Soho. When I rejoined our firm, I found out they'd had major rucks on the tube with West Ham, Forest and Bristol City among others.

WHO'S THE BEST RIVAL FIRM YOU'VE EVER SEEN?

Possibly the best single firm I've seen come to Derby was Chelsea in September 1982 when they were officially banned. They still brought about 500 and all were intent on finding trouble. There had been so much recent trouble that Derby's chairman at the time, snooker supremo Mike Watterson, advised all real football fans to boycott the match in an interview he gave to the tabloid press on the morning of the match. As a consequence only thugs turned up for the Wednesday night Second Division fixture. The gate was only 8,500 and I'd spent all day at work seething at the pre-match tabloid coverage.

I got in a car straight after work and we drove round looking for Chelsea's mob. We knew they'd come and I quickly found them at the Florence Nightingale pub on London Road. Although near the train station, it's a pub where you'd never expect to find visitors. This was in the days before mobile phones, and yet so many of their mob had found the pub that they were spilling on to the street. They all looked rough and ready, as though they'd just come straight from building sites. Man-for-man they looked old enough and hard enough to better your average mob of teenage vandals that I'd sometimes seen from Chelsea.

WHO ARE YOUR BIGGEST RIVALS TEAM-WISE?

Even as a young kid, I've always hated every other team in the Midlands. I have grown up to hate Leeds and Man. United at least as much. In the early '70s Derby's arch rivals were Leeds, largely fuelled by Brian Clough's personal and very public dislike for their reputation. This spilled over into violence on and off the pitch between players and fans alike. Who can forget Frannie Lee and Norman Hunter in 1975? I hate Man. United with a passion and cannot even bring myself to support them in European competition. If I can bear to watch at all, I'll always support their opposition. Man. United are run as a business and their players are commodities. I can't get excited about watching England any more because of the arrogance of their representatives in the team.

Local rivalry was almost non-existent as both Forest and Leicester were struggling in the First Division in the early '70s and posed little threat to Derby. My personal hate for Leicester grew from the '80s and far exceeds any feelings I may have about Forest. Most Derby fans hate both as a matter of duty, without understanding the lack of history between the clubs.

WHO ARE YOUR BIGGEST RIVALS FAN-WISE?

Much the same as hated teams, but for different reasons! I particularly hate Leicester as I was arrested against them for three successive seasons in '82, '83 and '84. Arrest would have been less likely had they stood, but they preferred to run off. I never rated them and it irks me when people give them any respect. In the mid-'80s their mob grew and they got a reputation for blades and playing dirty.

We took a mob of 200 there for a night match that coincided with the inner-city riots of 1985 and were met by 300 of them in the city centre before the match. Some naive suckers among our mob were taken by surprise and ran, and we were split not even in half as twenty of our best lads were stranded at the front on our own. Leicester went after the runners and we were probably saved from a hiding. After the match the Highfields Estate used the diversion as an opportunity to bring out their petrol bombs and it was 12.30 a.m. before the police could get us off the streets and out of Leicester.

Our skirmishes with Leeds and Man. United have been among the biggest and most frequent over the last 35 years, and their contempt for each other is as rabid as mine is for them both. In addition to my further contempt for Midlanders I should add Scousers, both Liverpool and Everton – but who wouldn't?!

HAVE YOU EVER JOINED UP WITH ANOTHER TEAM'S FIRM?

Over the years I've joined up with Crystal Palace, West Ham, Millwall, Tottenham and Arsenal. I would have been supporting them as second teams at the time when the crack would've found me rather than the other way around. I once went in against Arsenal while at Tottenham, the night the new East Stand was opened to replace the Shelf. There'd been a couple of pitch invasions during the match and at the end Tottenham chased Arsenal off the pitch right into the terrace I was standing in. I couldn't back off, so chinned the first one that came near me. About fifteen Tottenham blacks behind me then piled in. I bumped into the same crowd again outside on the High Road. They recognised me, and came over. I had some chips by then and stuffed them into the first geezer's face. Tottenham, on the other side of the road, saw this and piled in yet again.

DID YOU EVER FOLLOW ENGLAND AND WOULD YOU PUT ENGLAND BEFORE YOUR CLUB?

I went to every England match home and away, except when disposed at Her Majesty's pleasure from 1981 to 1986. I have gone to selected matches since then, but not recently. I've always put club before country then and now. I resent much about the modern international game today and the adverse effect the media overkill of the European Champions League and the Premier League has on sport development and the wealth of the clubs in lower divisions. Too many greedy and crooked businessmen, agents and players have taken pot loads of money out of the game and put nothing back into it. Ultimately football will consume itself and the decline has been rapidly picking up momentum in the last few years. The banks will eventually put a stop to it or take over the clubs themselves. England weren't a corporate commodity when I supported them and now they're yet another brand name.

WHICH WAS THE BEST ENGLAND ROW?

There have been many, but I'll always have fond memories of the European Championship qualifier in Greece in 1982. After riots involving England fans in Basle, Oslo, the 1982 World Cup in Spain and then the first European qualifier against Denmark in Copenhagen in September 1982, the authorities were supposedly prepared for us in Greece in November. They'd already arranged the fixture to take place in Salonika because the police there were more used to dealing with large-scale crowd control. At the time Aris Salonika were considered the Man. United of Greek football and their ground held 44,000. In Athens, Panathinaikos were more like the Millwall or West Ham of Greek football. Panathinaikos ground held 25,000 and their lads over there told me they had 25,000 hooligans. Having seen them in action I can believe it, and the police wouldn't have coped at the Olympic Stadium.

Phil, a West Ham fan that was with us, had been born to an English serviceman based on the island of Paphos and spoke fluent Greek. We were to find this useful in many respects. The Greeks were hyped up for the match by their own TV news coverage showing recent England riots and telling them what we were going to do to them. They were expecting the return of Hannibal or Ghengis Khan, and our hotelier asked if we were the 'English hooligans'. Although the Greeks wanted to have a go, they gave us plenty of respect. Remember, this was just after the Falklands War and I just happened to be travelling in an old army combat jacket. You couldn't buy such things in Greece and they told me they thought I was in the Army. They were also cautious of Phil's size as he kept flexing his biceps at them. After our welcome the night before I was ready for anything, but quite simply we had to fight our way into the ground. I have never seen anything like it! It was too outrageous to even be frightening!

Having eventually got through the turnstile we stood in awe watching these idiots swinging off the ledge above the tunnel we had to walk through to get to the terrace. Some minutes passed before the police could calm the situation sufficiently for us to attempt to get on to the terrace. Inevitably blows were exchanged but we all made it, only to be bombarded by fireworks the moment we got on to the terrace. The police tried to make a feeble excuse for an away enclosure with a piece of tape. Somebody counted 129 England fans inside the pen. The bombardment never ceased and seemed to erupt all the more every time further England fans arrived and battled their way through the tunnel. Some fans were hit by fireworks. When one exploded right through the collar of a West Ham motorcyclist's jacket we all decided to rear up ourselves.

We didn't get very far before the police decided the best alternative was to get us out of the pen and lead us round the pitch to where the England Under-21s were sitting behind the England bench. We actually sat with the players. It was clear they'd been told not to speak to us because I asked John Barnes and Gary Bailey how the Under-21s had done the night before and the best John Barnes could manage was to mouth the score to me.

The senior squad went on to win their match 3–0 and all remained quiet until we attempted to leave the ground at full-time. The trouble we had entering the ground erupted again and it took us an hour and a half to fight our way out of the ground. Every time we made an attempt at walking away from the ground, we were ambushed from all sides and were fought back to where we had started. The police were standing about watching this happen and didn't seem to mind if we got picked off one at a time, but they weren't happy when we all piled in mob-handed to sort the bastards out. They eventually held us back and made us get on a bus they'd provided for us to get back into town.

HAVE YOU EVER SUPPORTED OR LOOKED OUT FOR ANOTHER TEAM'S RESULTS?

As a kid I remember asking my mum exactly where I was born in London so I could pinpoint the location to the nearest football club. It was actually in the middle of a triangle between Crystal Palace, Fulham and Millwall. Looking for a pet second team I chose Crystal Palace and had a soft spot for all London teams except Chelsea. Although many London firms had reputations, I thought Chelsea's reputation was spoiled by teenage vandals.

My family originate from east London and I was the first born south of the river. My grandfather was an avid West Ham fan and went to the first Wembley FA Cup Final against Bolton in 1923. While at the National Sea Training College in Gravesend I started supporting Crystal Palace, West Ham, Millwall, Tottenham and Arsenal during my Saturdays off in London. This continued when I was on ships berthed in Tilbury. When I came back to Derby I would support those teams if they played at Forest or Notts County on mid-week nights.

When I moved to Suffolk in 1989 I found it difficult to get passionate about Ipswich. I started by occasionally supporting those same London teams either in London, or if they visited Ipswich or Norwich. As I lived there for eight years I owed it to the area to show some loyalty and eventually got quite into supporting Ipswich and Norwich against teams I already hated. I could get quite motivated by that and inevitably I still wish these teams every success. My relationship with these fans will always depend on whether our association is business or pleasure. I've always made this clear to England fans I may have befriended on my past travels – just so there are no embarrassing situations in future mob conflicts.

NAME YOUR TOP FIVE FIRMS, IN ANY ORDER.

Man-for-man I'd have to say Millwall and West Ham in the '70s and '80s, possibly even earlier, but I wasn't around London grounds to comment on the '60s. For sheer numbers Man. United could swamp most firms in the '70s and could do a lot of damage. They had the potential to take ends at away grounds, but for the most part it was the Cockney firms that had the end-taking culture – or, to put it another way, the balls! Chelsea certainly had that and were the predominant force in the England-away crews of the '70s and '80s. They were such frequent visitors in the 'wrong' enclosure at away grounds that we used to look for them at Derby. Even better than that was the cunning way the Cockneys, especially Chelsea, could slip through police roadblocks en masse and cause havoc among home fans before anybody had sussed them. This deserves the greatest respect.

Tottenham also deserve a mention. It's a rough part of London and Derby has had some extremely violent recent history with them. It started harmless enough, with firms getting done in pubs, but then got out of hand with stabbings and even sword fights taking place on non-match days. I think all of London knows what I'm talking about! I think it was in 2000 when we last tried to get a mob down Tottenham High Road. The police intelligence knew everything and an overwhelming presence at Scratchwood Services meant our coach

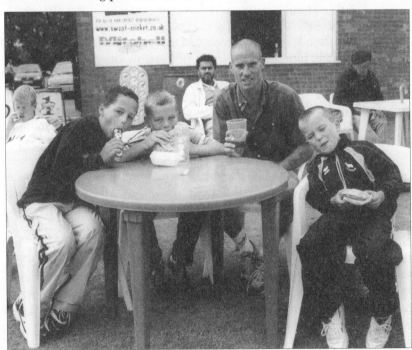

went no further. Everybody was searched and questioned. Some of us legged it, but I was the only one that made the match. You should have seen the look of surprise on the face of Derby's police intelligence officer when he saw me leaving a pub near the ground!

I wouldn't like to put any of these firms in a particular order and don't intend to give any respect to the likes of Leeds, Stoke, Birmingham and Wolves, who have had their moments over the last 30 years.

WHICH IS THE WORST GROUND YOU'VE EVER BEEN TO AND WHY?

This is easy, as I've only just been there for the first time. The Bescot Stadium, Walsall, reminded me of some of the worst facilities I came across in the old Second and Third Divisions in the 1980s. I suffered the ignominy of paddling in my own piss in the toilets for the first time since Oakwell, Barnsley, in the mid 1980s. There are no pubs for half a mile around the Bescot Stadium and there's no bar in the visitors' end. There is one small kiosk window to place your bets and another to get your pies and drinks. I arrived at the ground an hour before the kick-off and circled the outside for something to do. I then had little alternative but to enter 35 minutes before kick-off. There was already a queue twenty yards long simply for the refreshment kiosk. The toilets were flooded and I could think of better places to spend a Saturday afternoon.

WHICH IS THE BEST STADIUM YOU'VE BEEN TO?

My European travels have taken me to Milan and I found the entire sports complex of the San Siro most impressive. There is a horse-racing course and a cycling velodrome beside the football stadium shared by AC and Inter Milan. The spiralling corkscrew appearance of the stadium as you approach is most striking. Unfortunately, further ground developments for the World Cup in 1990 has meant the close proximity of the towering stands to the pitch has been slowly killing the grass.

WHO ARE THE FAIREST COPPERS YOU'VE COME ACROSS AT A MATCH?

Fresh in my mind is my only arrest this season (2002/3) at Preston, after only ten minutes at Preston's Deepdale. It was still 0–0, but I went for a walk around the stand and shouldered a police intelligence cameraman down three rows of seats (camera and tripod included) and then a steward down a flight of stairs for getting in my way. I was out of order really, but there was nowhere to sit in the side of the stand my mates and I had entered. I suppose I should have legged it out of the ground, but I just found somewhere to sit until about ten coppers came to remove me. They asked me to come down the back of the stand, which I did asking on the way for Nick, a good mate of mine, to come with me (as a witness). They explained what they believed to have happened and I gave my version, which suggested there was no intent. In the meantime I was arrested pending further enquiries. I was taken to Preston police station, but released just after 5.30 p.m. The police accepted what I had said and no charges were pressed.

AND THE WORST OLD BILL?

Stoke and West Ham were two of the roughest places to visit in the '70s and yet they had some of the least tolerant police forces. You could be nicked at both for swearing inside the ground, which is more common elsewhere today. In the early '80s South Yorkshire and the West Midlands forces had easily the worst reputations in law enforcement generally.

South Yorkshire Police seemed to incite more trouble than they prevented and failed to cope with thousands of Scouse gatecrashers that ultimately were responsible for the Hillsborough tragedy in 1989.

WHAT WOULD HAVE STOPPED YOU GETTING INVOLVED WITH THE BOYS AT MATCHES?

Staying in Cornwall at the age of nine would certainly have led to an interest, if not a career, in Rugby Union – a national sport in Cornwall. My mother was the matron of a girls' remand home and I lived in with her. Camborne Rugby Club used to play at the bottom of our grounds and I used to run up and down the touchline with the linesman. Redruth also played nearby, but on the other side of town. I quickly became a football fanatic when I moved to Derby and Brian Clough was solely responsible for the resurgence of Derby County and football passion in the area. Even in my hooligan days, no law would have prevented my participation.

DESCRIBE SOME OF THE METHODS AND TACTICS USED BY THE POLICE AND AUTHORITIES TO STOP FOOTBALL VIOLENCE, AND DO YOU THINK THEY WORK?

I think the turning point for thugs inside the grounds was the introduction of all-seater stadiums and in particular numbered seating that prevents you from moving around or sitting with your mates. Improved police intelligence shared between forces on the movements of known hooligans has made escape from arrest outside of the ground far less likely, even if the police are not around when the offence is committed. It's the ultimate downer getting pulled after the event when you think you've got a result. The police can even identify who is attending matches by sharing club information on ticket sales. Segregation inside grounds had an effect, but only created a new challenge for determined thugs to overcome, and fences only had a limited success even before the Hillsborough tragedy led to their removal. CCTV inside and outside of grounds has been more effective as a deterrent.

HAVE YOU EVER BEEN SICKENED BY SOMETHING YOU'VE WITNESSED AT A GAME?

We had played Man. City and we had a mob out expecting them to reciprocate. I believe they did before the match, but the police kept us apart and we never even saw them. After the match we had lads in a number of pubs between Pride Park and the city centre. I was in Strutt's when we got a call that there were some suspects in the Colosseum, which was the next pub from us. About half a dozen of us went to check it out and there were about fifteen blokes in there, some playing pool and others at the bar. We stood next to them at the bar as we ordered our drinks. They had southern accents and were certainly not Man. City fans. They seemed all right and their conversation was typically about sex and the like, so I took no further notice of them. Soon afterwards more of our less easily satisfied crew came into the bar and straight away one of them called out, 'Who's City in here?' I couldn't believe it. Oh no, I thought.

Everybody looked round and those just entering the bar immediately started on the pool players. Bearing in mind they were already tooled up with pool cues, and many had glasses in their hands, the carnage that followed was inevitable. A glass was thrown at the pool players and one of them was dropped. They were pinned into the recess that accommodated the pool tables and had nowhere to go. I've never been a fan of pub fights because of the tendency people have to grab the nearest bottle or chair. These pool players and their mates were cornered with no alternative but to fight their way out of it. It was also a fight that never should have happened. I was determined not to get involved and started to step away from the flying debris. I was manoeuvring myself along the bar with my own pint still in hand. The pool players were pushing their assailants back towards me so the missiles were getting closer. I decided to step outside and inevitably the fight followed me out into the tabled patio. The police will be here any minute, I thought, and continued to move away. The whole incident was out of order. I could hear a police siren in the distance, but that could've been going anywhere. I still couldn't see any police coming.

I looked back at the pub to see the Derby lads spilling out into the patio after me. The pool players followed brandishing their pool cues above their heads. I saw one Derby lad, whom I later found to be known as Scotty, squaring up at the front. He took one pool cue on the front of his head and began to fall backwards. He stopped about another three blows from pool cues on his way down to the floor. I didn't know it at the time, but he also hit his head on the edge of one of the tables. He may also have hit his head on the floor and was clearly unconscious before hitting the ground. He would've been finished off without drastic intervention.

There were still no police in sight so I threw my now empty pint glass into the middle of Scotty's attackers and charged into them myself with all guns blazing. I was quickly able to fight them away from him, sufficiently far enough to give emergency first aid. Two other lads steamed in with me and we tried to lift Scotty from the scene. I had hold of him from under his arms and the other two had a leg each. We had great difficulty moving him because the tables were too close together and were bolted to the ground. In trying I managed to pull his coat over his head, which didn't help, so we put him back down. He was beginning to gurgle blood out of his mouth, so I put him in the recovery position and put two fingers into his mouth to make sure he had a clear airway. Although seemingly unconscious, he then bit down on my fingers and wouldn't release his jaw from me. At this point the pool cues came back at us and I was caught in a defenceless position with my right hand stuck in Scotty's mouth. The cues were on that side of me, so I had to reach across with my left hand to defend myself. I thought this was curtains for me, because I couldn't protect my head. I shouted out, 'No, not now – stop, please stop.'

I still had two helpers at my side and a combination of their efforts, good luck and the arrival of Derby's police intelligence officer wielding his riot stick held them at bay. The officer forced them back into the pub doorway, taking a few kicks himself. This allowed me time to safely keep Scotty stable, but I still couldn't get my fingers out of his mouth until the ambulance arrived.

As more police arrived all the pool players were arrested and a couple from Derby for starting it. However, the police were more concerned with Scotty's injuries and their questioning was based around his assault. Scotty spent the night at Derbyshire Royal Infirmary, but the extent of his neurological injuries meant he was transferred to a specialist unit in Birmingham and remained there for over six weeks. He was in a coma for much of the time and would have been kept in hospital longer but for discharging himself. I didn't know him before and haven't seen him since, but those that do know him have said he's not the same person now and he recalls little of the incident. We later found out that the party of pool players were actually a stag night from Southend. They did all right for themselves under the circumstances, but not all of us joined in and most of us now accept that it was a fight that never should have happened.

WHAT'S YOUR FAVOURITE FOOTBALL SONG OR CHANT AND WHICH IS THE WORST YOU CAN RECALL HEARING FROM ANOTHER TEAM?

In the good old days you couldn't beat 'You'll Never Walk Alone' with scarves swaying overhead. Youngsters today wouldn't know what that was all about, but the culture died when it became unfashionable, particularly among the thug element, to wear your colours. Hooliganism became far more covert and only the rowdiest would advertise their presence by singing or wearing team colours. I must confess to liking a good 'Swing Low, Sweet Chariot' sung by England rugby fans and their rendition of the National Anthem is far superior to England football fans, who always sing too fast. Not many football fans can remember a song beyond a couple of verses, so there have been plenty of naff songs over the years that I'm happy to have forgotten.

WHAT WAS YOUR FAVOURITE BAND/RECORD DURING YOUR FOOTBALL DAYS?

My part in football culture was never reflected in my taste of music. In the late '70s and early '80s I was very much into electronic futurist and new wave music. Gary Numan was, and still is, my favourite singer. He's always had a loyal following that has grown old with him. I still try to see as many dates as possible when he tours and for many years I haven't bothered to see other bands I used to like. Gary Numan is the best live act I ever saw and I've seen many others over the years. Among my many favourite single recordings would be 'Are Friends Electric' and 'Complex' (both 1979), and live recordings would be 'Me, I Disconnect from You' (1979) and his remix of the Drifters' 'On Broadway' (1980).

WHO WAS YOUR ALL-TIME FAVOURITE PLAYER?

When I first started going to Derby matches I fell for the unsung hero of Brian Clough's team – Ron Webster. He was the most underrated fullback never to play for England. He was a model professional – consistent and fair. He was very athletic for a defender and I remember when Atletico Madrid came to Derby with their Argentine sensation of the early '80s, Ruben Ayala. We had heard how quick he was, but Ron Webster skinned him for pace down the flanks.

Personally I thought Charlie George was Derby's best striker. He left Arsenal to join Derby, the reigning champions in August 1975, just in time to make his debut in the Charity Shield against West Ham at Wembley. Derby won 2–0 and it was one of the best all-round team performances I've seen from Derby. Charlie George remained a favourite with Derby fans through the good and bad days that followed. He survived Tommy Docherty's destructive clear-out of the late '70s and spent at least a season as a lone striker up front.

My favourite all-time player was Sandro Mazzola of Inter Milan who was a star of the Italian side during the 1970 World Cup. I think the Brazilians that beat Italy in the Final are the greatest team ever and the England team that met the Brazilians in the group stage were the best-assembled England team ever. The video of that match, including Banks's wonder save from Pele, is a coaching lesson in itself.

WHERE DO YOU THINK THE NEW ENGLISH NATIONAL STADIUM SHOULD BE BUILT AND WHAT ARE YOUR THOUGHTS REGARDING THE WEMBLEY FIASCO?

I have always supported Wembley as the home of the England football team. The West Midlands only want it for status. I wish we could have a multi-sport venue, as funding would have been easier. The Football Association chose to go it alone and ignored plans to accommodate an athletics track at Wembley. Money was wasted in the planning and silly money is being quoted now. We should have something that is the envy of Europe with a capacity of 100,000, like we had before the old ground became all-seated. If we are to compete on the world stage with the likes of Italy, Spain and Germany, we should have stadiums of this size in the North, South and the Midlands.

I thought the old Wembley gave poor views, particularly from behind the goals. In 1980 it cost £3.50 to stand at the ends for a Wembley England international. Over the last ten years of use the stadium ticket prices became obscene, particularly to those choosing to take their family. The day out would cost over £100. Cup Final tickets reached £60 and I don't think any match in the world is worth more than £25. I think the new Wembley will give the FA an excuse to cash in, with prices that will exclude the likes of myself, the working classes and families, in an attempt to sell out to corporate hospitality. At the end of the match, you have to remember that you've only seen ninety minutes of quite mediocre entertainment and not the Royal Opera in Covent Garden or La Scala in Milan.

MARTIN KING MEETS

GILROY 'GILLY' SHAW

CLUB: WOLVERHAMPTON WANDERERS

GILROY 'GILLY' SHAW

THE MEET

I first came across Gilly on a BBC2 programme, *Hooligans*. I had been asked to appear on it as a so-called expert on football hooliganism. One, I'm no expert and don't profess to be, and two, it followed hard on the heels of the Donal Macintyre exposé fiasco on my mate J. My gut feelings about the show were well founded after I agreed to meet a couple of the production staff – a real pair of Roland Rats. Things just didn't add up and I declined their unbelievable offer of not getting paid for my services – how thoughtful of them! I'm not that desperate to appear on telly, unlike some I could name. Anyway, Gil was trapped on the programme by a couple of reporters with hidden cameras and boy did they stitch him up. They even gave him the new name of Lenny.

While researching this book, Gilly's name cropped up on more than one occasion and I managed to track him down through my mate in Cardiff, Tony Rivers. He gave me Gil's phone number and I gave him a call explaining who I was and that I'd like him to be in this book. He was a little bit unsure at first but with a bit of gentle persuasion and coaxing he agreed to meet me. Wolves were playing at Pompey the following weekend and Gil told me that he and his mates were stopping off in Southampton on the way to Portsmouth. So, after numerous mobile phone calls on the day, and a bit of cat and mouse, we arranged to meet outside a pub down by the docks.

When I pulled up in the car I noticed Gil standing outside with another couple of people and as I crossed the road to meet him I noticed one of them was a rather attractive girl. I introduced myself, we all shook hands, then headed round the corner to a boozer where about a hundred of the Wolves boys were drinking. I was introduced to a few faces and we ordered a drink – well, I did. Gil told me he doesn't touch alcohol so he had Coke. Not the sniffing type, the liquid – he told me doesn't do drugs either. We settled down in a quiet corner and a few of his close friends gathered round the table as I fired these questions at him. Before I started, Gil explained he'd like to study criminology and sociology one day and put his years of rucking at football to good use. I wouldn't bet against seeing a Professor or Dr Gil at university in the West Midlands in the not-too-distant future. Here's what he told me.

BACKGROUND

I was born in 1968 into a Romany family. I went to Molesey Park School in Bilston, a suburb of Wolverhampton, and left there with

'O' levels in art and geography, and CSEs in maths and English. I've done various jobs, including a YTS in bricklaying.

The first match I ever went to was with my stepfather in 1979/80. I saw Liverpool beat Wolves 1–0 at Molineux. The stars of that Wolves team then were John Richards and Kenny Hibbit. In the mid-'80s I started going to matches with my mates until 1988, when the police mounted one of their infamous dawn raids. This operation was code-named 'Growth', which stood for 'Get rid of Wolves troublesome hooligans'. It was one of the biggest undercover police operations ever seen involving football fans. There were 68 arrests, many receiving prison sentences after being convicted of violent disorder. I was remanded on bail and received community service. The only reason I got off lighter than the others was that I once attempted to rescue a man from a house fire and that went in my favour. The Old Bill were gloating at what they thought was the end of our firm. Many of the boys when released moved on to the then flourishing rave scene.

WHAT'S YOUR FAVOURITE TERRACE FASHION?
When I first started going with the boys I suppose it was Lyle & Scott, Pringle, Fila and Tacchini that first caught my eye. The Cockney lads definitely had the lead in the fashion stakes.

WHAT'S THE WORST FASHION YOU'VE EVER SEEN ON THE TERRACES?
Now it's got to be Burberry – every fucker's got it. It was all right the first time round [at this point the pub explodes with laughter as they point out to Gil he's wearing a Burberry scarf around his neck]. The same with the people wearing the Stone Island gear. They think if they pull on a Stone Island jumper or jacket then they're a hooligan or one of the faces – Stone Island Warriors I call them. The scene's become more like a fashion show.

DESCRIBE YOUR WORST FEELING AT A GAME.
The 2001/2002 season, when at one stage we had an eleven-point lead. With just eleven games to go, we looked odds-on to get into the Premiership and we threw it away. On the last game of the season we needed to win away to Sheffield Wednesday and our rivals, West Brom, had to lose. We drew 2–2 after taking a first-minute lead in front of 12,000 travelling Wolves fans. We just collapsed that day. West Brom beat Crystal Palace 2–0 and gained automatic promotion. We made the play-offs but were beaten by Norwich over two legs, who then went on to be beaten by Birmingham City, another of our hated rivals, in the final in Cardiff.

HAVE YOU EVER INCURRED ANY SERIOUS INJURIES OR BEEN BADLY BEATEN UP AT A MATCH?

Two of the best rows I've ever been involved in, where there were plenty of injuries and people were badly beaten, were with Birmingham City fans. The first happened just before Christmas, after their home game with Stockport at St Andrews. About sixty of us got back to Birmingham New Street train station after our away game at Walsall. About fifty Blues faces were drinking in the Bar St Martins and we happened to land on them. One of our lot was also in the bar and overheard the Birmingham boys ringing their mates on the mobiles telling them to get over to the pub quick as we had arrived. They came out of the boozer and we smashed them to pieces. Only a couple of Old Bill were there and could do nothing to stop it. Finally more police arrived, rounded us up and put us back on the Wolverhampton train. A result for us.

Later in the 2001/2 season, we were away to them in the league on April Fool's Day. One of the boys had hired a double-decker bus and 120 of us squeezed on board. We arrived at the Breeze Bar in Balsall Heath and called them up, telling them of our whereabouts. About half-past one I was sitting outside the pub sipping a Coke with a couple of my mates from Plymouth, who've come up for the game, when I saw a mob of about fifty coming towards the pub from my left. And it was their main firm, by the looks of it, with not many white faces among them. Off to the right they had another mob of about a hundred. 'They're here,' I shouted, and the rest of our boys poured out of the pub and got straight into both mobs. I went left and a few flares fired by one of our lot landed in among them and they backed off. But, give them their due, they came back into us. But we never budged an inch – it was toe-to-toe fighting.

People were getting knocked to the ground and stayed down. Some were unconscious. The street was alight with coloured smoke and flames from the flares. They'd get run and get backed off a few times, but then they'd come at us again from another side. But we held strong, we battered them. One of our boys was cracking skulls with a pool cue. It went on for a good twenty minutes before the Old Bill arrived. They took so long to get there because they'd been policing a march in the city centre that day and were short of manpower. At one point there was someone lying in the road out cold – my mates thought it was me. He was still there when we were finally moved on. He turned out to be one of our lot. He'd been hit over the head with a house brick and was in a coma for three weeks. His assailant later received a four-year jail term. From that day on, after we flogged them, I think we had the respect of the Blues mob and the Zulu Warriors.

HAS YOUR OWN SIDE EVER BEEN INVOLVED IN A FULL-SCALE RIOT?

The ruck in Birmingham I've just described I'd say was a riot. It was on a par with anything seen on our TV screens from somewhere like Northern Ireland. Three lanes of traffic were brought to a standstill with car windscreens smashed and cars damaged. Glass and prostrate bodies littered the street.

DESCRIBE THE BEST TAKING OF AN END YOU'VE EVER WITNESSED.

In about '87 six of us went into Wigan's end and cleared it. A good result for half a dozen nineteen-year-olds.

WHICH WAS YOUR OWN TEAM'S POPULAR END?

The South Bank was where all the singers and the shirts went, and a section of that end was set aside for away supporters. The opposite end was the North Bank, which was a sort of family section.

WHERE DID YOU STAND OR SIT IN THE GROUND?

The John Island Stand, named after one of our former players. I don't remember him – he was a bit before my time.

CAN YOU RECALL A BATTLE YOU HAVE BEEN INVOLVED IN, EITHER INSIDE OR OUTSIDE A GROUND?

Birmingham was by far the best.

CAN YOU RECALL THE BEST EVER MOB YOUR TEAM HAS PUT TOGETHER?

The best all-round support I've ever seen following Wolves was against Burnley at Wembley in the Sherpa Vans Final in 1998. We won 2–0 and there were 55,000 fans cheering us on to victory. When it comes to boys, we once took a massive mob to Wrexham and numbers-wise we took over 300 to a game at the Hawthorns.

WHO'S THE BEST RIVAL FIRM YOU'VE EVER SEEN?

That has to be Millwall. They turned up for a mid-week night game 300-handed and were a pretty formidable force. Chelsea turned up in the John Island Stand one season and a couple of hundred of them stood up and sang 'One Man Went to Mow'.

WHO ARE YOUR BIGGEST RIVALS TEAM-WISE?

West Brom.

WHO ARE YOUR BIGGEST RIVALS FAN-WISE?

West Brom and Birmingham City.

HAVE YOU EVER JOINED UP WITH ANOTHER TEAM'S FIRM?

We team up with Plymouth Argyle for certain big games. We got together through following England.

DID YOU EVER FOLLOW ENGLAND AND WOULD YOU PUT ENGLAND BEFORE YOUR CLUB?

Yes, I have followed England abroad – it's the elite. And yes, I would put them before my own club. Following England's about national pride and passion.

WHICH WAS THE BEST ENGLAND ROW?

Holland. We murdered them. Chelsea had a top mob out that day.

HAVE YOU EVER SUPPORTED OR LOOKED OUT FOR ANOTHER TEAM'S RESULTS?

I look out for Plymouth's results.

NAME YOUR TOP FIVE FIRMS, IN ANY ORDER.

The biggest has to be Manchester United, then Middlesbrough who smashed us to pieces once at Molineux, Cardiff, Millwall and at the moment the Yids. In the '80s I'd say West Ham and Chelsea were the top boys, with Arsenal being the most disappointing to come to our place. I don't rate the Gooners one bit. Their big black man turned up at our place in a stretch limo with a few of his pals and took a bit of a slap.

WHICH IS THE WORST GROUND YOU'VE EVER BEEN TO AND WHY?

Halifax. It's a shithole. I'd put it on a par with Shrewsbury's Gay Meadow.

WHICH IS THE BEST STADIUM YOU'VE BEEN TO?

Old Trafford. It's a massive stadium.

WHO ARE THE FAIREST COPPERS YOU'VE COME ACROSS AT A MATCH?

It has to be the Southampton Old Bill. We played Southampton in the FA Cup and I was arrested, and my mates refused to go home without me so the gathers let me go without a charge. Just shows you what loyal mates I've got.

AND THE WORST OLD BILL?

West Midlands plod. I've had my head split open a couple of times by them. And I was out in town on my birthday, celebrating with some of the boys, and a group of them came in the same pub. A fight broke out and they had me arrested, and I was taken to court. The pub's CCTV showed they'd started the fight so it was thrown out. A mate of mine was out shopping with his young daughter and one of them tried to pick trouble with him – called him scum and other names. We send the club's football liaison officer a Christmas card and present every year. One year we sent him a pair of pink furry handcuffs. The following year it was a box of chocolates. He loves us really.

WHAT WOULD HAVE STOPPED YOU GETTING INVOLVED WITH THE BOYS AT FOOTBALL?

Prison.

DESCRIBE SOME OF THE METHODS AND TACTICS USED BY THE POLICE AND THE AUTHORITIES TO STOP FOOTBALL VIOLENCE, AND DO YOU THINK THEY WORK?

The video camera.

HAVE YOU EVER BEEN SICKENED BY SOMETHING YOU'VE WITNESSED AT A GAME?

No, but clubs that bash fans in shirts, that's not on. Fair play should come into it. Rules of combat apply – only fight like-minded people.

WHAT'S YOUR FAVOURITE FOOTBALL SONG OR CHANT AND WHICH IS THE WORST YOU CAN RECALL HEARING FROM ANOTHER TEAM?

Birmingham City's 'Keep right on to the end of the road' is very intimidating. That stupid fucking hymn West Brom fans sing has got to be the worst, along with that 'Slap a Dingle' chant, which is aimed at us lot – they call us Dingles or Yam Yams. That's from a crowd who think it's trendy to wear shell suits!

WHAT WAS YOUR FAVOURITE BAND/RECORD DURING YOUR FOOTBALL DAYS?

Favourite record has to be by Harry J. All Stars – 'Liquidator'.

WHO WAS YOUR ALL-TIME FAVOURITE PLAYER?

That's easy – the legendary Steve Bull and Paul Gascoigne. Bully because of the loyalty he showed the club, and his goals. He could have moved on and even played in Italy but he stayed. And Gazza because he was pure genius.

WHERE DO YOU THINK THE NEW NATIONAL STADIUM SHOULD BE BUILT AND WHAT ARE YOUR THOUGHTS REGARDING THE WEMBLEY FIASCO?

I think they should have kept Wembley Stadium for something else and built a new national stadium somewhere in the Midlands – somewhere easily accessible to football fans from all over the country.

CASS PENNANT MEETS

JOHN WESTWOOD
CLUB: PORTSMOUTH

© Julia Rowley

JOHN WESTWOOD

THE MEET

I was introduced to John by Rob Silvester, the co-author of *Rolling with the 6.57 Crew*. John met me in his hometown of Petersfield, Hampshire, and took me to his local pub and also to his flat above a lingerie and piercing shop. Inside, the place was a shrine to Pompey Football Club with everything Pompey blue or engraved with the club crest. Wearing a blue wig, blue Dr Martens, a top hat and waistcoat, John himself looked like a '70s glam rock star. Covered in Pompey tattoos, he really is Mr Pompey. Forget about Biley, Dickinson, Walsh, Wittingham, Merson and all the other legends from the past and present – this man is right up there with them. He's the mad bell-ringer and Pompey bugler. He has blue blood running through his veins, and his band of eccentric disciples are a landmark at every game – you're often likely to find a stuffed gorilla and crash dummy beside him. In the stands, John has achieved celebrity status among the local and national press. He has taken his support of the club to another level that only real football fans would understand. Here he tells of his exploits following Pompey.

BACKGROUND

I've changed my name by deed poll to John Anthony Portsmouth Football Club Westwood. I've always loved the club so I thought it was a natural progression. I went and saw a couple of solicitors and did the business, then went home and told the missus, who wasn't at all impressed. That was in 1989 and I'd only been married three months. I'd met her five years previously, so she knew what I was like and what Pompey meant to me. I've been divorced six years now, so the football got the better of her in the end. I started going to Pompey with my mates in '76. They were my local club and I wasn't really a big football fan at the time but after my first game I was hooked. I just loved the atmosphere and the singing and chanting. I was hooked for life.

WHAT'S YOUR FAVOURITE TERRACE FASHION?

I've never been into fashion, really. I tend to do my own thing clothes-wise but I did once own a Pringle jumper. The original skins always looked good.

WHAT'S THE WORST FASHION YOU'VE EVER SEEN ON THE TERRACES?

The Scummers in their team shirts. It turns my stomach. Them red-and-white stripes – sends a shiver down my spine.

DESCRIBE YOUR WORST FEELING AT A GAME.

When there's been a ban on away fans at Millwall and we've had to go up to London to buy tickets for the game and go undercover, so to speak, just to watch our team without getting sussed out. I was rumbled one year when a bloke smiled at me and nodded. I nodded back – I thought he was one of ours – and he came over and asked me quietly if I was a Pompey fan. 'You know I am,' I said with a huge friendly grin. With that he hit me, so I laid into him. We carried on fighting and I was getting the better of him until he shouted out, 'Pompey fan here!' Everyone came towards me, so I legged it and hid among the crowds.

HAVE YOU EVER INCURRED ANY SERIOUS INJURIES OR BEEN BADLY BEATEN UP AT A MATCH?

A minibus load of us stopped at Rotherham on the way home from a game up at Huddersfield. Me and the rest of us, including a couple of girls, had a good drink and a laugh with the locals in one of the town's pubs. Come closing time we decided to move on to a nightclub. We were out on the dance floor causing no trouble, and not looking for any, when this group of lads steamed in to us for no reason. I was hit over the head with a bottle and knocked to the floor, then kicked and stamped in the head. I became dizzy and faint. I was covered in blood and thought for a moment I was going to die. It was only the actions of the bar staff dragging me under the serving hatch

© Solent Newspapers

that saved my life. The two girls with us were held up against the wall and threatened, and my mate Dave had his ribs broken. We had caused no trouble that night. I was dressed in my wig and top hat but they had no reason to attack us. It turns out that the fellas that done it were Sheffield locals.

HAS YOUR OWN SIDE EVER BEEN INVOLVED IN A FULL-SCALE RIOT?

In the early days there were plenty. In '83 when Plymouth were going for promotion and we won 1–0, there were 11,000 Pompey fans there supporting the team. We went on to the pitch and ran the home fans everywhere. That day we were more like the home side.

DESCRIBE THE BEST TAKING OF AN END YOU'VE EVER WITNESSED.

The best, without doubt, was Huddersfield away in the mid-'80s. Fifty Pompey boys came in the side terrace and cleared it.

WHICH WAS YOUR OWN TEAM'S POPULAR END?

The Fratton End – that's where all the vocal support came from. Them terrace days, you just couldn't beat singing and dancing 'Knees Up, Mother Brown' then falling over in a heap of bodies and having complete strangers helping you back to your feet. And pissing where you stood, so a big gap would open up around you with fellas frightened to get splashed. Also there'd be inter-town fighting – say, a fella from Gosport would clash with someone from, say, Leigh Park – and when it finished everyone would get back to watching the game. Often you'd get these private wars breaking out.

WHERE DID YOU STAND OR SIT IN THE GROUND?

The Fratton End.

CAN YOU RECALL A BATTLE YOU HAVE BEEN INVOLVED IN, EITHER INSIDE OR OUTSIDE A GROUND?

Being a coward, I tended to keep out of the aggro. I've been caught up in the odd skirmish but that's about it.

CAN YOU RECALL THE BEST EVER MOB YOUR TEAM HAS PUT TOGETHER?

We've gone to Millwall on occasions with local geezers who've gone just for the row.

WHO'S THE BEST RIVAL FIRM YOU'VE EVER SEEN?

Cardiff ... Chelsea, who once brought 12,000 fans down to our place. But I'd have to say Millwall – they've got some boys.

WHO ARE YOUR BIGGEST RIVALS TEAM-WISE?
The Southampton Scummers.

WHO ARE YOUR BIGGEST RIVALS FAN-WISE?
The Scummers.

HAVE YOU EVER JOINED UP WITH ANOTHER TEAM'S FIRM?
No, never. I'm Pompey until I die.

DID YOU EVER FOLLOW ENGLAND AND WOULD YOU PUT ENGLAND BEFORE YOUR CLUB?
Yes, I went to the World Cup '82, Euro '96, World Cup '98 and Euro 2000. And I'm an England Supporters' Club member. But it's club before country for me. I've only missed five or six England games in 23 years and that's because Pompey were playing.

WHICH WAS THE BEST ENGLAND ROW?
I follow England abroad and I keep away from the trouble – it is possible if you want to.

HAVE YOU EVER SUPPORTED OR LOOKED OUT FOR ANOTHER TEAM'S RESULTS?
No.

NAME YOUR TOP FIVE FIRMS, IN ANY ORDER.
West Ham, Millwall, Cardiff, Leeds and Chelsea.

WHICH IS THE WORST GROUND YOU'VE EVER BEEN TO AND WHY?
Oxford's old Manor Ground – it was a right khazi.

WHICH IS THE BEST STADIUM YOU'VE BEEN TO?
Apart from Fratton Park, I'd say Old Trafford. We were up there this year in the FA Cup and it's on another planet. We got the lift up to save walking up all those stairs and it's so plush it's better than some hotels.

WHO ARE THE FAIREST COPPERS YOU'VE COME ACROSS AT A MATCH?
I'd say Crewe. They're quite pleasant up there.

AND THE WORST OLD BILL?
That's a hard question because I could mention so many. But I'd say the north-east Old Bill are fucking obnoxious. They give you no respect and treat everyone like animals. They'd look at you, and arrest

you for nothing. Birmingham's another. They just stare at you, looking to nick you. The Met's got some bastards but I'd say Sunderland Old Bill are by far the worst.

WHAT WOULD HAVE STOPPED YOU GETTING INVOLVED WITH THE BOYS AT MATCHES?

I'm a fan and don't really like violence but I suppose tougher sentences and bigger fines may have stopped it.

DESCRIBE SOME OF THE METHODS AND TACTICS USED BY THE POLICE AND AUTHORITIES TO STOP FOOTBALL VIOLENCE, AND DO YOU THINK THEY WORK?

Millwall away – I've never seen so many lines of Old Bill as you approached the ground.

HAVE YOU EVER BEEN SICKENED BY SOMETHING YOU'VE WITNESSED AT A GAME?

Coventry away last year. There was fighting in the seats and some disabled fans got caught up in it. One lady in a wheelchair was helpless as missiles rained down around her. It was a sickening sight.

WHAT'S YOUR FAVOURITE FOOTBALL SONG OR CHANT AND WHICH IS THE WORST YOU CAN RECALL HEARING FROM ANOTHER TEAM?

The worst has got to be 'When the Saints Go Marching In'. That isn't a football song, it's a joke. The chant of 'Play up Pompey' is a very passionate song. It makes the hairs stand up on the back of my neck when the crowd sings it full blast. I think it's one of the oldest songs or terraces chants. Apparently it stems from the trenches in the First World War.

WHAT WAS YOUR FAVOURITE BAND/RECORD DURING YOUR FOOTBALL DAYS?

Mike Oldfield's 'Portsmouth'. It was played as the team ran out.

WHO WAS YOUR ALL-TIME FAVOURITE PLAYER?

Paul Merson. He took a wage cut to come to us and the way he has conducted himself and helped the younger players – well, he's a real star. He's the catalyst of this club I really respect him. He always gives 100 per cent on the pitch and he loves his football – I just love him.

WHERE DO YOU THINK THE NEW ENGLISH NATIONAL STADIUM SHOULD BE BUILT AND WHAT ARE YOUR THOUGHTS REGARDING THE WEMBLEY FIASCO?

It should have stayed at Wembley. The stadium is known by fans the world over. The twin towers has a place in all football fans' hearts.

CASS PENNANT MEETS

TREVOR 'T' TANNER
CLUB: TOTTENHAM HOTSPUR

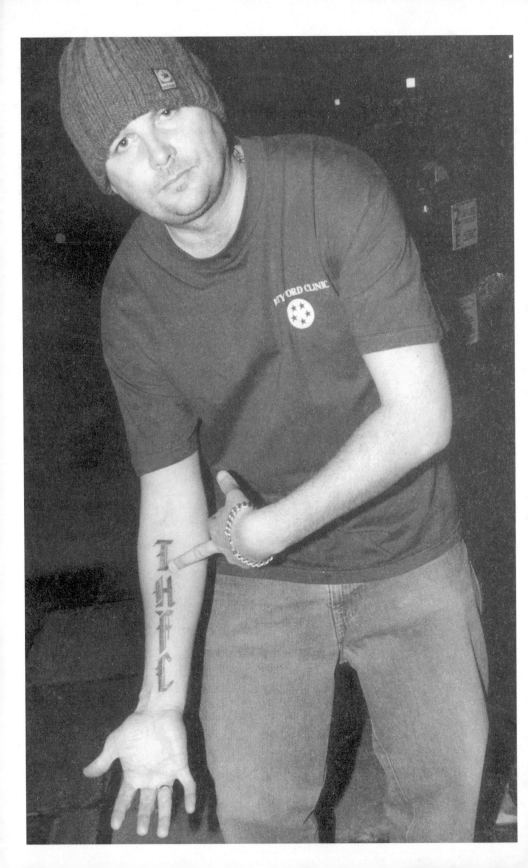

TREVOR 'T' TANNER

THE MEET

My idea of a Tottenham legend dates back to the time of the Crombie-overcoat-wearing boys that held the Park Lane and Paxton Road Ends of White Hart Lane. Those were the days when you could walk all around the ground. The days of Skivesy, Big Jim, Brixton and Vic Donkin. Tottenham, in the casual-look '80s, sort of lost their way in the capital but come the '90s they were up there with the best of them. They had a top firm but I wasn't aware of the emergence of a new name over at Spurs.

I was sitting in a quiet backstreet boozer in London with my QPR mate who was showing people a cutting from the *Evening Standard* newspaper about the latest hoolie film to hit the screen, *The Football Factory*. I'd been interviewed in depth about this film, based on the infamous Chelsea Headhunters firm. The name Pennant was very prominent in the piece by journalist Matt Hughes. A few old acquaintances were gathering by the bar and in their company was a younger face who was speaking loudly about the article we'd been looking at only moments earlier. This young gun was launching a torrent of abuse about everyone featured in the article within earshot of myself. He was running his fingers along the page shouting out extracts from my piece. The face nearest the bar raised an eyebrow and shook his head. Being diplomatic, and to spare the fella any embarrassment, I went off for a leak. On my return he was standing next to my drinking partner, who was chuckling away to himself, and a quick introduction explained a lot to him. And as he passed over a bottle of Bud the THFC tattooed on his arm explained a lot to me. He held out his hand – 'Trevor Tanner.' 'Cass Pennant,' I replied, and we both laughed. 'T', as he's known by close friends, went on to tell me about his days at Spurs.

BACKGROUND

I've lived in south London and north London so I guess you can call me a man of two rivers. I got my name by taking over the THFC firm from 1990 to the present time. I support Spurs for personal reasons. My job then, believe or not, was in the Merchant Navy. Now I've come full circle as a mature student studying computers. If you want to shorten my name, many simply call me 'T'.

WHAT'S YOUR FAVOURITE TERRACE FASHION?

I would have to say during the early to mid-'90s I was a walking advertisement for Stone Island, but I like to think I have my own unique and individual style, as clothes have always been a major part of my life. Quite simply, you wouldn't catch me in Stone Island now. I now see it as strictly a northern snide-merchants thing, preferring Maharishi and obscure funky labels to more conventional, mass-produced gear.

WHAT'S THE WORST FASHION YOU'VE EVER SEEN ON THE TERRACES?

Tight faded jeans and Burberry hats and scarves, fake or real. What the fuck is all that about? It's predominantly northern, but I've seen a lot of that shit this side of the 'Gap' as well. Fucking sad!

DESCRIBE YOUR WORST FEELING AT A GAME.

The worst feeling is always if the firm has a bad day at the office.

HAVE YOU EVER INCURRED ANY SERIOUS INJURIES OR BEEN BADLY BEATEN UP AT A MATCH?

On a personal level there were two. One was the night before the FA Cup semi-final against the Gooners in a backstreet pub a few miles from Tottenham. It was supposed to be an organised celebration drink, but it didn't turn out that way. The pub was a right mix of Herberts. This little mug fronted a pal of mine, so silly bollocks here dived in, knocked the little prick down, and while I was rolling around the floor with him, one of his brave pals decided to stick a bottle into the back of my head. I had long hair then, and was seriously pissed off with the thought of having it cut. So I went to a pal's house and I'll never forget filling his bath with blood, as it was all matted in my hair. I never let them cut my hair, so now I have a six-inch scar in the back of my head, which is clearly visible now that my hair is cropped. I should add that the little cunt took a good hiding.

The second time was similar. I knocked the geezer down, then some cowardly mug (you know who you are) decided to make a patchwork quilt out of the back of my neck with a sharp object.

HAS YOUR OWN SIDE EVER BEEN INVOLVED IN A FULL-SCALE RIOT?

Ifield Tavern, just round the back of Chelsea's ground, in the 1991/2 season. A lot of bollocks has been written about this, and it's good to have the opportunity to put the record straight. It's well known that Tottenham organised this one, so I know what I say is the truth. We met at Earl's Court, left four different boozers at approximately 1.30 p.m. and marched past the tube on to Ifield Road. The Chelsea firm were at the bottom of the road, in and around Ifield Tavern. We charged straight down the road and confronted two firms, inside and out. The main window went through with a dustbin and I tried climbing through it. Our other boys were having it in the main doorway. The pub got fucking annihilated and the firm outside the pub got run back twice. There were 200 on Chelsea's manor, and no Old Bill. The back page of the London *Evening Standard* newspaper reported: 'Ten mad minutes, Spurs and Chelsea go to war.' Enough said.

DESCRIBE THE BEST TAKING OF AN END YOU'VE EVER WITNESSED.

Before my time, from 1977 to 1982, Spurs took the Arsenal North Bank regularly. But in the present day, during the 2002/3 season, it was Birmingham away, when Spurs met in The Toad, a Zulu pub in the town centre, at eleven o'clock, 200-handed. Then, during the game, with ten minutes to go, Tottenham's firm kicked their way out of the ground by the emergency exit and charged around to get right underneath Birmingham's main stand, but were removed by the Old Bill. But, on the whole, these things very rarely happen in the '90s. There are too many cameras. Nowadays the trouble's always out on the street.

WHICH WAS YOUR OWN TEAM'S POPULAR END?

The Shelf.

WHERE DID YOU STAND OR SIT IN THE GROUND?

The Shelf.

CAN YOU RECALL A BATTLE YOU HAVE BEEN INVOLVED IN, EITHER INSIDE OR OUTSIDE A GROUND?

The best ever row could easily be the Ifield Tavern, but I'm going to say Manchester United at home, just before I got three years, and while we were all on bail for Chelsea–Tottenham at the Three Kings pub on North End Road. This row involved 45 of us running the Mancs' main firm, including Cockney Reds, out of the Somers Town Estate in Euston, and even through the station itself. It was fucking unbelievable. And all the Reds know this is true. We even had a Scouser with us that day, and you can imagine his joy in confirming that. I know that night sent shock waves round the North West of England.

CAN YOU RECALL THE BEST EVER MOB YOUR TEAM HAS PUT TOGETHER?

I would have to say Millwall, early '90s, and Millwall again, pre-season 2001. Both were unstoppable firms of 200-plus, but made up of the right people. You just know that no one's going anywhere. Again, a lot of shit has been said about the last encounter as well. Same thing – I know who organised it and, hand on heart, we took the fucking piss from eleven in the morning till eleven at night, and we were on their manor causing havoc. At eleven o'clock, we were 200-handed on Jamaica Road. Enough said.

WHO'S THE BEST RIVAL FIRM YOU'VE EVER SEEN?

Man. United at home, early '90s. There was mayhem and I got nicked, and bitten by a police dog in Tesco's, would you believe? A lot of the other boys got nicked. Old Bill were falling off horses – it was fucking mad. To top it all, the fucking police dog got a bravery medal for ripping my arm to shreds. What's that all about?

WHO ARE YOUR BIGGEST RIVALS TEAM-WISE?

The Gooners.

WHO ARE YOUR BIGGEST RIVALS FAN-WISE?

Chelsea, no question.

HAVE YOU EVER JOINED UP WITH ANOTHER TEAM'S FIRM?

Yes, we have a partnership going back years with Aberdeen. Big respect to the Aberdeen Massive.

DID YOU EVER FOLLOW ENGLAND AND WOULD YOU PUT ENGLAND BEFORE YOUR CLUB?

Yes I do, but I wouldn't put them before club.

WHICH WAS THE BEST ENGLAND ROW?

Sweden, in the European Championships '92. I was very nearly in a lot of shit there. After the game I was nicked near the flyover. It was going off with everyone – local immigrant stallholders, the Swedes, every fucker. One Swede was in a bad way, and they thought I'd done it, which I hadn't. I was held in a Swedish prison for a few weeks, and then I got bail on a technicality. There was only five of us held back out of the whole England support and, just as a nice touch, on my return flight as I was being deported I found out that I was splashed all over page 12 of the *Sun*, under the headline 'England's Foulest'.

HAVE YOU EVER SUPPORTED OR LOOKED OUT FOR ANOTHER TEAM'S RESULTS?

No.

NAME YOUR TOP FIVE FIRMS, IN ANY ORDER.

Aberdeen, West Ham, Chelsea, Man. United and Cardiff City. This is probably the hardest question to answer. I'm trying to be totally unbiased here, and speak strictly from personal experience. I would say Millwall, Boro and Birmingham could easily be among those, and I do respect each and every one of those firms.

WHICH IS THE WORST GROUND YOU'VE EVER BEEN TO AND WHY?

The Dell, Southampton, because it was a little shithole, and I hope Pompey wreck their new ground next season. I fucking hate Southampton. We've had plenty of rows with them during the '90s and smashed 'em every time.

WHICH IS THE BEST STADIUM YOU'VE BEEN TO?

Old Trafford – it's a magnificent stadium. But for a fun day out, Norwich away. We had a few great days out in Yarmouth, and a few naughty rows with Norwich as well. We actually had a riot in the nightclub district of Yarmouth, King's Road, one year, which was all over the local news and radio. I ended up doing bird in Norwich years later, which wasn't so funny.

WHO ARE THE FAIREST COPPERS YOU'VE COME ACROSS AT A MATCH?

None.

AND THE WORST OLD BILL?

Chelsea, Fulham CID – the same Old Bill that got me banged up for three years.

WHAT WOULD HAVE STOPPED YOU GETTING INVOLVED WITH THE BOYS AT MATCHES?

At the time, nothing.

DESCRIBE SOME OF THE METHODS AND TACTICS USED BY THE POLICE AND AUTHORITIES TO STOP FOOTBALL VIOLENCE, AND DO YOU THINK THEY WORK?

Having my front door kicked off at 5.30 in the morning, being dragged out of my house and then given three years' imprisonment at Knightsbridge Crown Court for steaming into Chelsea outside the Three Kings pub in North End Road, and being filmed the whole time, club in hand. A life ban from Tottenham and a five-year worldwide FIFA ban. I found all that to be pretty fucking effective!

HAVE YOU EVER BEEN SICKENED BY SOMETHING YOU'VE WITNESSED AT A GAME?

No, anyone who plays the game knows the rules. I know that sounds hard, but that's the way it is.

WHAT'S YOUR FAVOURITE FOOTBALL SONG OR CHANT AND WHICH IS THE WORST YOU CAN RECALL HEARING FROM ANOTHER TEAM?

Leave it out!

WHAT WAS YOUR FAVOURITE BAND/RECORD DURING YOUR FOOTBALL DAYS?

I've been into dance music and soul since I can remember. Favourite dance track is 'There For the Grace of God' by Fire Island, plus 'Ain't No Stopping Us Now', which we adopted as our unofficial anthem in the early '90s.

WHO WAS YOUR ALL-TIME FAVOURITE PLAYER?

Paul Gascoigne. For a while he was the best in the world.

WHERE DO YOU THINK THE NEW ENGLISH NATIONAL STADIUM SHOULD BE BUILT AND WHAT ARE YOUR THOUGHTS REGARDING THE WEMBLEY FIASCO?

It's nothing short of a national disgrace what the FA and the government have done to Wembley. And I believe the new stadium will go up when I see it with my own eyes.

CASS PENNANT MEETS

ANGUS NUTT
CLUB: BRISTOL CITY

ANGUS NUTT

THE MEET

I met Angus through Chris Brown, or Browner as he's known. Chris is the author of *Bovver*, a right good read about his time following Rovers.

The first thing that struck me about Angus was that he didn't look anywhere near his age. Dressed in an Aquascutum jumper, he looked years younger than fifty. I also noticed he wasn't very tall. As I expected, he's a man of his word and a gent. He's one of the old school – he gives respect and gets plenty back.

After the interview about fifty of us, including the Bear (see page 137) and a few mates, ended up in a pub near the dock area. It was a nice atmosphere, with fans from both clubs sitting around chatting with the two legends whose clubs were once sworn enemies – and still are. You could see the younger ones among us looking at them both, hardly believing they were sitting in the company of the great men themselves. Suddenly the pub emptied. What the fuck's going on here, I thought. A shout went up that Sheffield United's mob had turned up a day early for their play-off final game against Wolves in Cardiff and were looking for a row with the locals and they got one. I was sitting watching it all unfold through the pub window. I gathered up my gear and headed back to London with the chant of BBC echoing around my head.

I had a fantastic day in Bristol with both sets of lads. Here's what Angus had to say about his days following Bristol City.

BACKGROUND

I was born in Hartcliffe, south Bristol, which in geographical terms makes me a City fan. I got my nickname Angus after I played a character of the same name in a school play. I started going to games with my dad when I was about nine and from then on it just kicked in and I always went – I never changed. I first started going with the boys in the skinhead days of '69. I left school and became an apprentice carpenter.

WHAT'S YOUR FAVOURITE TERRACE FASHION?

In the '70s it was the skinhead stuff – you know, the Levi's Sta-Prest, Crombies and the Harringtons.

WHAT'S THE WORST FASHION YOU'VE EVER SEEN ON THE TERRACES?

The worst has got to be the gear worn by Rovers and Cardiff. They were bikers, punks and general scruffs. They lost the plot when it came to fashion.

DESCRIBE YOUR WORST FEELING AT A GAME.

Getting nicked at Luton in '75, the year we were promoted to the old First Division. We got cornered by the Old Bill and that was the end of my day. I had to travel back to Luton to appear in court at a later date.

HAVE YOU EVER INCURRED ANY SERIOUS INJURIES OR BEEN BADLY BEATEN UP AT A MATCH?

Stoke City away in a Cup replay on a Wednesday night. We took a coach up there and arrived early, and took a few liberties. It went off a little bit in the ground, but afterwards we came out and three of us steamed into about fifty of them, and we got caught right out. I had a broken jaw and a smashed eye socket. I was well fucked. I was off work for seven weeks drinking soup through a straw. I lost weight, though! The only good thing was we won 3–1 and ended up going to Anfield in the next round.

HAS YOUR OWN SIDE EVER BEEN INVOLVED IN A FULL-SCALE RIOT?

There's two really. One was at Reading away in the mid-'80s, when they were top and we were second. We took about six thousand fans there and for some reason it just went mental and kicked off. The pitch was covered in bottles, bricks and debris. There were 32 arrests, many of them resulting in prison sentences, and the game was abandoned for fifteen minutes until order was restored.

Then Millwall at Aston Gate was quite a famous battle. They arrived early and smashed up the Black Horse pub near Temple Meads. They arrived tooled up and smashed it to smithereens and, luckily for us, none of our lot were in there at the time. Later on that day the two mobs bumped into one another along by the river. It went toe to toe and there must have been 200 to 300 on each side. Thing is with Millwall, you knew they'd turn up and mix it – they always had this reputation.

DESCRIBE THE BEST TAKING OF AN END YOU'VE EVER WITNESSED.

That'll be when we took the Tote End at Rovers. The night before the game a couple of the lads went up to their ground and cut the padlocks and chains off of the gates leading into their end, and replaced them with a new set which a few of the City boys had keys to. A lot of our boys got in the Tote End early – we just sort of let ourselves in for free, and were mingling with the Gasheads. We had a big turn out and one of the boys, Maurice, ended up getting four years for his part in this ingenious plot. However, it worked. We really took the piss that day.

WHICH WAS YOUR OWN TEAM'S POPULAR END?

East End. It's all changed now because everyone sits in different parts of the ground.

WHERE DID YOU STAND OR SIT IN THE GROUND?

The Dolman Stand. It's an old stand where the boys used to meet and it was in a nice position to weigh up the away support.

CAN YOU RECALL A BATTLE YOU HAVE BEEN INVOLVED IN, EITHER INSIDE OR OUTSIDE A GROUND?

Millwall at home. They jumped over the railings and on to the pitch and came right up into the Dolman Stand where we were sitting. The battles were up and down the steps, with the Old Bill unable to control it, and outside in the streets it was a running battle. I remember a milk float and there was crumbled glass everywhere. There was bottles flying through the air. It was Agincourt with glass. It was bedlam. This was in the '80s.

CAN YOU RECALL THE BEST EVER MOB YOUR TEAM HAS PUT TOGETHER?

The biggest firm the City Service Crew took away was down to Plymouth in the early '90s. We'd heard talk they were going to turn out big style and sort us right out, and weeks before the game word on the streets was that all our old faces would be turning out for this one, and in the end 600 of our finest made the trip. We hunted high and low for their Central Element mob. We tried the pleasure park and turned up at the Britannia pub, which is their main boozer, but they didn't show. I remember a big car showroom getting smashed to smithereens, and there was thousands and thousands of pounds' worth of damage.

WHO'S THE BEST RIVAL FIRM YOU'VE EVER SEEN?

Millwall in the '80s.

WHO ARE YOUR BIGGEST RIVALS TEAM-WISE?

I fucking hate Rovers, they annoy me. And I fucking hate Cardiff as well – in that order.

WHO ARE YOUR BIGGEST RIVALS FAN-WISE?

Cardiff, for the simple reason we've had some lively encounters lately. Last year we took near on 600 there and it was even-stevens.

HAVE YOU EVER JOINED UP WITH ANOTHER TEAM'S FIRM?

Yeah, twenty to thirty of us have been to a few Leicester games. We went to Southampton away, Cardiff away and Swindon away. It came about when we played them in a friendly at Ashton Gate and one of our lads got friendly with one of theirs. I think it was a bit of respect on both sides but we made a mistake going to Cardiff with them because they got well fucked there. They got run everywhere and this was in the early '70s and the skinhead era.

DID YOU EVER FOLLOW ENGLAND AND WOULD YOU PUT ENGLAND BEFORE YOUR CLUB?

I've only been away with England once and that was to Holland, and I'd put my club before England.

WHICH WAS THE BEST ENGLAND ROW?

I've never seen one because nothing happened in Holland. We had a big English firm out there but there was nothing doing. There's usually a good hundred City fans at the England games and it seems that us and Pompey have the hardcore of fans. It's funny, we get on at the England games but, when we play against each other, we hate one another on the day.

HAVE YOU EVER SUPPORTED OR LOOKED OUT FOR ANOTHER TEAM'S RESULTS?

No.

NAME YOUR TOP FIVE FIRMS, IN ANY ORDER.

Millwall, West Ham, Spurs, Pompey, Man. United – any order, that is.

WHICH IS THE WORST GROUND YOU'VE EVER BEEN TO AND WHY?

Twerton Park, where Rovers used to play. It was awful, terrible. We called it 'Trumpton'. It was a southern league ground and I think the capacity was only about 7,000. It was the home of Bath City.

WHICH IS THE BEST STADIUM YOU'VE BEEN TO?

Liverpool. We went there in '94 and we won 1–0. Anfield was brilliant. I've been to Old Trafford, but the sound of the Kop was something else.

WHO ARE THE FAIREST COPPERS YOU'VE COME ACROSS AT A MATCH?

Merseyside Old Bill. From my experience, they seem fair.

AND THE WORST OLD BILL?

Definitely West Midlands. It's just the way they treat everybody. You're scum. Everyone's an animal and you're treated like shit.

WHAT WOULD HAVE STOPPED YOU GETTING INVOLVED WITH THE BOYS AT MATCHES?

Nothing, I don't think … no, nothing. I've been married twice and I'm still going. If I stopped going I'd lose my mates and I don't want to do that. I like being part of it, being part of the firm.

DESCRIBE SOME OF THE METHODS AND TACTICS USED BY THE POLICE AND AUTHORITIES TO STOP FOOTBALL VIOLENCE, AND DO YOU THINK THEY WORK?

Zero tolerance, as practised by the West Midlands Police. It's always been the same up there. If it's Walsall or Coventry, it's zero tolerance and you're treated like shit.

HAVE YOU EVER BEEN SICKENED BY SOMETHING YOU'VE WITNESSED AT A GAME?

The hooligan programme that was on the BBC when they showed a mob of Millwall fans attacking a single Pompey fan walking back to his car. He was given a hiding and that was awful – a sickening sight.

WHAT'S YOUR FAVOURITE FOOTBALL SONG OR CHANT AND WHICH IS THE WORST YOU CAN RECALL HEARING FROM ANOTHER TEAM?

The best song from the '70s was the classic: 'We don't carry razors, We don't carry lead, We only carry hatchets to bury in your head.' The worst is 'Goodnight Irene', a '50s song adopted by Bristol Rovers. In the '70s when they started to sing this crap, we used to chant back 'Irene is a stripper'.

WHAT WAS YOUR FAVOURITE BAND/RECORD DURING YOUR FOOTBALL DAYS?

Mine's all the '70s reggae stuff, Chairman of the Board, George McCray and Brian Ferry. 'Rock Me Baby', by George McCray, was a favourite of mine.

WHO WAS YOUR ALL-TIME FAVOURITE PLAYER?

My all-time favourite player in the world is Alan Shearer. I just think he's 100 per cent – he's the best at his job. As for club players, I'd go for Andy Cole when we had him here, and Paul Cheesley.

WHERE DO YOU THINK THE NEW ENGLISH NATIONAL STADIUM SHOULD BE BUILT AND WHAT ARE YOUR THOUGHTS REGARDING THE WEMBLEY FIASCO?

I think it's a good idea to take the international games around to various stadiums as it lets everybody have a shout. I think closing Wembley was a right old balls-up. Let the Geordies have a few games up there – they're fanatics, aren't they?

CASS PENNANT MEETS

ANDY 'THE BEAR' PHILLIPS

CLUB: BRISTOL ROVERS

ANDY 'THE BEAR' PHILLIPS

THE MEET

Most football fans would have been to one of the Bristol clubs, at some time or another, so I felt it right to include the blue half of the city in this book. Who better to ask and to point me in the right direction than my old mate Browner. I drove down to Bristol to meet the legend 'Bear' and interviewed him in his home. Later all the boys went for a drink – not just Rovers lads but City's main boys as well – which was a first. But that's the power of the pen for you. Andy's a smashing fella who made me feel more than welcome. Here's what he said about his days at Rovers.

BACKGROUND

I've been a regular at Rovers since the age of about ten. I used to go with my father and brothers, but my mum tells a story that when she was pregnant with me in 1950 she was queuing up for tickets for an FA Cup game against Newcastle United, so I was more or less born blue and white. I left school and worked for a firm that made and erected marquees all over the country.

WHAT'S YOUR FAVOURITE TERRACE FASHION?

I was never really into fashion. That's why we were known as 'the Tramps'. A lot of the guys at the time were into the mods and rockers gear, and I once wore a leather jacket with studs on, and I got some stick off the boys. I also once had a pair of black flared trousers with a white diamond on the bottom, topped off with a pair of winkle-picker boots. I hated the skinhead fashion. I suppose I'd describe myself as a bit of a greaser.

WHAT'S THE WORST FASHION YOU'VE EVER SEEN ON THE TERRACES?

Skinhead and suedehead gear – I hated it.

DESCRIBE YOUR WORST FEELING AT A GAME.

Losing to Huddersfield in the play-off final at Wembley. That was when the Wembley play-offs first started. It was a sickening feeling.

HAVE YOU EVER INCURRED ANY SERIOUS INJURIES OR BEEN BADLY BEATEN UP AT A MATCH?

At Shrewsbury, in the mid-'70s, when I had my nose broken. I was standing on the terraces, I looked around and, crack, I felt and heard my nose go. I tried to catch the bloke but he shot off a bit lively. The following year we played them at their place and we turned up team-handed. We went into their end and there he was. I punched him that hard I knocked him across the barrier and give him a right pasting.

HAS YOUR OWN SIDE EVER BEEN INVOLVED IN A FULL-SCALE RIOT?

Two coach loads of us stopped in Mansfield on the way back from a game at Chesterfield in about '74 and a full-scale riot developed. Windows were smashed as we clashed with Liverpool fans on their way back from a game, and gangs of locals. It went on for most of the night, with Old Bill everywhere.

DESCRIBE THE BEST TAKING OF AN END YOU'VE EVER WITNESSED.

I suppose that would be Aston Villa in about '71. We got into the Holt End early and we were doing well. We were in control for half an hour and then their mob came in and took their end back. Outside, on the park, it was going right off. There was about 45,000 at the game – not bad for a Third Division fixture actually. We've had some good punch-ups with Villa and it was Villa fans that gave me the nickname 'the Bear'. They asked a mate of mine, 'Who's the big geezer that looks like a bear?' Since then the name's stuck. Chelsea fans also know me as 'the Bear' because we used to have a few run-ins with them.

WHICH WAS YOUR OWN TEAM'S POPULAR END?

The Tote End. That's because around the edge of Rovers' pitch was a greyhound track and we stood on the terraces where you could have a bet on the tote – hence the name. We are also known as 'the Gas' or 'Gasheads' because of the gas works next door to the ground.

WHERE DID YOU STAND OR SIT IN THE GROUND?

The Tote End.

CAN YOU RECALL A BATTLE YOU HAVE BEEN INVOLVED IN, EITHER INSIDE OR OUTSIDE A GROUND?

Leeds away in the FA Cup. We were in their pub before kick-off and as we came out it went off, and I punched this bloke. It was like a Desperate Dan thing. Where I'd punched and jumped into this bloke by a corrugated iron wall it left his imprint in it.

Stoke at home, again in the FA Cup, that was another good one. Gordon Banks was in goal for them and I think they won 4–2 and run us in the Tote End – one of only two real firms to do so. We had a real good punch-up there that night and it was going on all day and all night.

CAN YOU RECALL THE BEST EVER MOB YOUR TEAM HAS PUT TOGETHER?

The Tote End Boys of the early '70s.

WHO'S THE BEST RIVAL FIRM YOU'VE EVER SEEN?

The Stoke City mob I've just mentioned was very impressive. They had a bloke with them that must have been eight feet tall. He was enormous, and they had to squeeze and push him through the turnstiles to get him in, he was that big. Birmingham also came in the Tote End in the late '60s and Rovers and City joined up to take them on.

Another time we stopped in Ashby de la Zouche on the way back from a game. All the roads were blocked off in the town centre because there was a street fair. We weren't there long when we saw a mob 100-strong chasing another mob and it turns out it was Man. United chasing Leicester fans. Everyone hates United so we joined up with the Leicester boys and give the United fans a good kicking. It was a good time and a good night.

WHO ARE YOUR BIGGEST RIVALS TEAM-WISE?

Bristol City and Aston Villa.

WHO ARE YOUR BIGGEST RIVALS FAN-WISE?

Bristol City. We never got on with them and still don't. It's quite boring, really, but they're from a different part of the city. Funny thing is, I live among them now.

HAVE YOU EVER JOINED UP WITH ANOTHER TEAM'S FIRM?

Yeah, Leicester and, even though we hated them, Bristol City. We even used to share a pub. It would be City in one bar and Rovers in the other, and we never once fell out. If a big London team came down, we'd join up together and be Bristol against the invaders.

DID YOU EVER FOLLOW ENGLAND AND WOULD YOU PUT ENGLAND BEFORE YOUR CLUB?

I didn't go to many games. I went to Cardiff once and it went off with the Welsh in a pub near the ground. England would never come before my club, no – no way.

WHICH WAS THE BEST ENGLAND ROW?

Wales v England. We never used to get on with the Welsh – still don't.

HAVE YOU EVER SUPPORTED OR LOOKED OUT FOR ANOTHER TEAM'S RESULTS?

No, just Rovers for me.

NAME YOUR TOP FIVE FIRMS, IN ANY ORDER.

Stoke City, Walsall, Leeds, Chelsea, West Ham. You might think, Walsall? But, believe me, at one time they were quite tasty. They were a little club with a nice hard-core mob. Every time we played them it was always a good punch-up, even though Birmingham fans would be with them, and God knows who else.

WHICH IS THE WORST GROUND YOU'VE EVER BEEN TO AND WHY?

I'd say Workington's ground when they were in the football league.

WHICH IS THE BEST STADIUM YOU'VE BEEN TO?

Goodison Park – it's awesome. We played Everton in the Cup up there and I was skint, so I pinched some money from the scrapyard I worked in. The next day I came back into work and was nicked. They kept a couple of Alsatian dogs in the yard and there was only a couple of people who could get near them, and I was one, so the finger pointed at me nicking the money. We lost the game and I lost my job.

WHO ARE THE FAIREST COPPERS YOU'VE COME ACROSS AT A MATCH?

Halifax. In them days there was only one copper on duty and he didn't want to get in the way of a punch-up so he'd just say, 'Carry on, do what you've got to do.'

AND THE WORST OLD BILL?

That would be Bolton. We were rowing with their boys outside and their Old Bill just stood and watched as some of their lot threw bricks and bottles at us. They just didn't do a thing about it – not that we wanted them to, but I didn't think a lot of them.

WHAT WOULD HAVE STOPPED YOU GETTING INVOLVED WITH THE BOYS AT MATCHES?

Nothing at all – it's in the blood.

DESCRIBE SOME OF THE METHODS AND TACTICS USED BY THE POLICE AND AUTHORITIES TO STOP FOOTBALL VIOLENCE, AND DO YOU THINK THEY WORK?

I go back to Everton again. We played most of our football in the old Third Division so when we played a First Division team there was fan segregation, police, dogs and horses – things we didn't find in our league – and it stopped the potential for trouble.

HAVE YOU EVER BEEN SICKENED BY SOMETHING YOU'VE WITNESSED AT A GAME?

Two things. One was watching Heysel unfold on TV. I think that shocked a lot of people. The other was Rovers fans coming back from an away game and fighting at a wedding reception in Gloucester. They spoiled this poor couple's day. They gatecrashed it and basically ruined their wedding. I didn't go a lot on that.

WHAT'S YOUR FAVOURITE FOOTBALL SONG OR CHANT AND WHICH IS THE WORST YOU CAN RECALL HEARING FROM ANOTHER TEAM?

My favourite is 'I was born under the Tote End bar' sung to Lee Marvin's 'I Was Born Under A Wandering Star'. The worst is 'Red Robin', City's chant. I fucking hate that, it gets right up my nose.

WHAT WAS YOUR FAVOURITE BAND/RECORD DURING YOUR FOOTBALL DAYS?

Favourite band was Deep Purple and favourite record was John Conga's 'I'm Going To Step On You Again' – it's a classic song.

WHO WAS YOUR ALL-TIME FAVOURITE PLAYER?

Alan Warboys and Bruce Bannister at Rovers. In the '70s they were called 'Smash and Grab' because they went in where it hurt. Also, Mick Jones at Leeds – he was a very underrated player.

WHERE DO YOU THINK THE NEW ENGLISH NATIONAL STADIUM SHOULD BE BUILT AND WHAT ARE YOUR THOUGHTS REGARDING THE WEMBLEY FIASCO?

I think England should always play at Wembley, not all over the country – they should play in one place. Wembley was always a sacred ground. It's taken the magic away from the game.

MARTIN KING MEETS

MAC
CLUB: CARDIFF CITY

MAC

THE MEET

I arranged to meet Mac at a pub near Kew Bridge in London. He was in town to watch a doorman who works for him in a boxing match later that evening. I've met Mac before, when I was in Cardiff for the Chelsea v Arsenal Cup Final. I was introduced to him while drinking in one of his bars and I found him a right nice fella. He made me and my mates more than welcome – he was the perfect host.

On the day of the interview he phoned me to tell me was running late. About half an hour later he pulled up in his sports car with the personalised number plate – you can tell Mac's now a successful businessman. As he stepped from the car I could see he'd lost some weight. We shook hands. 'Fuck me, Mac, you look well. You've done some weight?' 'Yeah, I know, three stone in all. It's all that gym work and running I've been doing.' We got a drink, sat down and began to natter.

BACKGROUND

I went to my first match with my dad in 1970 when Cardiff were in the old Second Division. I went with the old man regularly for a few seasons, then in 1974/5 I started going to games with my younger brother. I remember when I was about ten and Man. Utd came down with about 10.000 fans and covered the Bob End – I was shitting myself.

After I left school I trained as a butcher, which was handy for me because the terrace fashion at the time was white butchers' coats with the names of the team and players written all over them. We had a fella called Frankie who was the Cardiff leader. He was a legend in those days – the fans on the terraces used to sing songs about him. He was the gamest man I've ever seen at football but a real gentleman with it.

WHAT'S YOUR FAVOURITE TERRACE FASHION?

I like the classic labels like Boss, Prada and Lacoste. In the '80s I'd go suited up. I remember a cup game at QPR and I was on the pitch having a row in my Armani suit.

WHAT'S THE WORST FASHION YOU'VE EVER SEEN ON THE TERRACES?

It must be Stone Island – some of the quality is piss poor. If I wear a jumper or jacket of theirs, I take the badge off. Another label that makes me cringe now is Burberry – there's so much fake stuff about. Oh yeah, and shell suits still favoured by some Scousers.

DESCRIBE YOUR WORST FEELING AT A GAME.

There's two. The first was against Stoke City in the 2001/2 season's play-off semi-finals. We'd beaten them away in the first leg and everyone had great expectations. The club was moving forward at long last but we lost in the return and were knocked out. The other was the Third Division play-offs against Northampton. If we had won and our fierce rivals Swansea had won, which they did, we would have met in the final at Wembley. That game would have been nigh on impossible to police.

HAVE YOU EVER INCURRED ANY SERIOUS INJURIES OR BEEN BADLY BEATEN UP AT A MATCH?

Wolves in '88. It was the old First Division. They were top and we were second, and we won 4–1. I was sitting in the front of a minibus with about fifteen of us stuck in traffic waiting to pull out of a car park. We'd had a bit of a result before the game when a mob of ours had run Wolves outside the ground, so perhaps we were a little too confident or complacent. Next thing we were spotted and a mob of about 200 of their lot surrounded the van and smashed all the windows, and began attacking the boys stuck inside with bits of wood and scaffold poles. It was really frightening – I thought we were going to die.

A breeze block was thrown through the window and hit me in the guts. I felt faint and in a lot of pain – it felt like my ribs were broken. The driver managed to get up on the kerb and speed off along the path to escape. We got halfway home and I was in a lot of pain. We pulled up on the motorway and an ambulance was called. I refused to get in, saying there was no way I was going into hospital miles from home. We arrived back in Cardiff about half-past ten at night and went straight to the hospital's accident and emergency. Within minutes I was on an operating table, the doctors saying I was very close to death. I had internal bleeding, a ruptured spleen, several broken ribs and other internal organs were damaged. It was the most frightening day of my football life.

HAS YOUR OWN SIDE EVER BEEN INVOLVED IN A FULL-SCALE RIOT?

Swansea in the FA Cup in 1991 was the most memorable. It seemed that every window in every pub and shop was smashed to pieces. About 1,000 of us got there early and just wrecked the place. We'd been looking forward to this game for weeks. The Old Bill just couldn't handle it – our mob was too big. We smashed their boys. That day we would have done any firm – we were too big and too powerful.

DESCRIBE THE BEST TAKING OF AN END YOU'VE EVER WITNESSED.

It must be the Cup game against Everton in '77. They'd been given half of the Bob Bank End and our boys came in from the other side and ran the Everton fans right out of the ground. I was with my old man that day watching from across the other side of the pitch. Another time was at QPR in 1990. There was a big queue to get into the away-fans end so three of us walked round to the other side of the ground and went into the Rangers end. We let them know who we were and they just backed off. A big gap opened up around us but we stayed in there until half-time. Then we decided to jump the wall to stand back up at the other end with the main bulk of the Cardiff fans. As we walked round the edge of the pitch we got a massive round of applause from our lot.

WHICH WAS YOUR OWN TEAM'S POPULAR END?

It's been changed a few times. It's been the Bob Bank and the Grange End. Not many visiting ventured in there and came out in one piece.

WHERE DID YOU STAND OR SIT IN THE GROUND?

The Grange End.

CAN YOU RECALL A BATTLE YOU HAVE BEEN INVOLVED IN, EITHER INSIDE OR OUTSIDE A GROUND?

Millwall, first game of the season at our place in August 1999. We had a massive turn out by us and we'd been trying to get at them all day long but the police had it sewn up. There'd been one small row that morning when a small mob of about thirty Millwall fans got off one of the early trains and plotted up in a pub, but there were no real toe to toes. We had a mob of about 600 and the shout went up that 300 Millwall fans were coming our way. Two motorcycle Old Bill rode through the crowd and one was dragged from his bike – the crowd was in a hostile mood. At one stage a police helicopter landed in the park behind the ground to keep rival fans apart. So before the game it was a bit of a non-event. After the final whistle, we done the usual hanging around outside for the visitors. The Old Bill tried moving us on when a mob of about a hundred Millwall fans came out from a side entrance. We steamed into them and hammered them back into the ground. They were fighting one another to get back inside but, respect to them, they brought the fight to us and not many teams do that.

CAN YOU RECALL THE BEST EVER MOB YOUR TEAM HAS PUT TOGETHER?

Later on that season when we played Millwall at their place. We had a mob of about 700. Some of the faces out that day I hadn't seen for years. We were awesome that day.

WHO'S THE BEST RIVAL FIRM YOU'VE EVER SEEN?

Chelsea at our place in the early '80s – that was a cracking mob. And also Pompey, around the same time, showed up big time and impressed us. And Middlesbrough in the Cup in '93. About 100 of them showed up early and plotted up in a pub called The Albert. They were all old heads – no kids – and were well organised. We got to the doors and they drove us back, so we attacked again and they ran us. Walking up towards the ground our boys were gutted.

WHO ARE YOUR BIGGEST RIVALS TEAM-WISE?

Swansea and Bristol City.

WHO ARE YOUR BIGGEST RIVALS FAN-WISE?

Swansea and Bristol City. And I don't like the Yids either. When they were playing Blackburn at the Millennium Stadium I was working in town at one of my pubs. A bloke and his wife were looking for a certain pub, where they were meeting their friends. It was easier to show them than give them directions. We got to the pub and standing just inside the door was about seventy of Spurs' main boys. 'Oi!' one of them said. 'What's happened to your boys?' He must have recognised me from a BBC undercover documentary I'd recently had the misfortune to unknowingly appear in. I explained that if any of Cardiff's faces were caught in town on a Cup Final day they were likely to be arrested by the Old Bill. 'But why weren't Tottenham around last night?' I asked him. 'All our boys were out but you lot were in Swansea drinking with your Jack mates.' With that he took a swing at me and I banged him, and dragged him out the door with me. A few of them threw bottles and glasses at me, and followed me out on to the street. I stood there and called them on but they froze and didn't know how to handle the situation. The Old Bill appeared and moved me on. There wasn't a mark on me, the cowardly cunts.

HAVE YOU EVER JOINED UP WITH ANOTHER TEAM'S FIRM?

No, but I've been to watch Chelsea a couple of times. One of my doormen is a Chelsea fan so I've been with him. Also I've been up to watch Sunderland and Newcastle but purely as an observer.

© PA Photos

DID YOU EVER FOLLOW WALES AND WOULD YOU PUT WALES BEFORE YOUR CLUB?

I've been all over Europe watching Wales. I was locked up in Finland for three days and deported, and it got into all the local press. If Wales lose, I'm bothered for about ten minutes. If Cardiff lose, it fucks up my whole week. No, it's definitely club before country. My wife even looks out for the football scores so she knows what mood to expect me home in.

WHICH WAS THE BEST WALES ROW?

In Nuremberg, Germany, in the early '90s. A couple of thousand of our boys made the trip and put up a good show. Also in Belgium, at Anderlecht's ground, where again I was arrested and deported.

HAVE YOU EVER SUPPORTED OR LOOKED OUT FOR ANOTHER TEAM'S RESULTS?

One hundred per cent no.

NAME YOUR TOP FIVE FIRMS, IN ANY ORDER.

I'll steer clear of the ones everybody thinks I'm going to say – the likes of West Ham and Chelsea and other Premiership teams – when the simple fact is we've not played them for years. From personal experience and dealings, I'd say Millwall – I've got huge respect for them. Wolves – they're a top firm to match anyone on their day. Stoke – they can pull the numbers and are game. Portsmouth – because whenever we've played them they've been well game. And finally I was going to go for Hull City because they've turned up at our place the last few times we've met, and up there they turn out in huge numbers. But I'd have to go for Barnsley. We played them in the league in the 2002/3 and they turned up at our place eighty-handed and were as game as fuck. They held their own and have my respect. It's the same with a lot of the so-called smaller, lower-league clubs such as Chesterfield, Huddersfield and Burnley, and teams like Preston and Darlington – all tough northern towns. They don't necessarily travel well but one thing's for sure – never underestimate them.

WHICH IS THE WORST GROUND YOU'VE EVER BEEN TO AND WHY?

After years of playing in the lower divisions we've played at some shitty places – Halifax, Northampton's old ground and the Old Den, which wasn't so much a bad ground, just a nasty place. It had such a hostile atmosphere. I went there when I was seventeen years old and soon found out it was a rough place to watch football. But as for shitty grounds, I'm really spoiled for choice I've been to that many.

WHICH IS THE BEST STADIUM YOU'VE BEEN TO?

When I go on holiday abroad I always have a look around the local grounds, so I've had a look at the Nou Camp, Santiago Bernabeu and Olympic Stadium in Rome. All impressive stadiums – even when they're empty you get an incredible feel to the place. But my favourite has to be the Millennium Stadium. It's a beautiful big stadium smack bang in the middle of the city. It's not an eyesore and the travel facilities, shops and bars are right there on top of it.

WHO ARE THE FAIREST COPPERS YOU'VE COME ACROSS AT A MATCH?

Starsky and Hutch. No, only joking. I should say our own, down in Cardiff, but I don't want to push my luck because someone high up might say, 'Right, let's nick him', so I won't answer that question. One of Cardiff's main football intelligence officers was a mate of mine before he joined the force, and I was going to be Best Man at his wedding. But I'm under no illusion that, if he had to nick me, I'm sure he would. Plus I've never had any grief off the Met so I see them as fair.

AND THE WORST OLD BILL?

West Yorkshire. We've had loads of grief off them.

WHAT WOULD HAVE STOPPED YOU GETTING INVOLVED WITH THE BOYS AT MATCHES?

A banning order. A mate of mine has just got a ten-year one and that would kill me. I'd rather do six months inside than be deprived of watching football.

DESCRIBE SOME OF THE METHODS AND TACTICS USED BY THE POLICE AND AUTHORITIES TO STOP FOOTBALL VIOLENCE, AND DO YOU THINK THEY WORK?

It has to be cameras and CCTV. Years ago if you had a ruck and you weren't nicked on the spot, you'd gotten away with it. Nowadays they can come and kick your door in six months later and cart you away for something you'd been caught doing on film. At Millwall away we had a massive mob and when we got off the tube at Paddington, and made our way upstairs to the mainline station, there was a solid corridor of Old Bill with not a gap between them. It was wall-to-wall coppers. Even if you wanted to go elsewhere, there was no chance. So I suppose the excessive use of coppers seems to work. Tapping phones is another one of the techniques employed by the boys in blue.

HAVE YOU EVER BEEN SICKENED BY SOMETHING YOU'VE WITNESSED AT A GAME?

Not really, but I don't believe innocent people like women and kids should get hurt, and people like scarfers and shirts should be left alone. But generally most clubs adhere to the rules of combat.

WHAT'S YOUR FAVOURITE FOOTBALL SONG OR CHANT AND WHICH IS THE WORST YOU CAN RECALL HEARING FROM ANOTHER TEAM?

The worst have got to be the songs about Aberfan in Wales, where in 1966 young school children tragically lost their lives. And the songs about the Munich air disaster are sad. And, believe it or not, rival fans sing to the Scousers about the deaths they suffered at Hillsborough – there's certainly some sick bastards about. My favourite terrace chant has got to be the abuse about us being sheep shaggers. We've turned it around now and we call ourselves the sheep shaggers.

WHAT WAS YOUR FAVOURITE BAND/RECORD DURING YOUR FOOTBALL DAYS?

The Jam, The Clash. We still play them on our bus to away games today.

WHO WAS YOUR ALL-TIME FAVOURITE PLAYER?

Phil Dwyer who played for us between '72 and '85. He was a local lad, not blessed with the greatest of skill but he always gave 110 per cent. I later met up with him after he packed up the game. He stopped me for speeding – he's a copper now. In 1977 we had a player with us for half a season called Robin Friday. Honestly, he was fucking brilliant but as mad as a hatter. He looked like a gypsy – a real scruffy bastard. But he was so gifted – a sort of Peter Osgood or Rodney Marsh. Then he disappeared and later on in life he sadly died. I consider it a real privilege to have seen him play in the flesh.

WHAT DO YOU THINK OF THE MILLENNIUM STADIUM BEING USED BY THE ENGLISH FA FOR BIG GAMES?

It's been great for the City fans coming to a game and enjoying their stay so much that they come back again with their wives or girlfriends and make a weekend of it. But it's a shambles that the English FA can't get their act together and build a national stadium. It's a farce.

MARTIN KING MEETS

NEIL
CLUB: WREXHAM

NEIL

THE MEET

I'd been given Neil's number by my Cardiff mate Tony Rivers, who told me all about Neil and the reputation he had at Wrexham. I got in contact with him, and we spoke several times over the phone. Here's what he had to say.

BACKGROUND

I'm 39 years of age and the firm I go to football with is nicknamed the Front Line. A mate of mine, Big Rod, came up with the name in the early '80s because he said the boys that wanted to row put themselves on the front line.

WHAT'S YOUR FAVOURITE TERRACE FASHION?

I've been into clothes since about '78 when I used to go into Liverpool to buy my clobber. In the early '80s I was into Armani, Burberry and Aquascutum, and into the '90s it had to be Stone Island. Prada now seems to be the order of the day.

WHAT'S THE WORST FASHION YOU'VE EVER SEEN ON THE TERRACES?

That's got to be deerstalker hats. And, when the rave scene took off, everyone started wearing them multicoloured tops. I couldn't work out if they were going to an all-nighter or the match.

DESCRIBE YOUR WORST FEELING AT A GAME.

I'd say my worst feeling was when twelve of us slipped the police escort at an away game with our rivals, Shrewsbury Town. The dozen of us that slipped the net were all good boys and wouldn't let one another down. We were all up for it, so we knew if we bumped into Shrewsbury's mob we would give it our best shot and they would get it. As we got into the town centre I noticed the bizzies had seen us but had done nothing to stop us. We carried on walking and they followed about fifty yards behind. I had this feeling they knew something we didn't and we could be on some sort of suicide mission. We headed towards the station, where I expected their mob might well be in wait for us. I looked behind and noticed the police had stopped and we were now on our own.

The station came in sight and a roar filled the air as about forty of their lads piled around the corner and steamed into us. We went straight into them and it was a real row. We never backed off but the sheer size of their numbers was beginning to tell. From behind we could hear another mob bearing down on us. That's it, we're finished, I was thinking. At worst they'd do a clever pincer movement and they'd be stamping on us all night. But suddenly the Wurzels began to back off. There was a look of terror on their faces as another mob of our boys had come to our rescue. My feelings had never changed that fast. We chased them off and the bizzies arrived, and saved a couple of the locals from a good kicking. We were rounded up and surrounded by Old Bill with vans and dogs, and kept for about an hour before they released us in small groups without charge.

HAVE YOU EVER INCURRED ANY SERIOUS INJURIES OR BEEN BADLY BEATEN UP AT A MATCH?

Not really, but once I end up with fifteen stitches after a row with a mob of Cardiff. About seventy of us travelled to Belgium to watch Wales play in Brussels. About forty of us got off our coach and headed straight to the nearest bar, while the others went to the hotel. After about ten minutes one of our lot came in telling us some Cardiff boys were outside and they'd been giving him lots of grief. We all pushed outside. Standing there were thirty of Cardiff's finest – the Dock Boys, who can have a row.

They came straight into us, but the numbers favour us. It was toe to toe. Bottles were being used and thrown, and we grabbed a stack of wooden chairs. We had them on the run and chased them into a square. A bottle smashed on top of my head and I launched a chair into them. The riot police arrived on the scene and a baton hit the back of my head. I could feel the blood flowing down the back of my neck. I was dazed but stayed on my feet. I was handcuffed and thrown into the back of a police wagon, where they set about beating the living daylights out of us. We were then dumped at the local nick, where after more beating the injured ones were taken to hospital for treatment. After my stitches I walked out, and the rest were deported after two days. I'd call that particular fight with Cardiff's top boys one of our best all-time performances. A Cardiff lad described in a book his account of how he saw things. I know what I saw and was involved in, and this time victory was ours.

HAS YOUR OWN SIDE EVER BEEN INVOLVED IN A FULL-SCALE RIOT?

There've been a few nasty ones but Oldham away, last year, was one to remember. We've got a bit of history with their lot and I think it stems from them mobbing up with Stockport and Scotland's Hibs and the Shrewsbury Wurzels. Why do they have to mob up with other firms? Where's their pride? We agreed to get it sorted once and for all, and a meet was set up in a Manchester backstreet, away from the Old Bill and CCTV cameras. About fifty of us plotted up in a pub and it wasn't long before one of their lot came strolling in, telling us they were 300 yards up the road and that we should go to them. We knew full well they would be tooled up to the eyeballs, and that was why we had to move and not them.

We were fed up with waiting and headed in their direction, ammo in hand. Standing on the first corner were a group of Man. United fans who'd heard about the off and had came down to watch. We marched on and at the next crossroads about ten Oldham lads rained bottles down on us. At the same time about thirty of them poured out of a side road towards us. With no Old Bill about and no cameras, we gave it to them. We chased most of them back into a pub, where they thought they were safe. One was left stranded outside and he was punched to the floor. Soon every window was put in and broken glass littered the road. We steamed inside as their main boy tried to rally his troops and encourage them to get up from the tables they were hiding under. Someone smashed him over the head with a pump handle, which had been ripped from the bar. Some of them locked themselves in the toilets as their pals took a battering. We finished them off good and proper, only leaving the pub as we heard the police sirens approaching. We stepped over the prostrate body still lying motionless in the doorway and strolled off. Job done.

DESCRIBE THE BEST TAKING OF AN END YOU'VE EVER WITNESSED.
In the '70s and '80s me and a couple of mates would always go into the home team's end. At away games we'd either get sussed out by rival fans and a big gap would open up all around us, or the local plod would end up dragging us out and throw us down the other end, where the rest of our lads would be standing. I never saw anyone take the Kop End at Wrexham. I've seen plenty of teams try but no one ever stayed in there.

WHICH WAS YOUR OWN TEAM'S POPULAR END?
In the early days it was called the Town End or the Kop. Then all the boys sat to the right of the away supporters in the Yale Stand, recently renamed the Price Griffiths Stand.

WHERE DID YOU STAND OR SIT IN THE GROUND?
When I was allowed in, I'd say the Yale Stand, but I've just finished a five-year ban and now I'm on a three-year ban. Who knows when I'll be back.

CAN YOU RECALL A BATTLE YOU HAVE BEEN INVOLVED IN, EITHER INSIDE OR OUTSIDE A GROUND?
In the seats at Blackpool, in 1991. At the final whistle about 100 of

us steamed across the pitch into the home end and chased the crowd into the surrounding streets. Twenty-five of our lot were arrested after two pubs were smashed up and a copper was put in hospital.

CAN YOU RECALL THE BEST EVER MOB YOUR TEAM HAS PUT TOGETHER?

For a big local derby we've pulled 300 before now. Despite having thirty of our main boys banged up, we took a huge mob to Shrewsbury last time we played them. And during the 2001/2 season we took eighty top faces, all over the age of thirty, to QPR.

WHO'S THE BEST RIVAL FIRM YOU'VE EVER SEEN?

Birmingham up at Blackpool. One year they must have had a mob 1,000-strong.

WHO ARE YOUR BIGGEST RIVALS TEAM-WISE?

Chester City, when they were in the League. The last time we played them, on a Friday night in the FA Cup, I lost my £500 Stone Island jacket after a scuffle with a Chester mob. One of the Old Bill grabbed me and I squeezed out of my jacket, and had it away – but not before I was smashed around the head by a police baton and I ended up having it stitched back up in Wrexham Hospital. There were nineteen of our lads nicked that night. Months later the police launched operation 'Adhere' and a few of us got the dawn raid. I was charged with violent disorder and expected to be hit hard, but all they had on me was me and a mate gesturing at Chester City fans from behind police lines – no film of me doing a Harry Houdini trick. Ten months later we all appeared at Chester Crown Court, where nineteen of the boys received up to six months custodial sentences. Me and two mates got not guilty verdicts and walked away.

WHO ARE YOUR BIGGEST RIVALS FAN-WISE?

Chester and Shrewsbury Town.

HAVE YOU EVER JOINED UP WITH ANOTHER TEAM'S FIRM?

No, never.

DID YOU EVER FOLLOW ENGLAND AND WOULD YOU PUT ENGLAND BEFORE YOUR CLUB?

I'm Welsh but I have been to a couple of England games. No, it's club before country for me.

WHICH WAS THE BEST WALES ROW?

Cologne in '88. After the game a mob of Wrexham, Cardiff and Bangor lads got off the train at the main station and we made our way towards the city centre. We turned up a side road and two distress flares were fired at us from the top of a multi-storey car park. Both fell well short of the target as they exploded on to the road. A mob of about 100 Krauts came at us from the shadows. We steamed into them and scattered them everywhere. They regrouped and came at us again, and we ran them a second time. This happened again and again before the riot Old Bill turned up and kept the peace. A couple of years later one of our lot got talking to Ronald, a well-known German face. He's been with Chelsea, Arsenal, Millwall, Cardiff, Glasgow Rangers and most clubs in Europe. Anywhere there's going to be a row, you'll find Ronald. Well, he admitted that Wales had done the business that night and he was most impressed with our boys.

HAVE YOU EVER SUPPORTED OR LOOKED OUT FOR ANOTHER TEAM'S RESULTS?

No and I never will.

NAME YOUR TOP FIVE FIRMS, IN ANY ORDER.

Millwall, Cardiff, Birmingham, Spurs, Man. United.

WHICH IS THE WORST GROUND YOU'VE EVER BEEN TO AND WHY?

That has to be Shrewsbury Town's. They've not improved that place since the '70s.

WHICH IS THE BEST STADIUM YOU'VE BEEN TO?

I'd say Old Trafford or the Millennium Stadium. But I doubt if I'll see the inside of any football stadium for a long time as I'm banned at the moment and have to sign on at the police station.

WHO ARE THE FAIREST COPPERS YOU'VE COME ACROSS AT A MATCH?

Is there such a thing?

AND THE WORST OLD BILL?

Ours, when they done the dawn raids. We had inside info the day before so they found lots of lads moved out or not at home. The Midlands Old Bill – they'd nick you for smiling.

WHAT WOULD HAVE STOPPED YOU GETTING INVOLVED WITH THE BOYS AT MATCHES?

No violence.

DESCRIBE SOME OF THE METHODS AND TACTICS USED BY THE POLICE AND AUTHORITIES TO STOP FOOTBALL VIOLENCE, AND DO YOU THINK THEY WORK?

Old Bill who sit outside pubs watching the boys en masse.

HAVE YOU EVER BEEN SICKENED BY SOMETHING YOU'VE WITNESSED AT A GAME?

I've seen a Wigan lad knocked out cold and covered in blood, and I thought he was dead. But later I heard he recovered after a couple of days in hospital. One of our lot gave a slash to a Wolves lad, who received forty stitches and was jailed for five years. But the Old Bill arrested the wrong geezer – the lad who really done it wouldn't own up. It was awkward for a while, as they were both good mates of mine.

WHAT'S YOUR FAVOURITE FOOTBALL SONG OR CHANT AND WHICH IS THE WORST YOU CAN RECALL HEARING FROM ANOTHER TEAM?

None in particular.

WHAT WAS YOUR FAVOURITE BAND/RECORD DURING YOUR FOOTBALL DAYS?

Can't think of any.

WHO WAS YOUR ALL-TIME FAVOURITE PLAYER?

Wrexham's prolific goal scorer from the '90s – Gary Bennet.

WHERE DO YOU THINK THE NEW ENGLISH NATIONAL STADIUM SHOULD BE BUILT AND WHAT ARE YOUR THOUGHTS REGARDING THE WEMBLEY FIASCO?

No thoughts – I'm Welsh.

MARTIN KING MEETS

MR B
CLUB: BARNSLEY

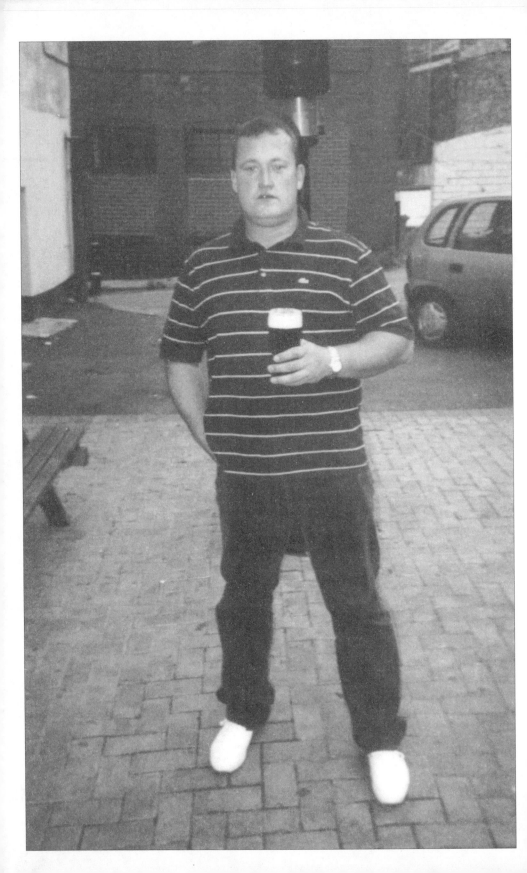

MR B

THE MEET

Now and again in football-hooliganism circles the name Barnsley would crop up. They were well known as a team that had a good little firm and over the years they had had some good results against firms from bigger clubs. Their reputation in the lower leagues has become somewhat legendary. Over the years I've been up there with Chelsea a few times and they never disappointed. Needless to say, I was well pleased when Nick, one of their faces, gave me a call and offered to put me in touch with their top boys. He'd heard about the book on the hoolie grapevine and wanted to know if I was interested in including the Barnsley boys in *Terrace Legends*. Of course I was. I jumped at the chance, and here, in his own words, is what one of their main chaps had to say.

BACKGROUND

I first started watching Barnsley when I was seven. I started going to games on my own at twelve and began knocking about with the older lads as a teenager in the early '80s. I joined the Army at sixteen, and was always going AWOL for the matches. All the skinheads used to stand in the corner of the ground near the away fans, and as I got older I started to get nearer and nearer to where they stood, eventually standing with them. They called themselves the Barnsley Beer Monsters. In the early '80s the fashions changed and the skinheads became Pringle boys. We started travelling in large numbers and began calling ourselves the Inter City Tykes, a rip-off of West Ham firm's name. This didn't last long and was changed to the Barnsley Casual Mafia, and more recently the Barnsley Five-O.

WHAT'S YOUR FAVOURITE TERRACE FASHION?

We weren't big on all this posing. All this Aquascutum hat and scarf stuff just makes firms look like prats – all in the same clobber and all that.

WHAT'S THE WORST FASHION YOU'VE EVER SEEN ON THE TERRACES?

Aquascutum hats and scarves.

DESCRIBE YOUR WORST FEELING AT A GAME.

When we lost the Division One play-off final to Ipswich at Wembley in 2000.

HAVE YOU EVER INCURRED ANY SERIOUS INJURIES OR BEEN BADLY BEATEN UP AT A MATCH?

We came unstuck outside the Old Den at Millwall. We'd just jumped out of a van and battered ten Millwall lads. We set off again but we got stuck in traffic and the ten had now become fifty. They smashed the van and then smashed us. I ended up getting a severe beating.

Middlesbrough 1983/4 was a bad one for injuries. We took a massive firm on the train – around two hundred – and we thought we'd take over, and we did. We were running the show and took over a boozer called The Wellington. The Boro lads were walking past the windows in twos and threes, putting their hands to their throats threatening to slash us, but we'd heard all this shit before, and carried on boozing. A few minutes later about thirty Boro appeared outside, so we charged through the doors and out at them. That was it. Out came the machetes and Stanley knives and seven of our top lads were cut to ribbons. One lad had to have over 100 stitches to a head and neck wound, and was lucky to survive. It was Ali Ali's Boro mob and we still hate the bastards now, fucking cowards. Another time was when we travelled to Oldham in the late '90s and a pub was smashed up. The police turned up and decided to let the dogs off. Me and my mate, Nicky, were savaged and our arms and legs were torn to bits.

My worst injury was probably when about thirty of us had a night out in Scarborough in the '90s and during a fight outside a nightclub I was slashed across my left shoulder and back, and the wound needed thirty stitches.

HAS YOUR OWN SIDE EVER BEEN INVOLVED IN A FULL-SCALE RIOT?

Bognor Regis. It hardly got a mention in the press as it was the same weekend that Leeds rioted in Bournemouth. We'd played Portsmouth away and we stopped off there. When the pubs shut our mob of about 100 was being policed by about thirty in two vans. One of our lads had had enough and decided to throw a bottle at them. They steamed straight in at us with their truncheons. We stood our ground and it turned into a full-on toe-to-toe with the police on the sea front, for about two hours. One of our lads, Albert, had a finger bitten off by a police dog. No reinforcements came because they were all dealing with Leeds fans in Bournemouth, just twenty miles away.

DESCRIBE THE BEST TAKING OF AN END YOU'VE EVER WITNESSED.

None really. The coppers were in control by 1980/1 when I started.

WHICH WAS YOUR OWN TEAM'S POPULAR END?

The Corner or the Ponty End.

WHERE DID YOU STAND OR SIT IN THE GROUND?
The Corner.

CAN YOU RECALL A BATTLE YOU HAVE BEEN INVOLVED IN, EITHER INSIDE OR OUTSIDE A GROUND?
Inside was at West Brom in the early '90s. About 25 of us had gone down on the train and we sat in their seats. Their lads were sat to the right of us and at half-time one of their lads came over mouthing at us. I jumped up and smacked him. He rolled over two rows of seats and, as this happened, both sets of lads jumped up and were at it about equal numbers. It spilled around the back near the refreshment bar, and at one point a large tea urn was thrown, hitting me in the head and scalding my chest. West Brom were getting the upper hand but the police moved in and we were quickly ejected via the police cells.

Outside a ground would have to be Everton at home, which has been mentioned in the book *Scally*, or on my stag do in November '92. One hundred and twenty of us went on a tour of Yorkshire, Harrogate, Huddersfield, Leeds and Wakefield. When we arrived in Huddersfield the word got round and Huddersfield quickly got a mob together and arrived outside the pub we were in. It immediately emptied and both sides were straight at it. The Huddersfield mob, who were outnumbered by us, were game as fuck and it was toe to toe, with neither side giving an inch for about thirty minutes. During the battle I was CS gassed and didn't see much after that. It took the police about an hour to gain control and running battles continued all over the town centre. The following day newspaper headlines read: 'Stag night turns into street riot' and 'Helicopter drafted in to quell town centre violence.'

CAN YOU RECALL THE BEST EVER MOB YOUR TEAM HAS PUT TOGETHER?
Middlesbrough away in 1983/4, as previously mentioned. More recently, the mob we took to Cardiff in February 2003. Although I wasn't there due to my banning order, a good 100 set off at 5.30 a.m. and travelled to Cardiff by train. They were in the city centre from 10.30 a.m., which is virtually unheard of for away teams to do in Cardiff. Although the police had the day sewn up, it did kick off twice during the day, the second being with the police and resulting in 25 of our lads being dawn raided and having court cases pending.

WHO'S THE BEST RIVAL FIRM YOU'VE EVER SEEN?
Man. City or Birmingham City in Barnsley in the '80s.

WHO ARE YOUR BIGGEST RIVALS TEAM-WISE?
None really.

WHO ARE YOUR BIGGEST RIVALS FAN-WISE?
Middlesbrough, Sheffield Wednesday, Sheffield United and Leeds.

HAVE YOU EVER JOINED UP WITH ANOTHER TEAM'S FIRM?
Never.

DID YOU EVER FOLLOW ENGLAND AND WOULD YOU PUT ENGLAND BEFORE YOUR CLUB?
I've followed England since a friendly in Germany in 1987. I went to Euro '88, the World Cup in '90, Holland in '93, Euro '96 and Euro 2000. But Barnsley comes first.

WHICH WAS THE BEST ENGLAND ROW?
Turin 1990, before the World Cup semi-final. About 2000 English lads were on the campsite, which had been set up in an athletics stadium. After the Italians lost to Argentina they came out in numbers and attacked the campsite. We smashed down the gates to get out at them and ran them all over the streets of Turin. The Italian Police arrived firing tear gas, so we retreated into the campsite and started a massive bonfire to keep them out.

HAVE YOU EVER SUPPORTED OR LOOKED OUT FOR ANOTHER TEAM'S RESULTS?
No.

NAME YOUR TOP FIVE FIRMS, IN ANY ORDER.
Man. United, Middlesbrough, Birmingham, Man. City and Huddersfield.

WHICH IS THE WORST GROUND YOU'VE EVER BEEN TO AND WHY?
The Old Den – very scary.

WHICH IS THE BEST STADIUM YOU'VE BEEN TO?
Oakwell, cos it's ours.

WHO ARE THE FAIREST COPPERS YOU'VE COME ACROSS AT A MATCH?
Man. United – crazy coppers.

AND THE WORST OLD BILL?
Peterborough – they let you do what you want.

WHAT WOULD HAVE STOPPED YOU GETTING INVOLVED WITH THE BOYS AT MATCHES?
Being good enough to play myself.

DESCRIBE SOME OF THE METHODS AND TACTICS USED BY THE POLICE AND AUTHORITIES TO STOP FOOTBALL VIOLENCE, AND DO YOU THINK THEY WORK?
I'm currently banned from all grounds and Barnsley town centre between eleven and nine on match days. I also have to hand in my passport when England play away. That's not a bad method of preventing violence, is it?

HAVE YOU EVER BEEN SICKENED BY SOMETHING YOU'VE WITNESSED AT A GAME?
Not really. We only fight lads who want to fight us Muppets. Whoever gives an innocent person a crack gets one back.

WHAT'S YOUR FAVOURITE FOOTBALL SONG OR CHANT AND WHICH IS THE WORST YOU CAN RECALL HEARING FROM ANOTHER TEAM?
N/a.

WHAT WAS YOUR FAVOURITE BAND/RECORD DURING YOUR FOOTBALL DAYS?
The Clash – 'London Calling'.

WHO WAS YOUR ALL-TIME FAVOURITE PLAYER?
Ronnie Glavin and Neil Redfearn.

WHERE DO YOU THINK THE NEW ENGLISH NATIONAL STADIUM SHOULD BE BUILT AND WHAT ARE YOUR THOUGHTS REGARDING THE WEMBLEY FIASCO?

Wembley.

My days of football violence have finally been stopped by the police but in twenty years I've had a great time. A lot of the books you read are one-sided and a lot of the firms writing them have never been done. What a load of bollocks. We've been done on many occasions but we've done many firms also. At the end of the day, it's all for a laugh!

MARTIN KING MEETS

LEE 'OATHEAD' OWENS

CLUB: MIDDLESBROUGH

LEE 'OATHEAD' OWENS

THE MEET

I got in touch with Oathead through Pat Dolan at Chelsea. Pat told me a great story about Oathead when Chelsea played Boro at Wembley and afterwards it all kicked off on Wembley Way. Pat reckoned he saw Oathead with about forty of Chelsea's firm hanging off him and they still couldn't get him down. I can't believe that – he doesn't look the type to get in any trouble.

Without losing your temper, Oathead, what's life like following Boro?

BACKGROUND

I'm 37 and was brought up on the Hardwick Estate in Stockton. In my youth I was a skinhead and I loved them times. I always seemed to be in trouble – my life revolved around violence. The first time I saw Boro's Front Line firm in action, I had to have some. I was hooked. The Boro boys were as game as fuck. Rucking at football is a buzz. You can't get the same buzz from drugs as you do at football. I've been everywhere with Boro and had some top rows. I respect every mob that turns out and has a go, regardless of the result. I hate these cyber warriors posting stupid fucking messages on hoolie websites. They claim to know everything that goes on, but do they ever go to games? The Front Line now includes some good decent lads from Stockton, Redcar, Thornaby and all the surrounding Middlesbrough areas. The Front Line always likes to oblige and we often turn up early at away games – Man. United, Spurs and Cardiff will vouch for that.

WHAT'S YOUR FAVOURITE TERRACE FASHION?

My favourite fashion used to be Dr Martens and a green pilot jacket, but nowadays I'm at home in a T-shirt, jeans and trainers. I can't see the point in paying £500 for a Stone Island jacket and someone rips it off ya back.

WHAT'S THE WORST FASHION YOU'VE EVER SEEN ON THE TERRACES?

Ain't really seen any. To me it's every man for himself.

DESCRIBE YOUR WORST FEELING AT A GAME.

When you've planned a row with another team somewhere and the Old Bill turn up.

HAVE YOU EVER INCURRED ANY SERIOUS INJURIES OR BEEN BADLY BEATEN UP AT A MATCH?

We played Sunderland in a night game at their place, and we got there early and took over their boozer, The Windmill. They plotted up in a club opposite and we came out, they came out and we ran them up the road. But then again, what do you expect? Sunderland are good at running. The Old Bill chased our lot back to the pub and somehow I found myself on my own, surrounded by a mob of

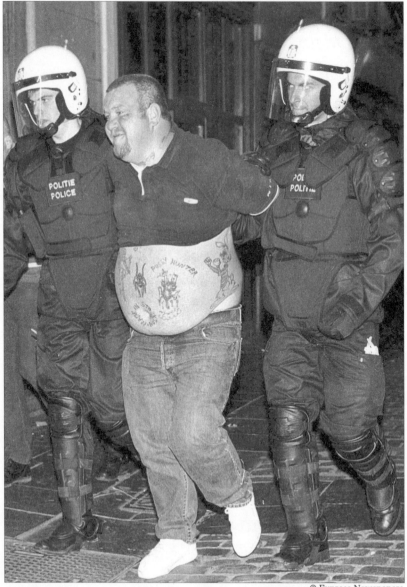

Sunderland. I just put my head down and went for it. I had thirty stitches in my tongue and other bumps and bruises, and Sunderland saw that as a result. Get real, you wankers. Thirty on to one and you still never put me on my arse.

HAS YOUR OWN SIDE EVER BEEN INVOLVED IN A FULL-SCALE RIOT?

In the '80s – Shrewsbury away, in Division Two. We were relegated and for ninety minutes we were fighting with the Old Bill, which resulted in twenty of our boys going to jail.

DESCRIBE THE BEST TAKING OF AN END YOU'VE EVER WITNESSED.

Boro at Carlisle. It was either Boxing Day or New Year's Day, but the way it happened was poetry in motion.

WHICH WAS YOUR OWN TEAM'S POPULAR END?

The Holgate End. 'You'll never take the Holgate.'

WHERE DID YOU STAND OR SIT IN THE GROUND?

The Holgate End.

CAN YOU RECALL A BATTLE YOU HAVE BEEN INVOLVED IN, EITHER INSIDE OR OUTSIDE A GROUND?

Everton at Goodison Park in the FA Cup in the '80s. Our lads went in their end and did okay. Outside it was mayhem as both sides were as game as fuck. It went toe to toe with no one giving an inch – it was a proper row. That was until their little urchins done the usual and got the blades out. We've had a lot of history with Everton but fair play to them, they give as good as they get. Nice one, lads.

CAN YOU RECALL THE BEST EVER MOB YOUR TEAM HAS PUT TOGETHER?

At home against Man. United. They'd won the title and there was a lot of hype surrounding the game. We had thousands out but in the end it was a non-event because the Old Bill were on top form.

WHO'S THE BEST RIVAL FIRM YOU'VE EVER SEEN?

Chelsea in the ZDS Final at Wembley. We had a big firm out that day but there was no real organisation and everyone was split up in different mobs. I was with about forty of our boys on Wembley Way, and hundreds of Chelsea appeared out of nowhere. They had a real tight mob and they looked awesome. The next time we played them at Wembley in a more serious Cup, we had hundreds out, but Chelsea didn't want to play.

WHO ARE YOUR BIGGEST RIVALS TEAM-WISE?
Sunderland, because of what the cowardly bastards did to me.

WHO ARE YOUR BIGGEST RIVALS FAN-WISE?
Who do you think?

HAVE YOU EVER JOINED UP WITH ANOTHER TEAM'S FIRM?
No.

DID YOU EVER FOLLOW ENGLAND AND WOULD YOU PUT ENGLAND BEFORE YOUR CLUB?
I've been all over the place watching England, but Boro come first.

WHICH WAS THE BEST ENGLAND ROW?
The World Cup in Marseilles. It went mental out in France.

HAVE YOU EVER SUPPORTED OR LOOKED OUT FOR ANOTHER TEAM'S RESULTS?
No, never.

NAME YOUR TOP FIVE FIRMS IN ANY ORDER.
Man. United, Cardiff, Spurs, Everton, Forest – in no particular order.

WHICH IS THE WORST GROUND YOU'VE EVER BEEN TO AND WHY?
The Shay, Halifax's ground – it's a right shithole.

WHICH IS THE BEST STADIUM YOU'VE BEEN TO?
Hampden Park when we play the Jocks. The buzz at that place is the tops.

WHO ARE THE FAIREST COPPERS YOU'VE COME ACROSS AT A MATCH?
I hate them all.

AND THE WORST OLD BILL?
Manchester. I think they've had enough of Boro over the years and they aren't very friendly towards us. I wonder why?

WHAT WOULD HAVE STOPPED YOU GETTING INVOLVED WITH THE BOYS AT MATCHES?
Having no arms and legs.

DESCRIBE SOME OF THE METHODS AND TACTICS USED BY THE POLICE AND AUTHORITIES TO STOP FOOTBALL VIOLENCE, AND DO YOU THINK THEY WORK?

The Belgian Old Bill at Euro 2000. They just got hold of anyone and locked them up.

HAVE YOU EVER BEEN SICKENED BY SOMETHING YOU'VE WITNESSED AT A GAME?

It doesn't really happen at Boro, but I hate to see a mob get someone down and give them a good kicking. If you're down and done, you're done, so no need to kick the shit out of anyone.

WHAT'S YOUR FAVOURITE FOOTBALL SONG OR CHANT AND WHICH IS THE WORST YOU CAN RECALL HEARING FROM ANOTHER TEAM?

Best song is 'No Surrender' and the worst is that stupid fucking Leeds song 'Marching On Together'.

WHAT WAS YOUR FAVOURITE BAND/RECORD DURING YOUR FOOTBALL DAYS?

Sham 69 and Angelic Upstarts are two of my favourite bands.

WHO WAS YOUR ALL-TIME FAVOURITE PLAYER?

Bernie Slaven, a great servant for Boro.

WHERE DO YOU THINK THE NEW ENGLISH NATIONAL STADIUM SHOULD BE BUILT AND WHAT ARE YOUR THOUGHTS REGARDING THE WEMBLEY FIASCO?

We should have kept Wembley as it's nice to go there for the day out, but it's also good to move it around the country and mix it up a bit.

MARTIN KING MEETS

DAVID 'SKEENY' SKEEN

CLUB: NOTTINGHAM FOREST

DAVID 'SKEENY' SKEEN

THE MEET

I met Skeeny through Martin Knight, my co-author on *Hoolifan*, and when I first spoke to him on the phone I felt like I'd known him years. He's a smashing geezer with a good sense of humour. He's also Monty's mate (Monty's one of the top faces, see Chapter 26) and holds a season ticket at Newcastle, even though he's a Forest fan. Work that one out.

BACKGROUND

I was born in Darlington in April 1956. My nickname's Skeeny. My first Forest game was in 1961 against Tottenham, which we won 2–0. I first started going with the Forest boys when I was still at school and we stood at the Trent End, which included loads of smaller firms like the Bernie Boot Boys, the Harper Boot Boys, the Town Lads, and a host of skinhead gangs – mine being Arnold. Gedling, Clifton and Bramcote also had good boys within the Forest mob. Before the skinhead scene we had a firm on the Trent End with some good boys like Kenny Grease, Big Howard Hall, Col White and Johnny Truelove, and they deserve the credit for putting us on the map. Also keeping the legacy going were the likes of Bernie, Johnny Harper, Marksey, Norwich, Snowy, Simon, Johnny L, Tony O'D, Dale C, Tony F, Simmo, Mick M, Brian B, Spider, Moggy, Kelv, Stabber, Mick R, Ronnie F, Bimbo, Paddy, Gary, all the Newark lads, Steve P, Gary C, all the Sutton lads, Measch, Johnny Martin and Jonah and Marshy and the boys. I left school and worked as a welder for the Coal Board. Now I'm a self-employed businessman and reasonably successful.

WHAT'S YOUR FAVOURITE TERRACE FASHION?

It has to be the skinhead thing in the '70s, with Harrington jackets, Crombies, Levi's Sta-Prest and Docs. It would still look wicked today. Also I loved them patchwork sweaters.

WHAT'S THE WORST FASHION YOU'VE EVER SEEN ON THE TERRACES?

That has to be me. I once bought a pair of white platform shoes from Chelsea Girl and wore them with a pair of 32-inch flared trousers that had a 7-inch waistband – what a fucking embarrassment.

DESCRIBE YOUR WORST FEELING AT A GAME.

Going to a night match with twenty of your mates and you've just heard about Stanley (knife, not the Park), and a Scouser comes up to you and says, 'Got the time, la?'

HAVE YOU EVER INCURRED ANY SERIOUS INJURIES OR BEEN BADLY BEATEN UP AT A MATCH?

In the 1979/80 season opener at Ipswich. Me and a few mates went to Great Yarmouth and I got into a fight with a rig worker and was stabbed seven times. After being given only a few hours to live a Navy surgeon saved me, God bless him – he knew his stuff. Also I was once hit with a road lamp by a Liverpool fan and that nearly cost me an eye. Another one, believe it or not, happened in the Welsh seaside resort of Rhyl. We played them in a pre-season friendly in 1973/4 and

won 9–0. The game had been nice and peaceful. I'd spent the match leaning against the goalpost talking to our keeper, Jim Baron. But later on, after the game, things turned nasty when we had to fight for our lives. We got into a fight with some locals and some fairground workers as we boarded our bus home. Two of our lot suffered stab wounds and three more were put in hospital. That's Great Yarmouth and Ryhl – two lovely holiday resorts. Sun, sea and stabbings!

HAS YOUR OWN SIDE EVER BEEN INVOLVED IN A FULL-SCALE RIOT?

The first year we played Derby when they came back into the First Division, which was about 1969, we had 200 to 300 lads on the 7 a.m. train. When we got there shop windows were smashed, and an army surplus store had its windows put in. Blokes were just marching out with handfuls of new boots and clothing. The Old Bill lost control. It was like a battle zone in Beirut. We never saw the Derby mob until just before the kick-off and by that time there were thousands of us – too many for them to handle. Derby never recovered from the humiliation of that day and even joined up with the wankers from Leicester City to plan revenge, and they formed the Derby Leicester Alliance. Now that's a fucking joke.

DESCRIBE THE BEST TAKING OF AN END YOU'VE EVER WITNESSED.

That has to be Sheffield United in 1977/8. I put my arm in a sling and hid a rubber mallet inside. We stormed into their end and cleared it in 30 seconds. Anyone who got a tap with the mallet was out cold. The police came in, moved us out and escorted us around the pitch to the other end.

WHICH WAS YOUR OWN TEAM'S POPULAR END?

The Trent End. Then we moved to the East Stand and the Kop, and then into A Block in the Main Stand.

WHERE DID YOU STAND OR SIT IN THE GROUND?

Besides the ones I've just mentioned, the South Bank at Wolves holds some fond memories for me. I once chatted up one of their birds who was dressed in a Crombie and monkey boots. As the battles raged around us she told me how the violence turned her on. One thing led to another and we ended up under a tarpaulin that was covering a pile of building sand under the main stand. We returned covered in sweat and sand. I stuck my sweet-smelling fingers under my mates' noses and they asked where I'd been. They all backed off when they got a whiff of the old bird's fanny. I think I had more of our lads on their toes than Wolves did that day, and I bet I gave her the best thirty seconds' worth of sex she's ever had.

CAN YOU RECALL A BATTLE YOU HAVE BEEN INVOLVED IN, EITHER INSIDE OR OUTSIDE A GROUND?

Tottenham away in the Fifth Round of the FA Cup, 1970/1. We had loads of football specials taking us down to London that day, and Norwich – one of the Harper Boot Boys' main faces – ran two coaches. One of the drivers ran into the bus in front of him and smashed the windscreen so they got down there late. Inside the ground Spurs were running us everywhere on the Shelf, with Alfie – a big, dopey kid of ours – being chased everywhere like a gazelle. It carried on all through the game, with them coming at us and us going at them. Afterwards, outside, Tottenham ran us all along the high road. We came to the coaches that had brought Norwich and his boys down and we made a stand. We picked up lamps and poles from some nearby roadworks and let the Yids have it. We laid into them and ran them back down the road from where they'd just chased us. To this day the Spurs boys will never admit what we did to them. Still, that's typical Yiddos!

CAN YOU RECALL THE BEST EVER MOB YOUR TEAM HAS PUT TOGETHER?

The 27,000 Forest fans that went out to Munich for the European Cup Final against Swedish side Malmo in 1979. In those days that was a record away support for an English team in Europe. I woke up the following morning with an almighty hangover and four German Deutschmarks in my pocket to get home with. Shit, I was nearly sick in my packet of pork scratchings.

WHO'S THE BEST RIVAL FIRM YOU'VE EVER SEEN?

It has to be Chelsea. Every year they'd come to Forest with thousands and once they pushed a police horse off the Trent Bridge into the waters below. That was the year the Old Bill put them in the Trent End and, contrary to popular belief, they didn't take it. Portsmouth's another team that one year came up in their thousands. I remember once, I was with Scarrott – one of our main loonies – down at Fratton Park and we'd been battered all day when he spotted this group of Pompey. He walked over to them and offered to fight the best man amongst them. One of them stepped forward and cracked him on the jaw, and he went down. He propped himself up on his elbows and said, 'I suppose you think that's funny?' The Pompey boys cracked up laughing, helped him to his feet and took us down the pub for a few pints.

WHO ARE YOUR BIGGEST RIVALS TEAM-WISE?

Derby and Leicester.

WHO ARE YOUR BIGGEST RIVALS FAN-WISE?
Derby and Sunderland – gobshites the pair of them.

HAVE YOU EVER JOINED UP WITH ANOTHER TEAM'S FIRM?
I went with West Ham to the League Cup semi-final at Hillsborough in 1972. That was some experience. They had a top firm out that day.

DID YOU EVER FOLLOW ENGLAND AND WOULD YOU PUT ENGLAND BEFORE YOUR CLUB?
I used to, but now it's all booked through the England travel club I don't bother.

WHICH WAS THE BEST ENGLAND ROW?
Frankfurt last year. Forest had a big mob out and we done well against some fierce numbers.

HAVE YOU EVER SUPPORTED OR LOOKED OUT FOR ANOTHER TEAM'S RESULTS?
Well, I've been living in Newcastle for the last five years and I've got to know some exceptional people, and I have every respect for them as a team and as a firm. They've got top lads and I'd like to say a big thank you for the way you've treated me!

NAME YOUR TOP FIVE FIRMS, IN ANY ORDER.
West Ham, Chelsea, Man. Utd, Millwall, Portsmouth.

WHICH IS THE WORST GROUND YOU'VE EVER BEEN TO AND WHY?
It has to be Hartlepool. I went there in 1975/6 for Cloughie's testimonial. You couldn't get a hot drink and the natives were well up for it. I had a new Mark 3 Cortina and I ended up lying across the windscreen to protect it with stones and rocks bouncing off my back.

WHICH IS THE BEST STADIUM YOU'VE BEEN TO?
Supporting Forest out in Cologne in the European Cup semi-final. We drew 3–3 in Nottingham so no one gave us a prayer for the return leg out in Germany, but amazingly we won with an Ian Bowyer goal. I've also visited the San Siro, Bernabeu and Bayern Munich's Olympic Stadium – all top-class stadiums.

WHO ARE THE FAIREST COPPERS YOU'VE COME ACROSS AT A MATCH?
There's no such thing.

AND THE WORST OLD BILL?
Definitely West Midlands, followed by Northumbria.

WHAT WOULD HAVE STOPPED YOU GETTING INVOLVED WITH THE BOYS AT MATCHES?
Nothing. What's in your blood is in your blood.

DESCRIBE SOME OF THE METHODS AND TACTICS USED BY THE POLICE AND AUTHORITIES TO STOP FOOTBALL VIOLENCE, AND DO YOU THINK THEY WORK?
Coventry Old Bill taking bootlaces out.

HAVE YOU EVER BEEN SICKENED BY SOMETHING YOU'VE WITNESSED AT A GAME?
I saw a Forest lad get a metal spike through his head out in Ireland. He wasn't a hooligan, he was just a normal fan and wasn't there for trouble. Also I find most hooligans don't pick on kids and don't bother people that aren't into the fighting. I was with the Middlesbrough lads out in Brussels in Euro 2000 and one of their main boys saw a woman struggling up some stairs with her pushchair, and he was the first person to help her. Next day he was deported and got a right slating in the press. It just goes to show and prove that some fans do have values.

WHAT'S YOUR FAVOURITE FOOTBALL SONG OR CHANT AND WHICH IS THE WORST YOU CAN RECALL HEARING FROM ANOTHER TEAM?
'We hate Derby' or:
'The River Trent is deep and wide,
With the City ground on the other side.
There ain't no finer team around,
According to the Trent End sound.
Oh we hate Bill Shankley and we hate St John,
And worst of all we hate Big Ron.
And we'll hang the Kopites one by one,
Along the banks of the Mersey.
Now to Man. Utd we sing this song,
You won't be top for very long,
Because in the papers you will read,
NOTTINGHAM FOREST ARE TOP OF THE LEAGUE.'

WHAT WAS YOUR FAVOURITE BAND/RECORD DURING YOUR FOOTBALL DAYS?
Any song off the *Tighten Up* albums, plus a bit of Northern Soul, The Jam and The Clash.

WHO WAS YOUR ALL-TIME FAVOURITE PLAYER?

It's a toss-up between the great Joe Baker – I think we would have won the league if he'd been fit in 1966/7 – and Stuart Pearce, who always gave his all.

WHERE DO YOU THINK THE NEW ENGLISH NATIONAL STADIUM SHOULD BE BUILT AND WHAT ARE YOUR THOUGHTS REGARDING THE WEMBLEY FIASCO?

Build it in the Midlands or improve Wembley, and the roads and trains that service it.

CASS PENNANT MEETS

GARY JOHNSON
CLUB: WOLVERHAMPTON WANDERERS

GARY JOHNSON

THE MEET
My good pal, Frasier Tranter, was behind the introduction for a recognised Wolves face. At six feet ten inches, if Frasier gives you some advice you tend to listen, and when he came up with the name of one of the Wolves old guard, that was good enough for me. He's been doing the security business up there for long enough and he knows and uses some top people. So enter Gary Johnson, one of the former leaders of the infamous Subway Army. Gary drove down to London to my house, where we spent the afternoon doing the interview. He was an interesting character who, once you'd jogged his memory, came up with some good stuff from the days when the Wolves lads were having their say.

BACKGROUND
I was born in 1964, I have three brothers, and I come from the Lowhill Estate in Bushford, an area of Wolverhampton. I started going to football with my mates when I was about seventeen. The top firm over there at the time were the lads that went with Roger Quinton and Ray Hickman, which including myself later became the original Subway Army. We had a good mix of black and white lads.

WHAT'S YOUR FAVOURITE TERRACE FASHION?
In '85 we were into Pringle and Farahs. Everyone was into the casual look. It was a nice colourful era.

WHAT'S THE WORST FASHION YOU'VE EVER SEEN ON THE TERRACES?
In the early '80s you'd get blokes wearing rolled-up leggings over the bottom of their stretch jeans, in a sort of *Fame* dance look. It must have been a Midlands thing.

DESCRIBE YOUR WORST FEELING AT A GAME.
Losing in the play-offs in '82 against Bolton. We won 1–0 at our place but lost the return 3–0. I could have cried that day – I was absolutely gutted. It was a long drive home.

HAVE YOU EVER INCURRED ANY SERIOUS INJURIES OR BEEN BADLY BEATEN UP AT A MATCH?
I've never been injured at a match but I did come unstuck at Birmingham in '85. Me and a mate of mine, Davo, bumped into about fifty Blues fans, who were supposed to come to our place early. They

hadn't turned up so we went by train, to see what had happened to them. They found us before we found them and we were saved by two traffic cops from getting a right pasting.

HAS YOUR OWN SIDE EVER BEEN INVOLVED IN A FULL-SCALE RIOT?
Wolves v Newcastle. There was fighting going on all around town. They come down mob-handed. There was fucking loads of them. It was like us kids fighting grown men but we did them in the end.

DESCRIBE THE BEST TAKING OF AN END YOU'VE EVER WITNESSED.
It wasn't us taking an end, it was up at Leeds and we smashed them and one of their pubs to bits. We turned up by coach and surprised them. I also remember going into Birmingham's end and clearing it. We started at the bottom and worked our way to the top before the Old Bill chucked us out and restored some order.

WHICH WAS YOUR OWN TEAM'S POPULAR END?
The South Bank.

WHERE DID YOU STAND OR SIT IN THE GROUND?
The South Bank.

CAN YOU RECALL A BATTLE YOU HAVE BEEN INVOLVED IN, EITHER INSIDE OR OUTSIDE A GROUND?
That has to be Newcastle in '85 at our place – the one I described earlier.

CAN YOU RECALL THE BEST EVER MOB YOUR TEAM HAS PUT TOGETHER?
Yeah, the Subway Army.

WHO'S THE BEST RIVAL FIRM YOU'VE EVER SEEN?
The Geordies weren't really organised but would turn up en masse. And West Ham for turning up and being well organised and giving us a good row.

WHO ARE YOUR BIGGEST RIVALS TEAM-WISE?
West Brom – they're shit.

WHO ARE YOUR BIGGEST RIVALS FAN-WISE?
West Brom. You're brought up just to hate them and that's it – I hate them. If you asked an Albion fan who they hate they'd say Wolves. It's as simple as that.

HAVE YOU EVER JOINED UP WITH ANOTHER TEAM'S FIRM?
No.

DID YOU EVER FOLLOW ENGLAND AND WOULD YOU PUT ENGLAND BEFORE YOUR CLUB?
I've never really been interested in watching England. My club always comes first and that's that.

WHICH WAS THE BEST ENGLAND ROW?
I've never been to watch England.

HAVE YOU EVER SUPPORTED OR LOOKED OUT FOR ANOTHER TEAM'S RESULTS?
When I was a little kid I remember watching the Arsenal–Liverpool Cup Final and wanting Liverpool to win, so I suppose I've a soft spot for Liverpool.

NAME YOUR TOP FIVE FIRMS, IN ANY ORDER.
West Ham, Newcastle, Liverpool, Millwall and Birmingham City.

WHICH IS THE WORST GROUND YOU'VE EVER BEEN TO AND WHY?
Wrexham – it's a shithole. It's falling to bits, but I hear they've recently spent a few bob on it.

WHICH IS THE BEST STADIUM YOU'VE BEEN TO?
Wembley. It's every team's dream to get there. We played Burnley in the Sherpa Vans Final. It was a great day out for all our supporters.

WHO ARE THE FAIREST COPPERS YOU'VE COME ACROSS AT A MATCH?
The QPR Old Bill were great and treated us well. They gave our fans respect and got it back in return.

AND THE WORST OLD BILL?
Bolton. Straight in and straight out of the ground – you're allowed nowhere else.

WHAT WOULD HAVE STOPPED YOU GETTING INVOLVED WITH THE BOYS AT MATCHES?
If my old lady had caught me that would have been it – she would have given me a kicking.

DESCRIBE SOME OF THE METHODS AND TACTICS USED BY THE POLICE AND THE AUTHORITIES TO STOP FOOTBALL VIOLENCE, AND DO YOU THINK THEY WORK?

It has to be cameras or ban away fans. It happened to us during the 2002/3 season at Millwall.

HAVE YOU EVER BEEN SICKENED BY SOMETHING YOU'VE WITNESSED AT A GAME?

Watching the Heysel Stadium disaster on TV. It was a free-for-all, with the police losing control.

WHAT'S YOUR FAVOURITE FOOTBALL SONG OR CHANT AND WHICH IS THE WORST YOU CAN RECALL HEARING FROM ANOTHER TEAM?

The best one I've heard is a song by the Wolves boys about an Asian guy and a corner shop. It's sung to the 'Everywhere We Go' tune. The worst is 'Keep right on to the end of the road', which the Birmingham fans sing. They've been singing it for years but they've only recently managed to make that song worth singing.

WHAT WAS YOUR FAVOURITE BAND/RECORD DURING YOUR FOOTBALL DAYS?

The Specials and The Beat, another band on the Two Tone record label, who came from Birmingham.

WHO WAS YOUR ALL-TIME FAVOURITE PLAYER?

Stevie Bull – he's a living legend. But the best player I ever saw was George Best.

WHERE DO YOU THINK THE NEW ENGLISH NATIONAL STADIUM SHOULD BE BUILT AND WHAT ARE YOUR THOUGHTS REGARDING THE WEMBLEY FIASCO?

The national team should play at Wembley but maybe build another stadium in the Midlands for Cup Finals and one or two internationals, and other big games.

CASS PENNANT MEETS

STEVE 'WING NUT' LYONS

CLUB: CHARLTON ATHLETIC

STEVE 'WING NUT' LYONS

THE MEET

In the past, most West Ham fans have had an affection for Charlton. I don't know if it's because of the two Woolwichs, with North Woolwich in East London's Dockland being home to many a Hammers fan, and Woolwich across the other side of the Thames a base for a good few Charlton boys. I myself would cross the old foot tunnel from the south and catch the 106 bus to East Ham Town Hall and walk to the ground as a teenager.

Steve was from the East End and, being a life-long Charlton fan, got untold stick off us West Ham boys. But he knew how to give it back, and he'd tell us stories of Charlton's escapades. People might say, 'Who the fuck are Charlton?' but I was there that day in the Fourth Round of the FA Cup when the Covered End boys took the back of the Arsenal North Bank, and they've always had my utmost respect. They even shared Upton Park with us for a while before they went back to the Valley.

Steve has followed Charlton through thick and thin. I met up with him not far from where Stanley Kubrick's *A Clockwork Orange* was filmed. As I walked into the packed pub where people were glued to the big screen, a roar went up as Rangers scored against Celtic and the roof nearly lifted up. A man in a kilt and Dr Martens – probably the only Jock in the place – looked pleased. The man behind the bar in the Rangers shirt was rushed off his feet as Steve introduced me to fans of almost every London club. A couple of Leeds fans came over to say hello, then me and Steve got down to doing the interview. I ended up staying all day and had a brilliant time. Here's what Wing Nut had to say.

BACKGROUND

I'm now 46, and known among the Charlton boys as Wing Nut, a nickname I was given for obvious facial reasons. I was born and bred in the East End of London but all my family were Charlton fans. In the '50s and '60s Charlton were one of the top sides. I grew up around Woolwich and, like most young men, started my working life in a factory. That was in the days when you could pack one job up on a Friday afternoon and start in another factory on Monday morning. Now I'm a builder.

The first game I went to was with the old man when I was eight years old. It was at the Valley – Charlton v Norwich. Most of my mates were West Ham supporters.

WHAT'S YOUR FAVOURITE TERRACE FASHION?

Early '70s – the original skinheads with the Ben Shermans, Levi's, Doc Martens and brogues. And then the Pringle casual gear. Everyone wore their best clobber. If you didn't, you were looked upon as a mug.

WHAT'S THE WORST FASHION YOU'VE EVER SEEN ON THE TERRACES?

The northerners in their baggy flares with loads of pockets. They looked right fucking idiots ... with their Northern Soul and the Wigan Casino.

DESCRIBE YOUR WORST FEELING AT A GAME.

To me it was going somewhere and you knew all the boys had to turn out because the team you were playing had a decent mob, and hardly any of your lot would bother to show up. If you went to somewhere like Newcastle you just had to get on with it, no matter how many of us were there. At the game the week before, the whole of the end had clapped their hands when we sang 'If you're all going to Newcastle, clap your hands'. It felt like everyone would be making the trip north. You'd turn up Saturday morning at the station and no cunt would be there.

HAVE YOU EVER INCURRED ANY SERIOUS INJURIES OR BEEN BADLY BEATEN UP AT A MATCH?

Leeds away, when ten of us got away from the police escort and went off to have a beer and within twenty minutes we had 200 Leeds firm on us. We were chased back to the station and three of us made it to the bar inside the station, where we bought ourselves a drink. The place was full of Leeds and not one of them was drinking. Within seconds they'd all come at us. They wanted us badly and had been up for a row all day.

The worst injury was following England out in Norway. We'd had a row with some Italians that lived out there and I broke the jaw of one of their boys. A few hours later the bloke came back with the Old Bill and picked us out. I was handcuffed and thrown in the police van. The rest of the England fans attacked the van and I escaped, but running with your hands behind your back is hard and I was collared again. I was thrown back inside the van face down and the coppers sorted me out. They kicked and stamped on me until I was black and blue. I had footprints embedded in my back and my ribs were bruised. They seemed to know what they were doing. I was deported and I ached for weeks afterwards.

HAS YOUR OWN SIDE EVER BEEN INVOLVED IN A FULL-SCALE RIOT?

Leicester City away in the early '80s. We packed into their pub near the ground called The Turnstile. About one o'clock their boys turned up and couldn't get at us because the Old Bill had surrounded the pub, so they started smashing all the windows. Next door to the pub was a bookies and we all went and had a bet on us to win, which we did. After the game twenty of us went to collect our winnings and as we walked back towards the station there was a mob of Leicester in front of us, following a police escort with the rest of the Charlton fans. We came up behind them and steamed into them, then backed them off as the rest of the Charlton boys broke through the police lines and steamed in with us. We battered Leicester everywhere.

DESCRIBE THE BEST TAKING OF AN END YOU'VE EVER WITNESSED.

The North Bank, Arsenal, which we took in the FA Cup in the early skinhead '70s. We had a mob and a half there that day. I was still at school and went with my cousin. I couldn't concentrate on the game because of the fighting going on around me – it was proper toe-to-toe stuff.

WHICH WAS YOUR OWN TEAM'S POPULAR END?

It's now called the North Stand but to us Charlton fans it's always been known as the Covered End, and some still sing songs about it to this day.

WHERE DID YOU STAND OR SIT IN THE GROUND?

I stood near the main stand on the edge of the Covered End so that we could spot any rival fans trying to infiltrate our end.

CAN YOU RECALL A BATTLE YOU HAVE BEEN INVOLVED IN, EITHER INSIDE OR OUTSIDE A GROUND?

Definitely – Sheffield Wednesday at home in the '70s. They were in the Covered End well early. We couldn't believe their numbers – there must have been 500 of them and most of them were skinheads. After the game they paid the price as we ran them outside down Anchor Lane all the way back to their coaches. Looking down the hill from Charlton Station, all you could see was a mass of bobbing heads being chased by our lot.

CAN YOU RECALL THE BEST EVER MOB YOUR TEAM HAS PUT TOGETHER?

Liverpool away in 1987/8. Most of us knew one another.

WHO'S THE BEST RIVAL FIRM YOU'VE EVER SEEN?

Sheffield Wednesday.

WHO ARE YOUR BIGGEST RIVALS TEAM-WISE?
Crystal Palace.

WHO ARE YOUR BIGGEST RIVALS FAN-WISE?
Palace. They never turn up. The amount of times they've called it on and not turned up, or turned up and run away … it's like chasing shadows.

HAVE YOU EVER JOINED UP WITH ANOTHER TEAM'S FIRM?
Only at England games.

DID YOU EVER FOLLOW ENGLAND AND WOULD YOU PUT ENGLAND BEFORE YOUR CLUB?
I've watched England home and away many times, and I would put England before Charlton. I'm very patriotic.

WHICH WAS THE BEST ENGLAND ROW?
England v Denmark in '79 where we won 4–3. As soon as we got there we had a bust-up with some Hells Angels in a bar and won that one. Then, during the game, we were rowing with the Old Bill and the Danes, and both were well fucking up for it. But it didn't stop there. Afterwards there was a NATO exercise in Denmark and we had a ruck with some US Marines. Some of our army boys got involved and so did the military police – it was fucking unbelievable.

HAVE YOU EVER SUPPORTED OR LOOKED OUT FOR ANOTHER TEAM'S RESULTS?
No. I would sometimes watch West Ham or Millwall if there was going to be a row.

NAME YOUR TOP FIVE FIRMS, IN ANY ORDER.
In London West Ham and Millwall, then Leeds, Portsmouth and Newcastle – in that order.

WHICH IS THE WORST GROUND YOU'VE EVER BEEN TO AND WHY?
Newcastle away. It's like going to another country. Every fucker hates you up there, whether a man, woman or child. They're mad. They've crammed into that Gallowgate End with steam coming off their bodies after it's been raining. You've also got geezers running around in kilts with no shirts on. You go for a drink and you have old men abusing you. They're definitely a different race.

WHICH IS THE BEST STADIUM YOU'VE BEEN TO?
Newcastle, just for the atmosphere. They're fucking mental.

WHO ARE THE FAIREST COPPERS YOU'VE COME ACROSS AT A MATCH?

I would say Charlton Old Bill. They've got us in British transport police clubs up north just to keep an eye on us.

AND THE WORST OLD BILL?

Bolton away in the FA Cup in 2000. They were fucking liberty takers – they all thought they were Robocop.

WHAT WOULD HAVE STOPPED YOU GETTING INVOLVED WITH THE BOYS AT MATCHES?

Nothing. I've been to court for criminal damage and offensive weapons, and I'm used to getting £10 fines. That was back in the old days. Now the Old Bill will come through your front door at five in the morning six months after you've had a row. I can do without all that old bollocks. I'm a family man now.

DESCRIBE SOME OF THE METHODS AND TACTICS USED BY THE POLICE AND AUTHORITIES TO STOP FOOTBALL VIOLENCE, AND DO YOU THINK THEY WORK?

CCTV and cameras. I don't like the idea of people with cameras filming you.

HAVE YOU EVER BEEN SICKENED BY SOMETHING YOU'VE WITNESSED AT A GAME?

Watching my TV at home and seeing the events and scenes from Heysel unfolding because it seemed the Liverpool fans were out for revenge that night after they'd earlier played in Rome, and lots of the Scousers were stabbed. In the end it all went sadly and terribly wrong. I think, if the Italians had fought back instead of panicking and running, no one would have died. I can honestly say I only ever fought other geezers that were like me and wanted it. That night was very sad for the whole of football – but on whose doorstep do you lay the blame? It put it out of fashion what went on that day. It went from being a laugh to something you don't want to be part of.

WHAT'S YOUR FAVOURITE FOOTBALL SONG OR CHANT AND WHICH IS THE WORST YOU CAN RECALL HEARING FROM ANOTHER TEAM?

My favourite's 'Valley Floyd Road' sung to Paul McCartney's 'Mull of Kintyre'. The worst is 'Munich '58' and taunts to Leeds fans about Istanbul.

WHAT WAS YOUR FAVOURITE BAND/RECORD DURING YOUR FOOTBALL DAYS?

My favourite bands were Roxy Music, Slade and The Clash. I particularly liked 'White Riot' by The Clash.

WHO WAS YOUR ALL-TIME FAVOURITE PLAYER?

Derek Hales (yeah, killer Hales). He used to get us in the players' bar. We fucking loved him – he was one of us.

WHERE DO YOU THINK THE NEW ENGLISH NATIONAL STADIUM SHOULD BE BUILT AND WHAT ARE YOUR THOUGHTS REGARDING THE WEMBLEY FIASCO?

Take it back to Wembley. It's the only place to have it.

CASS PENNANT MEETS

GINGER HOWARD
CLUB: PORTSMOUTH

GINGER HOWARD

THE MEET

When writing *Rolling with the 6.57 Crew* I'd asked a number of people involved with the book if they'd ever had a main leader. They were quite adamant that there never was a main leader, but older members told me about a man known as Ginger Howard, who was famed for putting his glasses in his top pocket before steaming in. 'Oh, Ginger Howard,' they would say, 'him with the trademark glasses and trilby hat.' Throughout the research for that book I tried to trace him but with little success – that was until Eddie, one of the Pompey lads, bumped into him while on holiday on the Greek island of Kos. 'Oi, mate, are you Ginger Howard?' he asked, and he knew as soon as he said it. Off came the trademark glasses and a little mischievous twinkle of recognition came into his eye, and then came the immortal words, 'Aye, I'll be Howard.' We now had the Fratton's End's first governor for our book. A quick exchange of phone numbers resulted in a meeting being set up at his brother's pub in Cosham just outside Portsmouth – and what a character. Here's what the man had to say for himself.

BACKGROUND

I was born in January 1947, which makes me 56. I got my nickname, Ginger, for obvious reasons. I was born and bred in Cosham and first started going to Pompey with my brothers. We're a big family – I've got seven brothers and five sisters. When I first started going to matches with my mates I was an apprentice butcher, and I now work as a warehouseman.

WHAT'S YOUR FAVOURITE TERRACE FASHION?

Skinhead gear, and my favourite Prince of Wales check trousers. I also used to wear a trilby hat with a Number Six cigarette coupon stuck in the side band. I was a longhaired skinhead – my ginger hair was down to my shoulders – and I also wore a Crombie overcoat or Harrington jacket. These were smart days.

WHAT'S THE WORST FASHION YOU'VE EVER SEEN ON THE TERRACES?

The northerners wore some shit. It took ages for the people of Manchester and Bolton to cotton on to the southern style.

DESCRIBE YOUR WORST FEELING AT A GAME.

We had a big battle in Norwich and we were well outnumbered as there was only about sixty of us, and we came unstuck. The coach driver wouldn't take us any further than London and threw us off. We had no money and we had to find our own way home.

HAVE YOU EVER INCURRED ANY SERIOUS INJURIES OR BEEN BADLY BEATEN UP AT A MATCH?

Millwall in the late '60s at our place. I was in Commercial Road on my own and I was recognised by a mob of Millwall that had seen me in the ground. I was beaten black and blue, and kicked senseless. Not a great day out.

HAS YOUR OWN SIDE EVER BEEN INVOLVED IN A FULL-SCALE RIOT?

We got in Cardiff's Grange End in about '73. We ran them, they ran us; it was back and forth. The Old Bill tried to get in between us and break it up, but in the end the coppers disappeared under the sheer numbers fighting.

DESCRIBE THE BEST TAKING OF AN END YOU'VE EVER WITNESSED.

Plymouth away. We took all three sides of the ground. I had my arm broken by a policeman's truncheon and was taken to hospital where it was set in plaster.

WHICH WAS YOUR OWN TEAM'S POPULAR END?

The Fratton End.

WHERE DID YOU STAND OR SIT IN THE GROUND?

The Fratton End. I loved it in there, the singing and swaying. I knew most people that stood in there or, should I say, most people knew me.

CAN YOU RECALL A BATTLE YOU HAVE BEEN INVOLVED IN, EITHER INSIDE OR OUTSIDE A GROUND?

There's been a few of them, and there's been some good ones. Millwall were standing at the back at the Fratton End and we came up from the bottom and steamed up the steps and retook our end. The Old Bill tried to hold us back but we were having none of it.

CAN YOU RECALL THE BEST EVER MOB YOUR TEAM HAS PUT TOGETHER?

Oxford United away in the early '70s. We went by train and took a top firm. I was in the pub before the game and I was rotten drunk and ended up getting three months. I was that drunk I was carried out on a stretcher as I couldn't walk. I went to football one day and came home three months later!

WHO'S THE BEST RIVAL FIRM YOU'VE EVER SEEN?

Looking back, I'd say Millwall as they always turned out. It was their docks against our docks.

WHO ARE YOUR BIGGEST RIVALS TEAM-WISE?

The Scummers, I hate them bastards.

WHO ARE YOUR BIGGEST RIVALS FAN-WISE?

Southampton, the Scummers again. The hatred's always been there.

HAVE YOU EVER JOINED UP WITH ANOTHER TEAM'S FIRM?

No, no, never.

DID YOU EVER FOLLOW ENGLAND AND WOULD YOU PUT ENGLAND BEFORE YOUR CLUB?

No, never been. It's Pompey first.

WHICH WAS THE BEST ENGLAND ROW?

Never seen one because I've never been.

HAVE YOU EVER SUPPORTED OR LOOKED OUT FOR ANOTHER TEAM'S RESULTS?

No.

NAME YOUR TOP FIVE FIRMS, IN ANY ORDER.

Millwall, Cardiff City, Barnsley, Sheffield United and Port Vale. These are from my own experiences.

WHICH IS THE WORST GROUND YOU'VE EVER BEEN TO AND WHY?

Wigan takes some beating – it was a mud bath.

WHICH IS THE BEST STADIUM YOU'VE BEEN TO?

Old Trafford. I went there when Bobby Charlton was still playing and the ground was a different class. We had a good day out up there. We lost 2–0 but had a great time.

WHO ARE THE FAIREST COPPERS YOU'VE COME ACROSS AT A MATCH?

Never met one yet.

AND THE WORST OLD BILL?

Norwich. They're fucking farmers. Don't mess with them.

WHAT WOULD HAVE STOPPED YOU GETTING INVOLVED WITH THE BOYS AT MATCHES?

Nothing would have stopped me. I loved it and I went all over the country with Pompey.

DESCRIBE SOME OF THE METHODS AND TACTICS USED BY THE POLICE AND AUTHORITIES TO STOP FOOTBALL VIOLENCE, AND DO YOU THINK THEY WORK?

We lost 4–1 against Liverpool at Anfield. There was about 13,000 of us up there, and the Old Bill escorted us to and from the ground. We were surrounded by Old Bill with dogs and horses. It was a forced march.

HAVE YOU EVER BEEN SICKENED BY SOMETHING YOU'VE WITNESSED AT A GAME?

I was at a game at Fratton Park in a pre-season friendly in '78 against Chelsea. Fighting broke out and a blind man was caught up in it and no one seemed to give a fuck about him. People were shouting 'Stop, stop, stop' and 'Hang on, hang on'. The warring parties ceased hostilities and I led him away to safety, and then we resumed steaming into one another.

WHAT'S YOUR FAVOURITE FOOTBALL SONG OR CHANT AND WHICH IS THE WORST YOU CAN RECALL HEARING FROM ANOTHER TEAM?

That's got to be 'Play up Pompey' and the Liverpool classic 'You'll Never Walk Alone'. The worst has got to be the song we sang to Dennis Edwards, the former Pompey player. He hated it when we sang, 'Daisy, Daisy, give me your answer do.' We used to go up to away matches on the same train as the players and you'd often hear a chorus of that when he'd been spotted.

WHAT WAS YOUR FAVOURITE BAND/RECORD DURING YOUR FOOTBALL DAYS?

'I'm Not In Love' by 10cc. I've got all their records but that track's my particular favourite.

WHO WAS YOUR ALL-TIME FAVOURITE PLAYER?

The old left-winger for Pompey, Micky Jennings. He was a skinny left-winger who used to fly up and down and get a lot of stick. He had lumps kicked out of him, but he never gave up. He was a legend. Also Bobby Charlton was a top player.

WHERE DO YOU THINK THE NEW ENGLISH NATIONAL STADIUM SHOULD BE BUILT AND WHAT ARE YOUR THOUGHTS REGARDING THE WEMBLEY FIASCO?

It's good the internationals are going all around the country because it gives everyone a chance to see the team. It costs fans a lot of money to get to Wembley, so moving it around gives everyone a chance.

CASS PENNANT MEETS

TERRY 'TESS' MANN

CLUB: NEWCASTLE UNITED

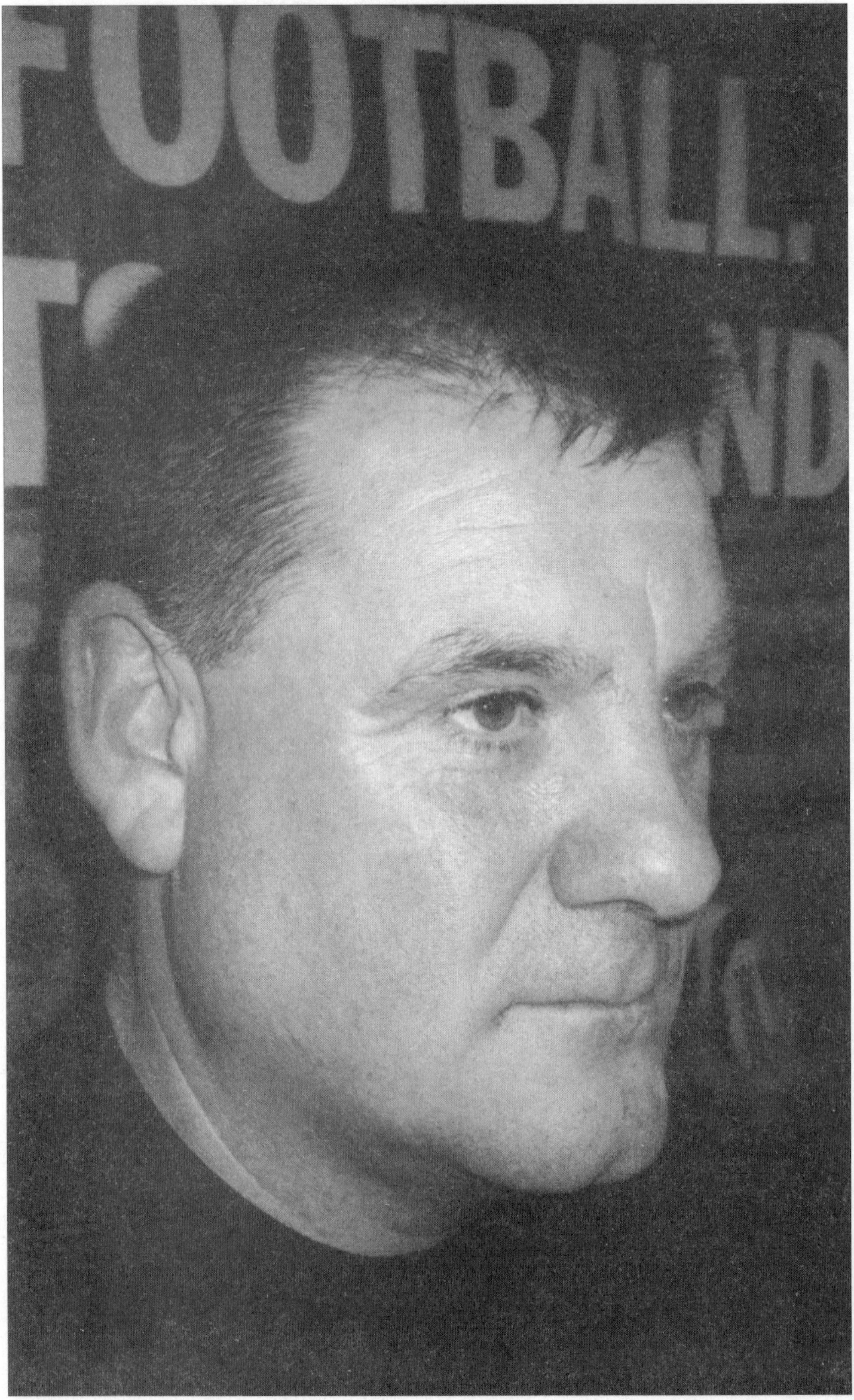
FOOTBALL,
ND

TERRY 'TESS' MANN

THE MEET

Terry had been on my list for months and, believe it or not, it was a Sunderland fan, Gary Lamb, that put me in contact with him. Coming from an arch-rival, it was a surprise to say the least.

I met Terry at Newcastle Central Station and headed back to his pub, The Adelphi, opposite the theatre. As soon as you walk in the place you can see why some people call him Mr Newcastle. Everywhere you look there's football memorabilia – it's a shrine to Newcastle United. Some estimates say it's worth near on a hundred grand, and I could well believe it. I took a picture of an etching of a gravestone of a fan that had passed away in 1900. The words all related to beating Sunderland on 1 September, 'The Magpie's Day Out'. Terry's followed the Toon Army everywhere and his regulars at the pub, young and old, always have a story to tell about the boys in black and white.

I bid Terry farewell and went in search of a bite to eat. I fancied a nice Italian meal so I headed back towards the station to look for a restaurant and ended up getting myself half lost. Then from out of a pub doorway a voice said, 'In here, Cass!' As I looked through the door there were some of Terry's regulars from The Adelphi. They had a beer on the bar for me and wouldn't let me leave before I'd downed a few more shorts. How's that for Geordie hospitality? They love their football and pint up there, in no particular order.

How times have changed. It was a far cry from the '80s when they were throwing petrol bombs at me and the rest of the ICF because we dared to turn up to watch West Ham play at St James's Park. Still, those were the days. Come to think of it, I never did get my Italian ...

BACKGROUND

I started supporting Newcastle in the mid-'60s and the first time I went to a match was with my dad. I used to live just across the road from St James's in Queen's Court, and as a kid me and my mates would offer to look after people's cars when they were going to the match. They'd give us two bob, and five minutes before kick-off we'd bunk into the ground. I made a bit of a living as a kid, car washing. I remember going with my dad to watch us play Stoke City, and George Eastham was on their side then. Later on I got the nickname of Tess or 'Little Legs'.

I now run The Adelphi pub in Newcastle city centre. It's a good old football bar where the walls are full of memorabilia. It's my pride and joy and must be worth in the region of £100,000. I used to keep the memorabilia in the house before I had the pub, but I think it's helped make the pub one of the most popular in Newcastle. We get every generation in here, from the young kids to the old men who tell all the old stories. It's amazing, we even get one or two players in, but most of them like to keep to the posh end of town.

WHAT'S YOUR FAVOURITE TERRACE FASHION?

Donkey jackets and steel toe-capped boots were my all-time favourite fashion, and Dr Martens. I liked the early '70s thing.

WHAT'S THE WORST FASHION YOU'VE EVER SEEN ON THE TERRACES?

The Stone Island Warriors walking around with their £250 jumpers on – it's like, 'Mind me arm!' Stone Island gets on my nerves. You see all the wannabes wearing it.

DESCRIBE YOUR WORST FEELING AT A GAME.

The worst feeling must be the fear of getting nicked. It's always in the back of your mind. You know what you're doing, you know where it's going to go off and you know it's going to happen. If you get a hiding, you get a hiding, but getting nicked is a different feeling.

HAVE YOU EVER INCURRED ANY SERIOUS INJURIES OR BEEN BADLY BEATEN UP AT A MATCH?

Newcastle were playing at West Ham and Leicester City were playing Spurs in the League Cup Final at Wembley. We got back to King's Cross about six o'clock and we went looking for one of our mates. We found the boozer and one of our lot told us that Leicester were drinking round the corner, so twenty of us walked round there. We turned the corner and there were 200 of them standing there. We couldn't run so we had to fight, and we went straight into them. We got fucking hammered and kicked all over the place, but such is life. Suddenly my jaw went boom and it was hanging down to my knees. My lips were cut, and the inside of my mouth was filled with blood. I was smashed to pieces by some cunt smashing me in the face with a big brick – but I'm still good-looking!

HAS YOUR OWN SIDE EVER BEEN INVOLVED IN A FULL-SCALE RIOT?

In 1969 when we played Glasgow Rangers in a Fairs Cup game. Honest to God, they brought thousands upon thousands down here. I was only ten years old at the time and I'll never forget it as it was going off all day and night. Inside the ground they were on the pitch fighting with the coppers, and there were bottles and bricks everywhere. Next day the papers were full of it.

DESCRIBE THE BEST TAKING OF AN END YOU'VE EVER WITNESSED.

I've been in the Fulwell and at Sunderland's Roker Park a few times when we've cleared it. It's a great feeling going through the turnstile, up the steps, and into their end. They back off, and we've had a right result. The Makems never once came in our end. It's a lovely feeling walking round the edge of the pitch with the job done – I'm five feet tall but now I feel twenty feet! Once we went to Cambridge in the old Second Division and went into their end. We had huge numbers but, respect to them, they didn't half give us a good fight. It went on for a good ten minutes. They came from everywhere and I take my hat off to them and respect them totally after that day.

WHICH WAS YOUR OWN TEAM'S POPULAR END?

The Leazes End.

WHERE DID YOU STAND OR SIT IN THE GROUND?

I used to like the Gallowgate End where I used to go with my dad, and all the kids were passed over people's heads to the front where we could see. Those were the days, at the proper old terraces. It was magic times.

CAN YOU RECALL A BATTLE YOU HAVE BEEN INVOLVED IN, EITHER INSIDE OR OUTSIDE A GROUND?

There's a few that spring to mind. Hibs in the late '70s in a so-called friendly. We had a good ruck with them – they just wouldn't stop fighting both inside and outside the ground. Man. United was another good barney where the fighting went on all day. So was Forest in 1974. It spilled on to the pitch and carried on outside.

CAN YOU RECALL THE BEST EVER MOB YOUR TEAM HAS PUT TOGETHER?

The 2002/3 season out in Rotterdam when we played Feyenoord in the Champions League. We met up in Amsterdam. It was all the old school – a good 500-strong mob. The Dutch boys are no mugs but the Old Bill out there have it all sewn up.

WHO'S THE BEST RIVAL FIRM YOU'VE EVER SEEN?

It was the 1984 season. I was standing in The Adelaide with a few mates having a quiet pint before our home match with Portsmouth when we saw a group of about fifty lads coming across the road towards the pub. They came straight into the bar and, bang, it went straight off. They had a lot of young kids with them and a few old heads, and the only thing that spoiled it was there was a couple of their lot taking pictures. Now, how can you have a row with some cunt pointing a camera in your face?

WHO ARE YOUR BIGGEST RIVALS TEAM-WISE?

In 1908 Newcastle and Sunderland fans were involved in a riot and since them days we have hated one another. Some say it was the first riot at a football match. It shocked the nation and since then the hatred has been handed down from our great-grandfathers to our grandads, to our dads and onwards. The hatred has been passed on, not just with the football clubs but in ship building, coal mining and other industries. It's in the history.

WHO ARE YOUR BIGGEST RIVALS FAN-WISE?

The Stinking Makems.

HAVE YOU EVER JOINED UP WITH ANOTHER TEAM'S FIRM?

Never. Well, I've never done it, but these days I've seen Newcastle join up with Nottingham Forest and vice versa. Don't get me wrong, they're all good lads, but in my day you could never do that. I've seen it at England v Scotland games and us Geordies are funny about who knocks around with us.

DID YOU EVER FOLLOW ENGLAND AND WOULD YOU PUT ENGLAND BEFORE YOUR CLUB?

I've been to a couple of England games. I went to Hampden Park and we ended up fighting with the Makems. We walked to the ground in one big mob and gave a Celtic mob a good scudding [beating] that day. But my club comes before England. I would expect everybody to be that way in Newcastle.

WHICH WAS THE BEST ENGLAND ROW?

Fighting with the Jocks at Hampden, and I'm sure Steve Bull of Wolves scored a couple that day. Anyway, we battered the Jocks.

HAVE YOU EVER SUPPORTED OR LOOKED OUT FOR ANOTHER TEAM'S RESULTS?

When I was a kid, Stoke City was my second team. They had a good side in them days with the likes of George Eastham in the team.

NAME YOUR TOP FIVE FIRMS, IN ANY ORDER.

Pompey have always had a good crew. And Millwall – you have to respect them, don't you? I'll also say West Ham and Everton cos they always get a good mob up and, in the last couple of years, Man. United.

WHICH IS THE WORST GROUND YOU'VE EVER BEEN TO AND WHY?

Walsall. I went there in the Cup years ago. It was absolutely disgusting – the pitch was like a mud bath. Bristol Rovers ain't much better and the worst is Roker Park definitely, because I hated the place.

WHICH IS THE BEST STADIUM YOU'VE BEEN TO?

That's easy – Old Trafford. The noise in the old days was fantastic. I've been to Cup semi-finals there and the place has been rocking.

WHO ARE THE FAIREST COPPERS YOU'VE COME ACROSS AT A MATCH?

Our own at Newcastle are fair, and very well organised, while West Ham Old Bill will let you wander off for a pint.

AND THE WORST OLD BILL?

Birmingham, they're the worst in the world. If the Midlands Old Bill smell drink on you, you're not going into the match. You're nicked, and that's it. Stand up or do anything, and that's it. The police are real horrible.

WHAT WOULD HAVE STOPPED YOU GETTING INVOLVED WITH THE BOYS AT MATCHES?

Nothing. I've been married for 24 years so the wife knew what I was like before I met her, so she wouldn't have stopped me. It's just the buzz. I live, eat and drink football. I can't wait for 16 August and Champions League football. Roll on the new season!

DESCRIBE SOME OF THE METHODS AND TACTICS USED BY THE POLICE AND AUTHORITIES TO STOP FOOTBALL VIOLENCE, AND DO YOU THINK THEY WORK?

The Newcastle Police seem to have it sorted now. They know everybody, and what bars we drink in. If there's a hint of trouble they're there and on top of it – they know every little thing. You get very little trouble on match days in Newcastle. They're well up on the ringleaders – they've done the dawn raids. God knows how many spotters they've got and how many cameras they use. It makes me wonder just how much money they spend. If we take a coach to an away game, I know for a fact the police will ask the bus company for a list of the names of those travelling.

CUP FINAL

WCASTLE UNITED

ARSENAL, 0

WEMBLEY 1952

ADELPHI

ADELPHI'S THE BAR, TERRY'S THE MANN
PICTURES ON WALLS, FOR THE TOON HE'S A FAN
HEART OF THE CITY IN SHAKESPEARE STREET
FROM TV AND STAGE THE FAMOUS YOU MEET

TEAMS FROM THE PAST, WOR JACKIE IS THERE
REMEMBER GINOLA, HIS PASSION AND FLAIR
GILLESPIE'S A SORE POINT, A NAME NOT TO MENTION
TERRY'S BLOOD BOILS, HYPER HIS TENSION

THOSE GLORY DAYS, RESULTS ON BRASS
FOR WOR FIFTIES HEROES, LETS RAISE A GLASS
FILLED IN NOW, THE STREETS OLD LOO
TO WIN A CUP, WHAT WOULD WE DO

ADELPHI STAND PROUD, WE KNOW YOUR NAME
GOOD CRACK, GOOD BEER, FOR YOU WE AIM
MANN IS NO ANGEL, BUT HE COULD BE A SAINT
FOR CHARITABLE CAUSES, THE TOWN HE WOULD PAINT

COMPLETE WITH FRAME ONE NAIL AND HOOK
ONE FOR THE WALL, THATS NOT IN MY BOOK!

HAVE YOU EVER BEEN SICKENED BY SOMETHING YOU'VE WITNESSED AT A GAME?

I saw Middlesbrough fans attack this bloke walking along with his son. They spat in his face and beat him up – it was disgusting. You don't do things like that. If he's a football fella and up for the row then that's fine, you know who's who. You don't pick up dads with their kids.

WHAT'S YOUR FAVOURITE FOOTBALL SONG OR CHANT AND WHICH IS THE WORST YOU CAN RECALL HEARING FROM ANOTHER TEAM?

The best is singing to Sunderland 'You're going to get your fucking heads kicked in'. The worst has to be Chelsea singing 'Old MacDonald had a farm', and Man. City fans singing that 'Blue Moon' – it goes on forever and you can't understand a word. And why are grown men singing about a farmyard? It's a fucking nursery rhyme.

WHAT WAS YOUR FAVOURITE BAND/RECORD DURING YOUR FOOTBALL DAYS?

Madness and UB40 – classic. They got you going for the match.

WHO WAS YOUR ALL-TIME FAVOURITE PLAYER?

Alan Shearer. He's a God up here. He always gives 100 per cent. There's no shit about him, he's like a boxer – he gets knocked down and gets up and gets on with it. He carries on and on and on. We've had some great players at the club, like Peter Beardsley and Malcolm Macdonald, but Shearer is a real lionheart. Every game's a battle with him.

WHERE DO YOU THINK THE NEW ENGLISH NATIONAL STADIUM SHOULD BE BUILT AND WHAT ARE YOUR THOUGHTS REGARDING THE WEMBLEY FIASCO?

The Wembley fiasco is absolutely ridiculous. Wales have built a great stadium and we're still humming and hawing. For years the Cup Finals have been at Wembley and that's where it should stay. It feels weird playing big games at Cardiff – it's just not right. Keep it in London, where it should be.

CASS PENNANT MEETS

FRANK WHEATLEY
CLUB: SUNDERLAND A.F.C.

FRANK WHEATLEY

THE MEET

I was standing outside The Village, one of my local boozers I use on match days, just chatting and passing the time of day with the pub's governor. Coming towards us were a swarm of red and white shirts, so he quickly made some excuse about changing the pumps or something. Three lads in Burberry caps pushed their way to the front but I was blocking their route in – 'I don't think so, lads.' I wasn't looking for bother or being confrontational, I had their best interests at heart. These lads were in the wrong part of town. The pub we were standing outside would be packed with the lads from the I.C.F. in the next hour.

The group parted and a man came to the front. I could tell by the twinkle in his eyes and by studying his features that this man was an old warhorse. He also spoke a language the young men in the Burberry caps had not yet learned. It turns out they were lost and had been walking around the east London backstreets looking for a watering hole. Typical Makems?

This was my first introduction to Frank Wheatley, or so I thought. But, as Frankie the old devil reminded me, it turns out we'd met each other before, when Sunderland were down at Chelsea in a mid-week semi-final Cup game in '85. West Ham were away to Wimbledon but stopped off on the way just to add some confusion to the night's events. There were clashes and battles going on in the backstreets around the ground before the game and many arrests were made in this classic hoolie encounter.

Since my chance meeting with Frank outside the pub I decided to get in touch with him through some contacts I knew, and it wasn't long before I found myself in the North East talking to him. He drove me around one of the bleakest housing areas in the country but the people were warm and friendly, though hard people hardened even further through having the heart ripped out of the community by the closure of the mines. A short drive and we were out into some beautiful countryside. We parked up and seemed to be walking in an empty field – that is, until Frank whistled and called out in his thick north-east accent, and a black cob appeared. It stopped short of us, probably sensing a stranger. Frank coaxed it and it came right up to him. Even the horses up there don't trust them Cockney wide boys. But it didn't stop it trying to eat my camera from out of my hand. I took a picture of Frank, the terrace legend, and his horse, and it showed me another side to the man. A sort of gypsy type, happy with life and at ease with the surrounding countryside and his well-loved animals.

I eventually left Frank, parting with one of his prized signed Sunderland shirts. I felt like Bobby Moore after swapping shirts with Pele. I found Frank to be a man with gypsies for friends and Geordies for enemies. He's a proud Makem who defends his friends and team with honour.

BACKGROUND

I'm from a coal-mining background. I left school at fifteen and worked as an electrician. In them days, around about 1971, I had a terrible stutter and was considered a bit of a softie, not a hard nut. I was in the pub with a few mates and someone suggested going to watch Sunderland play at Preston, so we said why not. We got down there about eleven o'clock and went for a drink. There must have been about 150 of us crammed in there. A lot of the people I worked with at the colliery were there and we were having a great time, all pit lads together. We came out of the pub about twenty to three to head off towards the ground, and as we reached some waste ground I could see a couple of our mob fighting.

Next thing I know this guy came from nowhere and cracked me on the chin. 'What've you done that for?' I asked, and then I got booted up the arse. That was it, I just got stuck in and it carried on inside the ground. Some of our lads were getting their heads kicked in at the other end and we steamed across the pitch, and flattened the Preston End. Afterwards we had a night out in Blackpool and had a fantastic time. That was it, I had the buzz. From that day on up until about '81 I never missed a game. Home, away, pre-season friendlies – I went everywhere.

WHAT'S YOUR FAVOURITE TERRACE FASHION?

The donkey jackets, which were free pit issue with NCB [Newcastle Coal Board] on them, Ben Sherman shirts and my old Levi's jacket. Dr Martens boots or baseball boots were all my favourites at the time. A few of the lads also wore Crombies and Sta-Prest, but not all, as half of us were mods and rockers. But when the '80s arrived it was Lacoste polo shirts and jeans.

WHAT'S THE WORST FASHION YOU'VE EVER SEEN ON THE TERRACES?

The purple-and-pink and other funny-coloured shell suits worn by the Scousers take some beating. I think you can still get them in Turkey.

DESCRIBE YOUR WORST FEELING AT A GAME.

The worst feelings are being relegated, or needing to win a match to stay up, or watching your club as a loyal supporter knowing your team's already down and not being able to find the words to speak to your mates about the game. That happened to me at Wimbledon. We took nearly 7,000 fans down there and we'd already been relegated. I can't describe how I felt. I was empty, drained. I wanted to cry, but my heart was empty. You don't feel like drinking. You're thrusting the beer down and you feel sick. Next day you don't want to do nothing. I couldn't face going to work, in fact I couldn't face the world. Another is being arrested and you're drunk. As you sober up you realise you're locked in a cell, all your mates have gone back home, and you think, how do I get home? You wake up to reality. It's happened to me in Swansea and Cardiff twice.

HAVE YOU EVER INCURRED ANY SERIOUS INJURIES OR BEEN BADLY BEATEN UP AT A MATCH?

Millwall away. The night before the game about thirty of us travelled down to London in a big old furniture van. We parked up at the Elephant and Castle and slept in the back. In the morning we came across this pub and, as we went to walk in, a shower of glass rained down on us and we were chased up the road. We stopped and held our own for a good twenty seconds. Next, we were running everywhere with every man for himself. I'd had enough and made my way to the ground, and went in. But unbeknown to me I'd gone in the wrong end and was standing with the home crowd. I was sussed out straight away and my only hope of survival was to get down the front and on to the pitch. As I walked down the concrete steps the crowd gave me a slow handclap. I was a sorry sight. Head bowed, I just had to take it.

Eventually I got to the away end and found my brother and a Cockney lad he knew. Just as I was feeling a bit safer, a mob of Millwall came surging towards us and somehow we ended up on the pitch. The police gave us a choice of either getting back on to the terraces with this mad Millwall lot or being arrested. 'Put the handcuffs on,' I said, offering the copper my wrists. We were taken away and held, but released at half-time, and we decided it would be safer to stand on the halfway line. In no time at all we had 200 Millwall around us. I told the Cockney lad, 'You do all the talking because of your accent and tell them we're deaf and dumb.' I started doing sign language to my brother who grunted and done it back. At the time my mum had been working with a deaf and dumb girl, and me and my brother had picked up a bit of the sign language. It worked a treat until after the game when we were chased all the way back to the tube station. On the platform were 200 Sunderland fans. A train pulled in, we all jumped on, the doors shut and every single window on the train was smashed in by the Millwall mob that had just chased us up the road. Was I glad to get out of there.

As for worst injuries, I've had my nose broken and been covered in blood, and in '81 in Loughborough a couple of dozen of us got into a fight with a Chelsea mob en route back to London. Chelsea had been fighting with the locals and sent word down to the pub we were in, asking to give them a hand. We turned up and were faced with fifty to sixty Chelsea. It turns out they wanted to fight us so I took my teeth out and off I went. I was glassed and my mate had his arm broken, another mate suffered a broken foot, and then we were arrested.

HAS YOUR OWN SIDE EVER BEEN INVOLVED IN A FULL-SCALE RIOT?

Yes, at a league game against Newcastle in about '87. A pub had opened up for us at half-five in the morning for a midday kick-off. Around the back of the bus station appeared a mob and a few of our lads came running towards us shouting, 'They're here!' I stopped and took a piss up against a wall, when bricks came raining down around me. We stopped in the road and went into one another. Everything you could think of was getting used – bottles, bricks, pieces of wood and fencing. It was toe to toe and next to me were two lads on the floor and they were getting a good kicking from our lads. One got up and ran and the other was still getting a good seeing to. 'Leave him, he's had enough,' I told the two blokes dishing out the beating.

I picked him up and asked if he was all right. 'Aye,' he said, 'I'll wait for me mob here.' 'Your firm's gone, mate. They've run and left you,' I told him. 'Don't be fucking daft, we don't run from no one,' he said. 'Mate, I've just saved your life,' I told him. 'Fuck off!' he said with plenty of attitude. 'Oh fuck you!' I said, and pushed him back down on the floor and the lads gave him another kicking. Then we went up the road and we just got chased all over. That day was the worst violence I'd ever seen between us – it was a mob fighting a mob toe to toe. There was even people getting their heads put through windows and it must have been a good half-hour before the police regained control.

DESCRIBE THE BEST TAKING OF AN END YOU'VE EVER WITNESSED.

Middlesbrough in the early '70s when we went in their Holgate End. We got run at first and then we held our own. It was a real buzz. We done well. Everyone stuck together.

WHICH WAS YOUR OWN TEAM'S POPULAR END?

The Fulwell End.

WHERE DID YOU STAND OR SIT IN THE GROUND?
At the back of the Fulwell.

CAN YOU RECALL A BATTLE YOU HAVE BEEN INVOLVED IN, EITHER INSIDE OR OUTSIDE A GROUND?
All the derbys against Newcastle, but the one where we beat them in the play-offs at St James's Park takes some beating. The fighting outside went on until the early hours of the morning.

CAN YOU RECALL THE BEST EVER MOB YOUR TEAM HAS PUT TOGETHER?
Newcastle away in the '80s. We took a top mob there that day and never got run or moved once. The boys like Stanley, Spinny, Mower and Parlo held everyone together, and we looked impressive coming up the road. A few Newcastle doormen I worked with even said we had a top firm that day. They said, 'Frankie, you've got a good squad here – untouchables.'

WHO'S THE BEST RIVAL FIRM YOU'VE EVER SEEN?
Chelsea at home in '76. They had a good 2,000 to 3,000 around the back of the Fulwell and chased a lot of our boys up the backstreets. They looked a good firm that day. Also West Ham at Upton Park. We had it with Bill Garner and the bloke with the hair lip outside the Boleyn pub. It was a good toe to toe.

WHO ARE YOUR BIGGEST RIVALS TEAM-WISE?

Newcastle, it has to be. We hate each other.

WHO ARE YOUR BIGGEST RIVALS FAN-WISE?

Newcastle, because they think they're harder than you and they think they're the bee's knees because they've got an active firm.

HAVE YOU EVER JOINED UP WITH ANOTHER TEAM'S FIRM?

We were coming back into Victoria on the way back from Brighton and we met a group of West Ham lads in the pub. They said, 'Have a drink first and then we'll have a fight.' There was about thirty of us and about twenty of them, so we had a drink with them and moved on to another pub called The Shakespeare, which around this time – '86/'87 – was a main meeting place for Chelsea's boys. We were well outnumbered and for a few moments it looked as if it was going to kick off. The West Ham boys turned up and said to the Chelsea lot, 'If you fight them, you fight us', which calmed the situation. We ended up teaming up with the West Ham boys and had a good night. They even held the train up for us at King's Cross so we could all get home together.

DID YOU EVER FOLLOW ENGLAND AND WOULD YOU PUT ENGLAND BEFORE YOUR CLUB?

England for me wouldn't come before Sunderland. You have to put club before country.

WHICH WAS THE BEST ENGLAND ROW?

England v France out in Paris in 1985/6. I was on the tube with a lass and some QPR blokes and the train was full of Frenchies who were talking in their language so none of us could understand them. A schoolteacher that spoke fluent French explained to me that they were planning to ambush us at the top of the stairs. I told the girl, 'When you get to the top of the escalator make your way outside and find the pub with the England fans in, and tell them we need help.' We got to the top of the escalator and they caught us out. I chinned a couple and they backed off, then the rest of the England boys came to the rescue with bottles and chairs. In the ground the French were paying 35 francs to get in and we were being charged 85 francs – typical French dirty trick. Inside the ground we charged down into the French and gave it to them, and afterwards we got stuck right into them. The English fans were pulling coppers off their motorbikes, shop windows were smashed, and blokes were pinching fur coats and watches.

HAVE YOU EVER SUPPORTED OR LOOKED OUT FOR ANOTHER TEAM'S RESULTS?

Between the ages of ten and fifteen I supported Tottenham, maybe because they were the glamour side of the day and they'd just done the double, but now I hate them.

NAME YOUR TOP FIVE FIRMS, IN ANY ORDER.

Millwall, West Ham, Chelsea, Newcastle and either Portsmouth or Sheffield United.

WHICH IS THE WORST GROUND YOU'VE EVER BEEN TO AND WHY?

Millwall's Old Den, it's just evil. I remember me and my brother fighting our way out of the door because everyone had fucked off and left us. It's just the worst ground to go to – every exit or way in is a dead end.

WHICH IS THE BEST STADIUM YOU'VE BEEN TO?

The old Wembley. The atmosphere and walking up Wembley Way makes you feel like crying, just because it's your team that's here. Also, when you stand there with everybody singing 'God Save the Queen', the whole place brings tears to your eyes and makes the hair stand up on the back of your neck. It's just a fantastic place.

WHO ARE THE FAIREST COPPERS YOU'VE COME ACROSS AT A MATCH?

I find the London Old Bill friendly, maybe it's because they're from all walks of life and from all over the country. At least you can talk to them, have a bit of banter with them, and take the piss, and they're all right about it.

AND THE WORST OLD BILL?

The three worst for different, but obvious, reasons are: Northumberland Police because most of them are Newcastle United supporters and they're working at the Stadium of Light which is why our arrest figures are high; Sheffield Police because it was the Yorkshire and Sheffield Police we were fighting during the miners' strike, and West Midlands because they aren't too keen on visiting fans.

WHAT WOULD HAVE STOPPED YOU GETTING INVOLVED WITH THE BOYS AT FOOTBALL?

Nothing, even if my wife had thrown me out, nothing would have stopped me.

DESCRIBE SOME OF THE METHODS AND TACTICS USED BY THE POLICE AND THE AUTHORITIES TO STOP FOOTBALL VIOLENCE, AND DO YOU THINK THEY WORK?

Brighton Old Bill making us take our boots off, a strange tactic, but maybe not, because in them days you could just jump in their End.

HAVE YOU EVER BEEN SICKENED BY SOMETHING YOU'VE WITNESSED AT A GAME?

I once saw a Sunderland fan take a walking stick off of a spastic and hit him with it. I found that disgusting and he showed his club colours up by pulling a stroke like that.

WHAT'S YOUR FAVOURITE FOOTBALL SONG OR CHANT, AND THE WORST YOU CAN RECALL HEARING FROM ANOTHER TEAM?

'Rule Britannia' is a favourite or 'God Save the Queen' at England matches, and a few years ago we made up our own 'Jack the Ripper' song. Everyone at the time was being stopped and searched so we came up with – 'Me brother's in Borstal, Me Ma's got the pox, Me sister's a whore down Hartlepool Docks, Me uncle's a pervert, me auntie's gone mad, And Jack the Ripper's me Dad'. La La La La etc. etc. The worst song has to be the one we sang to Middlesbrough fans after the Cleveland scandal. 'Where's Your Babies Gone? Where's Your Babies Gone?' we sang that after social workers took children away from their parents after claims of child pornography.

WHAT WAS YOUR FAVOURITE BAND/RECORD DURING YOUR FOOTBALL DAYS?

Dexy's Midnight Runners, we'd sing 'Come on Sunderland' instead of 'Come on Eileen', and The Jam were another band I liked.

WHO WAS YOUR ALL-TIME FAVOURITE PLAYER?

Kevin Ball for what he done for the club, all the fans loved him. Another favourite was Dickie Hord, he was a centre half. I met him and his wife and daughter-in-law for a drink after his testimonial, and we had a fantastic night.

WHERE DO YOU THINK THE NEW ENGLISH NATIONAL STADIUM SHOULD BE BUILT AND WHAT ARE YOUR THOUGHTS SURROUNDING THE WEMBLEY FIASCO?

I've seen England play at the Stadium of Light and the atmosphere was fantastic, and I've seen England at Liverpool against Paraguay and the atmosphere was shit. I think it's fair to take international games around the country, but we do need a national stadium, or a revamped Wembley.

MARTIN KING MEETS

ALAN 'MONTY' MONTGOMERY
CLUB: NEWCASTLE UNITED

ALAN 'MONTY' MONTGOMERY

THE MEET

I've met Monty on a few occasions and he's great company. He doesn't drink or smoke and he always keeps out of trouble! He's a good mate of Time Warp Tel's (nicknamed this because of his 60s and 70s fashion sense) so that says it all. Here's how he recalled his crazy days at football matches to me.

BACKGROUND

I was born in February '62. I first started going to football with my cousin, and we stood at the Popular Home End.

I left school with no qualifications. My first job was in a meat factory and for a laugh I nicked a whole pig's head and took it on the coach with us down to Millwall – it must have been around 1969/70. There was flies buzzing around and it fucking stank. Anyway, for some reason or other we stopped at King's Cross and bumped into some Spurs fans travelling up to their game at Forest. A row started and I launched this pig's head at them. They weren't too pleased – they were going fucking mad. In them days I used to keep a scrapbook of all the trouble but my dad found it and burned it. The Leazes End started as a mob around '67/'68 and was made up of different firms or areas such as Big Lamp, Scotswood, Long Benton, North Kenton, Heaton, Walker, West Denton and many, many others. From there evolved lots of other firms, such as the Bender Squad, Mental Central, NME to the Modern Day Gremlins. You also have to include the infamous ICD (Inter City Drunks) comprising myself, Mallabar, Johnny, Big Tony, Brooksey, Simmo (God Bless), Paddy the Jukebox, Boiler, Jimmy Chargesheet and (get this) Hitler's Butler. Now probably nobody has heard of the ICD outside Newcastle, but let me tell you, I once went to Arsenal and was that drunk I caught the 2 p.m. train home, and thought I'd been to the match and we'd won. Shit and I was the brains of the outfit! I now run a successful business.

WHAT'S YOUR FAVOURITE TERRACE FASHION?

In the 1970s it was a donkey jacket and steel-toe-capped boots. Today, I mix with the best – George and Top Shop … Seriously, Armani and Stone Island.

WHAT'S THE WORST FASHION YOU'VE EVER SEEN ON THE TERRACES?

Anything worn by anyone south of Watford – no dress sense!

DESCRIBE YOUR WORST FEELING AT A GAME.

The worst feeling I have ever had is the promotion play-off when we lost 2–0 to the Scum (S*********d) after drawing the first leg at Joker Park. They were 2–0 up when the ground totally lost interest and Newcastle fans started to invade the pitch from the Gallowgate End. The referee took the players off the pitch as the police tried to restore order, which they did eventually with dogs. At the final whistle I was totally sick as I never got near a Makem and we were out.

HAVE YOU EVER INCURRED ANY SERIOUS INJURIES OR BEEN BADLY BEATEN UP AT A MATCH?

This is hard to believe – well, maybe not – but this is how it happened. Newcastle had Shrewsbury away in Division 2 in the 1983/4 season. Going for a familiar bevvy before the game, we came across three-quarters of Newcastle Trees [shirts] who were having a hard time. So Kev from Gloucester and myself waded in to help them and they did a non-jolly helper and ran, which concluded with the two of us getting a mighty pasting. Now them that know me know I'm no film star at the best of times but the modelling jobs dried up for a while after that – no hard feelings, lads, it's all part of the job. I broke my arm at Millwall in 1978/9 on the first day of the season – well, I say Millwall but I actually broke it on the tube chasing some Arsenal fans even before I got there.

HAS YOUR OWN SIDE EVER BEEN INVOLVED IN A FULL-SCALE RIOT?

This one really is what got me hooked on the terrace scene. In 1974 we played Nottingham Forest in the Sixth Round of the FA Cup. I was thirteen years old and Newcastle invaded the pitch from the Leazes End while losing 3–1 (actually invading when they scored their third goal). That day there had been fighting for most of the match in the Gallowgate End and the third goal sparked the invasion. At the time this was a massive event as it rarely ever happened. On the day, we won 4–3 but the FA made us replay at Goodison and we eventually came out on top 1–0 after a second replay. But we were banned from home FA Cup ties the following season after the events at St James's.

DESCRIBE THE BEST TAKING OF AN END YOU'VE EVER WITNESSED.

Hey, if you had to take an end you had to leave their pub early – fuck that! Not many got taken within the pub hours, but we have forgone a few jars to take the Fulwell End on numerous occasions – especially as told to me by others in the late '60s, early '70s, 1984 and 1985. We've had a go at other ends on occasion but Newcastle always had a place in their hearts for Sunderland, so to speak.

WHICH WAS YOUR OWN TEAM'S POPULAR END?
Leazes End, then Gallowgate and anywhere we could find away fans.

WHERE DID YOU STAND OR SIT IN THE GROUND?
I've had some fantastic time supporting the lads but sitting in the clock stand with Malabar at Joker Park among all the Makems, and taking the piss out of them, has to be one of my favourites. I've also had good times in Bosnia during the 2002/3 season in the Champions League. There were about 150 of us but all the lads were there and, although we were in trouble, no one backed off. Then on to Milan ... We had 12,000 there and it was like everybody was together for once – really an unforgettable trip. There was no trouble but what a night! I was with the Adelphi Boys – all angels!

CAN YOU RECALL A BATTLE YOU HAVE BEEN INVOLVED IN, EITHER INSIDE OR OUTSIDE A GROUND?
Inside the ground we've had loads of rows but my favourite was a one on one I had with a Spurs fan who strayed on to the East Stand Paddock, down the back. I was with the lads but I don't believe in taking liberties so we had a straightener, which was broken up by the Old Bill – no arrests, just a few bruises and sore faces. Outside the ground I remember rowing with Chelsea at the back of the away end (Leazes Corner) in 1980/1. It happened about 3 p.m. and went on for about five minutes. The Old Bill eventually broke it up and I actually shook hands with the kid I had been fighting with – a great day. I could go on but these are the two that have stuck in my mind.

CAN YOU RECALL THE BEST EVER MOB YOUR TEAM HAS PUT TOGETHER?
We have taken some top firms away with us over the years, especially to London, Leeds and Manchester. We've won some, lost some and maybe had a few draws along the way but the one that stands out in my mind came during the 2000/1 season when we played Sunderland at the Stadium of Shite. The police had decided that everyone had to go on free buses from St James's but a lot of people came out of retirement that day, so we ended up taking a mob of 250 on the train. I would say their ages ranged from mid-30s up to early 50s. I'm not sure how the train pulled out of the station with all the weight it was carrying but it managed to get us to Sunderland, where their Old Bill struggled badly to protect the locals. It took them all of an hour to get us the ten-minute walk to the ground. After the match the Makems were scattered badly by the Wheatsheaf Pub – another bad day at the office for the Seaburn Casualties. It could have been worse for

them, had the police not arrested eighty of the Newcastle Gremlins in a Sunderland centre pub, but everyone came back extremely happy with the day's events.

WHO'S THE BEST RIVAL FIRM YOU'VE EVER SEEN?

Two very good firms came to Newcastle in the 1983/4 season. Chelsea brought thousands up and looked impressive, but the lads turned out equally good numbers on that day. Most of the fighting was between our lads trying to get at Chelsea and the Old Bill – there were over 120 arrests. Also Portsmouth caught everyone out by coming into the city centre and nobody really did that. It took a while for everyone to greet them properly and, yes, I was very impressed with the Portsmouth numbers.

But, out of everyone, one firm stands out above all. In 1979/80 West Ham came up for a league game. I was drinking in the Black Bull on Westgate Road when someone came in and said West Ham had arrived and he wasn't kidding. I went outside to confront what turned out to be 300-plus lads who were well up for it. There was hell on all day. Newcastle very quickly raised a mob that would have matched or beaten anyone that day. During the game a petrol bomb was thrown from the East Stand Paddock into the West Ham fans, who were in the Leazes Corner. As I said, I think this is the best mob I have seen come to Newcastle, however I think even West Ham will admit they were glad to get out of Newcastle that day. The reception we got at our next London game that season (QPR) confirmed they were after revenge big time, because they had come off second best up at St James's.

WHO ARE YOUR BIGGEST RIVALS TEAM-WISE?

Sunderland and Sunderland Reserves.

WHO ARE YOUR BIGGEST RIVALS FAN-WISE?

Sunderland and Man. United.

HAVE YOU EVER JOINED UP WITH ANOTHER TEAM'S FIRM?

I went to a few Hearts matches in 1985/86 and had a massive row with Celtic on London Road, leading to Parkhead. There were about 100 Hearts casuals and we were about to be rumbled, with loads of Celtics throwing Irn-Bru bottles at us. We went straight into them, then all of a sudden we were joined by hundreds of Hearts scarfers to finish the job off. All in all it was an experience. The local Old Bill in Edinburgh got slick and warned us off about bringing the English disease to the peace-loving Scottish people, but we had filled in some good gaps when the town had no game.

DID YOU EVER FOLLOW ENGLAND AND WOULD YOU PUT ENGLAND BEFORE YOUR CLUB?

I used to go regular to home games with Simon, but mainly for a drink. I've been to a couple of away games but Newcastle always comes first.

WHICH WAS THE BEST ENGLAND ROW?

In Edinburgh after a game against the Jocks in the '80s. I was drinking with West Ham when it went round that the Jocks were on Princess Street. When we went out there was a large mob. I can remember dropping this Jock in the middle of the road and all the lads were doing the same, and it was over quite quickly. The West Ham lads were a good firm to have around you – cheers, lads!

HAVE YOU EVER SUPPORTED OR LOOKED OUT FOR ANOTHER TEAM'S RESULTS?

I had a lot of family in Berwick, so I used to watch them. My first memory of a Berwick game was at the start of the 1971/2 season in a League Cup game against Hearts. I stood and admired the size of the mob that Hearts had, and I could see Berwick were having a go, but they had no chance. I was only a young boy watching but it stuck with me. I had many incidents watching Berwick over the years, and a couple of arrests to go with it. I do still go to the odd game – I think the last one was a Scottish League Cup game in 2000/1.

NAME YOUR TOP FIVE FIRMS, IN ANY ORDER.

Chelsea, Millwall, West Ham, Portsmouth and Middlesbrough.

WHICH IS THE WORST GROUND YOU'VE EVER BEEN TO AND WHY?

Joker Park and Antwerp – both were crumbling wrecks.

WHICH IS THE BEST STADIUM YOU'VE BEEN TO?

Nou Camp in Barcelona in 1997. We had over 10,000 there and we were already out. I don't remember too many details about the game as the silly twats kept serving bottles of wine to me, Mallobar and Mad Jimmy Chargesheet beforehand.

WHO ARE THE FAIREST COPPERS YOU'VE COME ACROSS AT A MATCH?

No such thing.

AND THE WORST OLD BILL?

Don't mess with the Scouse bizzies with the big sticks – ouch!

WHAT WOULD HAVE STOPPED YOU GETTING INVOLVED WITH THE BOYS AT MATCHES?

I don't regret it one bit. The buzz I got rowing at football can't be beaten. I decided to take a back seat six or seven years ago as I now have a successful business life and a family to look after. I still drink with all the lads and have remained good pals with them all. Oh, I forgot to mention – I got sick of sitting in the cells as well.

DESCRIBE SOME OF THE METHODS AND TACTICS USED BY THE POLICE AND AUTHORITIES TO STOP FOOTBALL VIOLENCE, AND DO YOU THINK THEY WORK?

I remember the Old Bill taking the laces out of everybody's boots at Ipswich in the late '70s.

HAVE YOU EVER BEEN SICKENED BY SOMETHING YOU'VE WITNESSED AT A GAME?

Not as such. Some people have got out of order but I stop when someone's had enough.

WHAT'S YOUR FAVOURITE FOOTBALL SONG OR CHANT AND WHICH IS THE WORST YOU CAN RECALL HEARING FROM ANOTHER TEAM?

'They call us the Newcastle United,
They call us the team of the land.
And here's to Bobby Moncur,
With the FA Cup in his hand.
We're better than Glasgow Rangers,
We're better than Celtic too.
And if you don't support us,
You must be a Sunderland Bastard.'

Also, 'Joe Joe Joe Harvey' and 'You're gonna get your fucking head kicked in!' And, of course, 'Harry Roberts is our friend' – this was a popular song at most grounds across the country in the 60s and 70s.

WHAT WAS YOUR FAVOURITE BAND/RECORD DURING YOUR FOOTBALL DAYS?

The Clash (Joe Strummer – RIP), 'I Fought the Law' and Fun Loving Criminals, 'Where the Bums Go' (say hi to Huey and Guy the Pink Punk).

WHO WAS YOUR ALL-TIME FAVOURITE PLAYER?

I have several – Wyn Davis, Malcolm Macdonald, Peter Beardsley, Alan Shearer, and the one thing I do like about Man. United – George Best.

WHERE DO YOU THINK THE NEW ENGLISH NATIONAL STADIUM SHOULD BE BUILT AND WHAT ARE YOUR THOUGHTS REGARDING THE WEMBLEY FIASCO?

Keep it in London. I enjoy the visits and catching up with old pals. If you haven't been mentioned, no disrespect. I don't want to incriminate anyone – you know who you are. Keep it up, lads, you're doing a good job. And I would like to dedicate this to Paul 'Simmo' Simpson – RIP.

CASS PENNANT MEETS

GARY 'SUNDERLAND AFC' LAMB

CLUB: SUNDERLAND A.F.C.

GARY 'SUNDERLAND AFC' LAMB

THE MEET

When you think of north-east football clubs you immediately think of fanaticism and obsession. In my book, the Makems have always had that type of supporter and in trips up to the new Stadium of Light in recent years I noticed the hostile atmosphere has all but disappeared, but the passion and their sense of humour still remains. 'You're just a small club in London,' they sang as they taunted the travelling band of West Ham fans. But, as I say, they've still got that unique brand of humour that seems to be prevalent in that part of the world.

While searching out a Sunderland fan for the book I had a mate of mine in mind. He's a real Sunderland nut and a right character to boot. He once brought a new Porsche sports car and had it sprayed in red and white stripes all over. He lives, breathes, eats but also does business with Sunderland Football Club, and because of that he didn't feel right about doing a piece for the book, but he did offer to introduce me to a special pal of his who's even more fanatical than him. 'Cass,' he proudly said, 'this bloke hasn't missed a game for near on thirty year.' So that's how I got to meet Gary Lamb, and my mate was right, he is special. He's a true fan and the real Mr Sunderland. Here he shows just how far you can go in the support of your favoured team.

BACKGROUND

I'm 43 years old and I was raised in Murton, a small mining village in the North-East. I went to my first match with a mate and his dad. I was ten years old at the time and up until then I was never really interested in football. That was in 1969 and I can remember the day like it were yesterday. I stood in the boy's section of the Roker End and the whole occasion just grabbed hold of me. As a ten-year-old I remember looking around and listening to people calling out the players' names and it made me wonder how on earth they could recognise and remember all those names – at that age, it was beyond me. We were beaten 2–1 by Sheffield Wednesday, but it was the first goal we'd scored so far that season. I bought myself a programme and studied it in detail and learned all the players' names off by heart. On the Wednesday we had Man. City at home and I was back for more of this new and exciting adventure.

In 1999 I changed my name by deed poll to Gary 'Sunderland AFC' Lamb. I dropped my little-used middle name of Norman, which came from my grandad. It seems there's a lot of people that end up with middle names that are never really used, or don't want to be used. It was all official – my bank cards, passport and driving licence all carry my new full name. In January 2002 I received a phone call telling me I'd won the Barclaycard 'Fan of the Month' but I told them they must have been mistaken as I hadn't entered any such competition. It turned out my daughter had put my name up. Next, Sky TV done a piece on me, then the BBC done a documentary called *Obsessions*, which I featured in, then the *Daily Star* newspaper did a two-page spread of us. Everything seemed to just snowball. A lot of it was to do with my devotion to Sunderland Football Club and how I've not missed a single game in 29 years. Home, away, pre-season friendlies, cup games – you name it, I've been there. The last game I missed was West Brom away in 1974, and I only missed that because I was in a car crash on the way to the game. On the documentary they covered my wedding to Jackie, which was on 17 March, St Patrick's Day. It was a Sunday and we weren't on Sky TV so I wasn't missing a game. I had a Sunderland player from the '60s, '70s, '80s, '90s and the present one came along, plus our vice chairman, John Fickling. It was a fantastic day.

WHAT'S YOUR FAVOURITE TERRACE FASHION?
Dr Martens, a pair of jeans up to the knees, braces and a Ben Sherman shirt. Add a Crombie with a handkerchief sticking out the breast pocket, and you had the look.

WHAT'S THE WORST FASHION YOU'VE EVER SEEN ON THE TERRACES?
Bristol City away in about 1974 sticks in my mind. The Bay City Rollers were in the charts and there were all these lads walking around with trousers up to their knees with tartan strips down the bottom and the sides, held up with a pair of braces. And they had sticking-up, Rod Stewart-style feather-cuts. I thought, why on earth are they wearing this gear? It's schoolgirls' and teeny-bop fashion.

DESCRIBE YOUR WORST FEELING AT A GAME.
Well, my worst fear or feeling is missing a game. With my attendance record for the last 29 years, I now have a bit of a reputation to uphold – people look out for me.

HAVE YOU EVER INCURRED ANY SERIOUS INJURIES OR BEEN BADLY BEATEN UP AT A MATCH?
I've never really been injured, but two instances stick in my mind. I can remember going to Eastville, the old Bristol Rovers ground. I was

about fourteen or fifteen at the time and everyone was together and having a good time, safe in the knowledge you had fellow supporters around you. Suddenly a Rovers mob burst in. The window next to where we were sitting in the corner was smashed from the outside, and me and my mate, Gillie, were showered with glass. We jumped behind our seats as all hell broke loose. In the silence that followed I heard a West Country accent: 'It's all right, lads, there's none of them Geordie bastards in here.' I had to laugh. Geordies – we hate them as well!

We waited until it went quiet then we gingerly left the pub, leaving our unfinished soft drinks on the table. We got three paces from the pub and a crowd of Rovers fans came storming towards us. That was it, we were off, and we didn't stop running until we reached Temple Meads train station, which was about four miles. They never caught us, so we took a deep breath and walked back to the stadium, where we missed fifteen minutes of the first half.

HAS YOUR OWN SIDE EVER BEEN INVOLVED IN A FULL-SCALE RIOT?
Well, I wouldn't say it was an actual riot, but I can remember a game at Portsmouth in about 1975. After the game we came out and headed back towards the station to get the Football Special back home. Thousands of Pompey fans swarmed out of the ground behind us, and a running battle ensued. Anyway, they started chasing us up the road and the Pompey fans that had left the ground early thought we were chasing them, so they start running until at one point they stopped and came into us. Now we were trapped and sandwiched between two mobs, and in the end it was everyone for themselves with people running in every direction.

DESCRIBE THE BEST TAKING OF AN END YOU'VE EVER WITNESSED.
Preston away in the '70s. About 1,000 of us arrived early and went straight into a deserted ground – everyone else must have been down the pub. It was only about one o'clock and someone suggested, probably through sheer boredom, to go up the other end into the Preston section. We just casually walked over the billboards, across the pitch and into their end, and the few home fans already there made themselves scarce and disappeared down the back of the stand. We stood there for ten minutes. Nothing happened, so we walked back across the pitch, back down to the other end.

WHICH WAS YOUR OWN TEAM'S POPULAR END?
The Fulwell End. It was the covered end behind the goal at the old Roker Park.

WHERE DID YOU STAND OR SIT IN THE GROUND?

The Fulwell because of the atmosphere in there.

CAN YOU RECALL A BATTLE YOU HAVE BEEN INVOLVED IN, EITHER INSIDE OR OUTSIDE A GROUND?

I can remember us playing a little village team just up the road from us. Let me think, it was something castle … Yeah, I know, it's come back to me. It was Scum Castle United. Just outside Roker was a pub called The Fork which, in its time, had a bit of a reputation. About fifty of their lot came down Roker Avenue and, as they passed the pub, a couple of young kids had spotted them and were shouting at them from the safety of a back alleyway – 'Come on, you wankers, you'll never catch us.' The Geordies gave chase but, unbeknown to them, a mob of Sunderland lay in wait and ambushed them, and for thirty seconds bricks and bottles rained down on them. It's the worst fight I've ever witnessed.

CAN YOU RECALL THE BEST EVER MOB YOUR TEAM HAS PUT TOGETHER?

I'd say when I was thirteen or fourteen years old and we'd go to pre-season tours up in Scotland and we'd have a top mob with names like Slosher, the Bear, Sammy the Chin and Gunner. They were real characters and game as fuck.

WHO'S THE BEST RIVAL FIRM YOU'VE EVER SEEN?

The late '70s at Old Trafford in the Scoreboard End. United at this time had a bit of a reputation. I was a kid and it was the first time I'd been to Man. United. We stood on the terraces chanting 'Sunderland!' when United fans surged into us from behind. The Stretford End sang, 'United aggro, hello, hello, United aggro.' Sunderland fans just scattered and I ended up standing on my own in the corner.

WHO ARE YOUR BIGGEST RIVALS TEAM-WISE?

Scum Castle United.

WHO ARE YOUR BIGGEST RIVALS FAN-WISE?

The same.

HAVE YOU EVER JOINED UP WITH ANOTHER TEAM'S FIRM?

No, as I say, I personally never got involved in the violence. You know, I saw it happening, and stuff like that, but I'm a football fan, not a fighter.

DID YOU EVER FOLLOW ENGLAND AND WOULD YOU PUT ENGLAND BEFORE YOUR CLUB?

I've only ever been to one England game and I said I'd never go again to watch England, and it's club before country. I went to the last game ever played at Wembley. We lost 1–0 to the Germans. I got into the finals of the 'Football Fan of the Year' competition held in conjunction with the *Sunday People* newspaper, and ten of us were invited to the game. We had a weekend in a top London hotel and stretch limousines took us to the game.

WHICH WAS THE BEST ENGLAND ROW?

Never seen one. I've just seen rival club fans going against one another.

HAVE YOU EVER SUPPORTED OR LOOKED OUT FOR ANOTHER TEAM'S RESULTS?

No, I went to my first Sunderland game at ten, and the bug's lasted.

NAME YOUR TOP FIVE FIRMS, IN ANY ORDER.

I'd say West Ham, Millwall, Chelsea – them three stick out straight away. And then I'd really have to struggle for an answer and say Cardiff and, believe it or not, Stoke, which was an awful place to go to.

WHICH IS THE WORST GROUND YOU'VE EVER BEEN TO AND WHY?

It's not actually in this country, it's Antwerp in Belgium. Their fans out there like to call themselves the Millwall of Belgium. You get in the ground and there's Man. United crests and emblems everywhere as it's actually a feeder club for Manchester United. How they ended up being a feeder club for anyone I'll never know, as our local Colliery Welfare Club's ground is in better condition. We sat on wooden benches, which were close to collapsing, and safety-wise I can't see how it passes any sort of test. This was only a couple of years ago, so I'd be surprised if it's still standing.

WHICH IS THE BEST STADIUM YOU'VE BEEN TO?

I'd say Sunderland's Stadium of Light, but, if I can't choose my own ground, I'd say Porto's stadium in Portugal. It's just a big, open-air, rose-bowl stadium and it made a big impression on me.

WHO ARE THE FAIREST COPPERS YOU'VE COME ACROSS AT A MATCH?

Liverpool coppers are always good for a laugh and a joke. They seem to have a sense of humour – something rare, as any football fan will tell you.

AND THE WORST OLD BILL?

Without a doubt it's the West Midlands, but Nottingham Old Bill run them close. We played Forest just after the miners' strike and the Old Bill were blatantly out for revenge. Lots of the north-east lads who were on strike came down to Nottinghamshire and went on the picket lines. Some Nottingham scabs worked through so obviously the Old Bill had real hatred for some of our lads. I remember sitting at the game with Forest and the Old Bill would steam into the crowd for no reason, and hit out with their truncheons. You could hear them shouting, 'This is for what you did during the miners' strike.' I've never witnessed anything like it in my life.

WHAT WOULD HAVE STOPPED YOU GETTING INVOLVED WITH THE BOYS AT MATCHES?

I've never been involved, but nothing would stop me following Sunderland AFC, nothing. The only thing that would stop me was if my wife and kids were on their deathbeds and then there'd be no choice. I take holidays, but I plan them around our pre-season friendlies.

DESCRIBE SOME OF THE METHODS AND TACTICS USED BY THE POLICE AND AUTHORITIES TO STOP FOOTBALL VIOLENCE, AND DO YOU THINK THEY WORK?

I suppose being banned and having your season ticket taken away must hurt. It also destroys the myth that hooligans are not interested in football.

HAVE YOU EVER BEEN SICKENED BY SOMETHING YOU'VE WITNESSED AT A GAME?

Hillsborough without a doubt. I was watching the aftermath on TV. Also, the Bradford fire when people were burned to death inside the ground. That tragedy helped bring in all-seater stadiums and the removal, and end to, wooden-structured stands.

WHAT'S YOUR FAVOURITE FOOTBALL SONG OR CHANT AND WHICH IS THE WORST YOU CAN RECALL HEARING FROM ANOTHER TEAM?

'I'm Sunderland 'til I die' just about sums everything up. The worst is anything sung by Scum Castle United. I hated it when they started singing to us in the 2002/3 season, 'We'll meet again, don't know where, don't know when.' I think it was rubbing salt into the wounds, and it sucked.

WHAT WAS YOUR FAVOURITE BAND/RECORD DURING YOUR FOOTBALL DAYS?

I've always been into heavy rock, but my favourite is an adaptation I wrote of the Boys' Own song 'No Matter What'. I actually rewrote the song and adapted the lyrics to us beating Scum Castle United 2–1 at their place two years running. It was close to being released – there was a lot of interest in it. Meatloaf, who wrote the original, put the block on it – he wouldn't let us change the lyrics.

WHO WAS YOUR ALL-TIME FAVOURITE PLAYER?

I can't give you one, it's got to be two – Kevin Ball and Gary Rowell. Kevin is 'Mr Sunderland'. He always gives 100 per cent, especially when you think he's a southern lad from the south coast. However, if I picked someone from another club it would have to be George Best.

WHERE DO YOU THINK THE NEW ENGLISH NATIONAL STADIUM SHOULD BE BUILT AND WHAT ARE YOUR THOUGHTS REGARDING THE WEMBLEY FIASCO?

I think the country that started football off must have a national stadium. We gave football to the rest of the world and we can't get our act together and build a stadium to rival the best in the world. That's quite sad.

MARTIN KING MEETS

PAT 'FAT PAT' DOLAN

CLUB: CHELSEA

PAT 'FAT PAT' DOLAN

THE MEET

I've known Pat, or Fat Pat as he's known to most people, for a good twenty years and he's a fellow Chelsea fan. Through following England, Pat has made many friends and he knows all the faces from clubs up and down the country. You see, Pat's that type of bloke. He'll chat to anyone, and some of the stories he tells are unique and very funny. He's a gentleman and a top bloke. He met up with me just after he'd come back from Thailand. I wonder what he got up to?

BACKGROUND

I was born in Shepherd's Bush, London, of Irish parents. I went to the Pope John Catholic School on the White City Estate, and then to the London Oratory, the same school Prime Minister Blair's son goes to. I left school with two O levels in History and English, and became a security man working on the Lisson Green Estate – I got used to being terrorised by the local riff-raff every day. I now work as a doorman in London.

I started going to football with my dad and the first game he took me to was QPR v Everton, which Rangers won 5–0. I was a Chelsea fan but he wouldn't take me there because he said Chelsea were too rough. I told my dad one Saturday I was going to watch Rangers, and me and a mate sneaked over to Stamford Bridge to watch Chelsea play Bristol City. I remember it clearly because Bristol tried to take the Shed.

WHAT'S YOUR FAVOURITE TERRACE FASHION?

The early casual look. I badgered my mum to buy me a Taccini tracksuit. Chelsea were playing Burnley away and I got caught up in a fight outside the ground, as usual. About fifty of us were taking on about 2000 of them and, as we were making a tactical retreat, some clever northern cunt hit me over the head with a full bottle of beer, and that's my worn-only-once tracksuit top fucked and ruined.

WHAT'S THE WORST FASHION YOU'VE EVER SEEN ON THE TERRACES?

The worst fashion – and it still makes me laugh thinking about it – was the ski jumpers tucked into tight jeans, as worn by our friends in the North. Also, the permed hair and the tashes sported by the Scousers.

DESCRIBE YOUR WORST FEELING AT A GAME.

I'd gone out to Germany to see Dortmund play Schalke and about twenty of us had got split up from the main Dortmund mob. We jumped on a tram to get out of the way and passed a bar with about 500 Schalke fans crammed inside and outside. A few of the Dortmund boys banged on the tram windows and I shouted, 'What the fuck are you doing?' Someone pulled the cord and we spilled off the tram. Hundreds and hundreds of Schalke's boys came from everywhere and launched anything they could lay their hands on at us. A petrol bomb landed at our feet and a bloke standing next to me was sparked straight out. Then a bloke came at me with a bike chain and I pulled out a bottle of squirt, which backed him up. We now had them on the run. Suddenly our lot stopped and we gave up the chase. 'What the fuck have we stopped for?' I asked, trying to catch my breath. I was told that two fellas we'd just chased up a side street were members of a Turkish street gang and that they'd run into their HQ to get help and back-up. That was it; we were on our toes, into the station and on to the train. The Dortmund geezers I was with began to dig out some Schalke fans that were little more than divs – they just stood there and took the abuse. One geezer had had enough of the stick and pulled out a gun and pointed it at his tormentors. Shit! People then dived for cover. The next stop was Dortmund and one of the boys got a call to say Schalke were on their way over, and by this time I'd had enough. I just wanted the day to end as even inside the ground at the game I'd got untold shit from a group of Turks who thought the badge on my Stone Island jumper was a right-wing symbol, and were giving me the slit-throat sign. What a fucking day.

HAVE YOU EVER INCURRED ANY SERIOUS INJURIES OR BEEN BADLY BEATEN UP AT A MATCH?

Newcastle away. We went up on Steve Hickmott's coach. I'd been up there the previous two seasons and we'd done well. This particular year we were drinking in the Trafalgar pub outside Gateshead Metro, which I knew was a bad move as the pub was all boarded up and had no glass in the windows. A few of us stood outside drinking with about forty more inside.

I noticed one of their main faces walk past, clock us lot and walk back into the Metro. I told everyone that they were going to be here soon and with that about 300 of them came bursting out of the station. One of our lot fired a distress flare into them and we ran the bulk of them back, but about thirty of their older lot stood firm and came into us with hammers and bats. That was it – we were fighting to get back in the pub with the others who hadn't bothered to even come out. I got caught in the doorway and was being punched around the head as the Geordies swarmed all over us. I looked around to see who was punching me and all I saw was a cricket bat coming towards me. I just couldn't get out of the way as it hit me full in the face. It broke my nose, split my eyebrow and I saw stars. I was taken to hospital, got stitched up and was back in the ground by half-time.

Afterwards, the main lot of the Chelsea fans came out of the ground and turned left. Our coach load turned right, the same as we'd done the year before. I'd had enough by now and was ten yards behind the rest and my bottle had gone – I just wanted to go home. At the top of the road there was a roar and people in front of me were running in every direction. I just wanted out of it as I was mangled, and looked like the Elephant Man. When I got home I told me mum and dad I'd been in a car crash. The old man believed me until he read the *News Of The World* and saw we'd been playing Newcastle.

HAS YOUR OWN SIDE EVER BEEN INVOLVED IN A FULL-SCALE RIOT?

Chelsea at Brighton's old Goldstone Ground. We ran all their supporters and the police off the pitch and for ten mad minutes the Chelsea hordes had control of the ground – the Old Bill had completely lost it. A couple of seasons ago we played Aston Villa away on the last day of the season and Villa fans came on to the pitch at the end to celebrate, as teams do. A 100-strong Chelsea mob joined them and cleared about 3,000 Villa fans back into the seats. It was like one of them BBC wildlife programmes where the gazelles are stampeded by hyenas. It was an amazing sight. I was sitting next to a big six-foot-six Villa fan who was nearly crying. 'I don't fucking believe it' he mumbled shaking his head and holding back the tears. I just sat there with a sly grin on my face. Job done.

DESCRIBE THE BEST TAKING OF AN END YOU'VE EVER WITNESSED.

There was a Friday night fancy-dress do at Stamford Bridge and we all met in the pub opposite the ground. One of our lot noticed a group of fellas in the corner that kept looking over. Curiosity got the better of one of our lot and he went over and asked who they was. 'We're QPR,' they replied. Silly answer because the fella who asked the question was a well-known Rangers fan and he did'nt know them from Adam. One of the other lads then remembered where he'd seen their faces before. 'West Ham, fucking West Ham, that's who they are,' he said. One of the lads that lived locally ran home, emptied his mum's cutlery drawer and handed out the weaponry. We steamed into them and ran them up the road. Elvis, Alvin Stardust, Robin Hood and Batman gave up the chase halfway up the Fulham Road.

The next morning 300 Chelsea met up at Liverpool Street

Station to catch a train to Stratford. It was good turn out for a New Year's Day and outside we were met by the Old Bill. Across the road were an assortment of West Ham faces and in among them was a well-known face sporting a newly acquired black eye from the previous night. The Old Bill informed us our game had been called off and we had two choices – either the Wimbledon v Portsmouth game at Plough Lane, or Highbury, where the Gooners were entertaining the Yids. 'Arsenal, please,' everyone agreed with a knowing smile, and we were escorted to Highbury where we were put into the Clock End.

Three hundred of us snaked across the terraces and the Yids parted like the Red Sea, and we took up a position just below the clock. We paused for a split second and let Tottenham have it. They were no match for us lot and ran in every direction, and after the Old Bill restored order we were surrounded with a sea of blue uniforms. 'Hello, hello, Clock End aggro,' sang the Arsenal fans on the North Bank. The final whistle went and the Old Bill cleared the Spurs fans from the terraces. They'd been humiliated but a few still shouted idle threats and abuse. Within minutes they were running back on to the terraces as a big Arsenal mob outside steamed into them and they were run back in. That day they were totally disgraced.

WHICH WAS YOUR OWN TEAM'S POPULAR END?
The Shed.

WHERE DID YOU STAND OR SIT IN THE GROUND?
I liked sitting in the West Stand seats, but in the '80s our home mob was humungous. We had a mob on every side of the ground: Gate 13 in the East Stand, our mob in the West Stand, the boys in the Shed, the mob in the benches at the bottom of the West Stand, and whoever could blag their way into the North Stand and have it with rival fans. We looked the business.

CAN YOU RECALL A BATTLE YOU HAVE BEEN INVOLVED IN, EITHER INSIDE OR OUTSIDE A GROUND?
Inside the ground I'd have to say West Ham at Stamford Bridge in the '80s. We met at 9 a.m. and West Ham were already attacking Chelsea at 8.30. Inside the ground West Ham's Brit mob got into Gate 13 with a load of moody tickets. The Canning Town mob were seated in the West Stand and the Beer Monsters went in the Shed and the North Stand. We had a good 1,000-strong mob out that day, but West Ham had double that – it was some firm they brought over. It's the only time I've seen fighting on three sides of the ground at the same time, and it was organised with military precision.

Outside of a ground the best fight I've ever seen was England v Scotland. About sixty of us turned into Leicester Square and we were made up of Chelsea and mainly northern fans. Across the road was a mob of about the same numbers who came straight across the road and into us. One of their boys at the front pulled out a blade and plunged it into one of our lot, but he was lucky as it missed his body and went through his coat and out the other side. They started chanting CCS so we knew they were a Hibs firm and we backed off. I hobbled into the Hippodrome nightclub as some cunt had kicked me in the shins. Cameras flashed, as the Japanese tourists loved it, and as they took pictures of the row. Slowly, slowly we backed Hibs off until we had them on the run. As we were dropping them, their mates would stop, pick them up and help them get away. In the end they were gone and we gave up the chase, but as we regrouped we gave each other a round of applause. That was the first and only time I'd seen or heard that, but fair play to Hibs – they were well game. They were a top firm.

CAN YOU RECALL THE BEST EVER MOB YOUR TEAM HAS PUT TOGETHER?

Man. United in the Cup Final at Wembley. Chelsea were drinking in the Lily Langtree pub, just off Kilburn High Road, and Man. United's firm were drinking about half a mile away. Five hundred of us left the pub and made our way through the backstreets towards them. We got within 200 yards of the Black Lion, where they were drinking, before we were brought to a halt by the riot Old Bill dressed in blue boiler suits, riot helmets and shields. I later spoke to two Mancs who were outside the pub, and they said that the Chelsea mob coming towards them looked like the start of the London Marathon. Another good mob Chelsea put together was Millwall away in the cup. There must have been about 1,500 of us getting off the packed train at Peckham.

WHO'S THE BEST RIVAL FIRM YOU'VE EVER SEEN?

Middlesbrough in the play-offs at Stamford Bridge. They came with a massive firm down the King's Road and looked the bollocks. Also, Millwall away at Man. City when they must have had a 1,000-strong mob – all geezers, all over forty.

WHO ARE YOUR BIGGEST RIVALS TEAM-WISE?

The Yids. I've always thought they were overrated as the only results they've had against Chelsea has been when we've been well out-numbered.

WHO ARE YOUR BIGGEST RIVALS FAN-WISE?

Newcastle for obvious reasons. A year after the cricket-bat saga, me, a mate from Stockton and another mate went over to Newcastle. We came out of the station and Newcastle were drinking in Yates's Wine Bar opposite. There must have been 300 of them and they'd seen us. They came spilling out of the pub but are stopped dead in their tracks as we'd all put our hands inside our jackets, like we were carrying a tool. 'Come on, cunts,' we growled. 'Why don't you fight with your fists?' hissed the Geordies. 'Well, tell 280 of your mates to fuck off and we'll have a straightener,' I replied.

There was a van full of Old Bill parked up and some of the Geordies went and told them we were tooled up, the fucking no-good grasses. The Old Bill leaped out, had us up against the wall and thoroughly searched us. The Geordies stood there smiling and laughing, the grassing cunts, but the Old Bill found fuck all and let us go. We turned to the Geordies and did a thumb on the nose to them. 'Get fucked!' I shouted and we bowled up the road with the cops in close attendance.

HAVE YOU EVER JOINED UP WITH ANOTHER TEAM'S FIRM?

Yes, QPR, Cardiff, Millwall, Sheffield Wednesday. I've seen Wednesday absolutely kill Barnsley. I've seen fifty QPR run 200 Leeds and hold their own against a top firm of Boro on the Goldhawk Road, and this particular year Boro were going through everybody. I also went out to Paris with Glasgow Rangers and about seventy of us smashed the Frogs everywhere.

DID YOU EVER FOLLOW ENGLAND AND WOULD YOU PUT ENGLAND BEFORE YOUR CLUB?

It's Chelsea before England, but I've followed England away to lots of big games.

WHICH WAS THE BEST ENGLAND ROW?

Poland away. The Poles came and attacked our hotel at eight o'clock in the morning. They put the front windows in as we were coming down for breakfast, and we went out and steamed into them. They all looked like Lech Walesa with big moustaches and knitted cardigans. It later went off over at the railway station on a bridge for a good half an hour. There was Chelsea, Boro, Wolves, Wednesday and Stockport fighting side by side when suddenly a Tottenham fan threw a stick of lighted dynamite into a mob of Poles.

They went apeshit – it was like a Tom and Jerry cartoon. And when I saw it land I thought, fuck me, there's going to be arms and legs and limbs and blood and guts everywhere, but it just fizzled out as these Poles just stood there waiting for it to burn out. The Old Bill pushed us back up the road and we found a tram load of Poles stuck in traffic. One of our lot gassed them through the window as the driver refused to open the doors. Inside the ground the Poles were fighting with one another and all you could see was hundreds of them wearing the green nylon flight jackets turned inside out to show the orange lining. It was a strange sight.

HAVE YOU EVER SUPPORTED OR LOOKED OUT FOR ANOTHER TEAM'S RESULTS?

I've always supported Chelsea but I have a soft spot for QPR.

NAME YOUR TOP FIVE FIRMS, IN ANY ORDER.

West Ham, Millwall, Arsenal, Middlesbrough, Cardiff. That's my all-time top five.

WHICH IS THE WORST GROUND YOU'VE EVER BEEN TO AND WHY?

West Ham's the scariest ground I've ever been to. In 1980/1 we put leaflets out in the Shed to get everybody to go together for the game at West Ham the following week. A mob of us got off at Upton Park and walked down to the ground. As we got outside the back of the South Bank we could hear 'Hello, hello Chelsea aggro' followed by an even louder 'Hello, hello West Ham aggro' as we were queuing to get in. A mob of West Ham steamed into us and we were run into the ground, many just jumping the turnstiles without paying. Inside, it was mental. A few West Ham were on the pitch down by the corner flag. Nearly everyone there had the green or blue flight jackets on so no one really knew who was who. West Ham was one hell of a place to go to in those days.

WHICH IS THE BEST STADIUM YOU'VE BEEN TO?

Turin, when England played Germany and we lost on penalties. That was some stadium. And also Wembley because I was there when Chelsea beat Man. City in the Mickey Mouse Cup. Still, it was a nice feeling to win a trophy after all those years.

WHO ARE THE FAIREST COPPERS YOU'VE COME ACROSS AT A MATCH?

In terms of organisation, it's got to be Fulham Old Bill. We never get a sniff of a row and, when we do, it's only by accident, although they did slip up once when we were playing Arsenal at home and nothing was happening, so after the game we headed over to King's Cross where we hoped to find the Yids.

A few of us went up in a car and as we pulled up outside the station we saw a mob of Leeds running Spurs up the road towards Euston. A geezer with his head split open ran past us and we grabbed him and bundled him into the car. When he found out we were Chelsea he shit himself and tried to get out the door but he had second thoughts when he saw the Old Bill hot on his friends' tails. Just then a mob of Chelsea about eighty-strong came round the corner. 'Want some more, Tottenham?' said a Leeds face standing in the road beckoning our boys towards him. 'Tottenham? We're fucking Chelsea,' we replied, and our boys steamed in running the bulk of the Leeds firm into King's Cross Station.

The Old Bill turned up and nicked a few and restored some order while we headed back to one of our usual boozers south of the river. We'd just sat down with a pint when Fulham Old Bill walked in. 'By all accounts, lads, they said smugly, 'you've just missed a blindin' row over at King's Cross.'

AND THE WORST OLD BILL?

The silliest has to be Huddersfield. We got there at eleven o'clock in the morning and were met off the train. Only about three of us got out of the escort, the rest were marched down to the ground and, to our surprise, they were just let go. The Old Bill even pointed out the way to the town centre because the stadium wasn't open yet. How fucking daft can you get? So there were 700 of us creating murder in the

town. Hickey turned up at the ground and took a mob of Chelsea into the Huddersfield end. They did well, but in the end had to get out. One of our lot lost one of his trainers so he paid to get back in to retrieve it. He worked his way through the crowds and spotted it lying there on the crumbling concrete terrace. Everyone around was oblivious to this trainer lying on the floor – it was like a Peter Sellers film! He got down on his hands and knees going over people's feet and through legs, and he was inches away. He went to grab it when a Huddersfield fan spotted him and kicked him under the chin, and broke his jaw in three places. Just before the end of the game we went back into their end and, just as we got in there, the final whistle went and we were swept outside on a tidal wave of bodies. There was fighting everywhere and in the darkness no one knew who was who.

We finally got back to the railway station and told the coppers we were Leeds fans, so they put us on a train to Leeds. Now Leeds were at home to Preston in the cup. We pulled in at Leeds and the Old Bill surrounded us and told us they knew what we were up to. The next train back to London was in an hour and it looked like we were fucked and stuck on the platform until someone kicked open a gate and we were out on the street – 300 of us roaming the backstreets of Leeds. We turned a corner and found Leeds drinking outside the Black Lion. They came out and we got into them and annihilated them. The Old Bill now had the right hump and battered us back into the station. Only one of our lot got done and that was Greenaway. He'd been to an off-licence and bought a crate of beer and he'd been attacked by Leeds fans who kicked and punched him all the way up the road, but he refused to let go of his treasure!

WHAT WOULD HAVE STOPPED YOU GETTING INVOLVED WITH T HE BOYS AT MATCHES?

Nothing, I lost my ex-girlfriend and my daughter because of football, something that, as I've got older, I've regretted. It's in my blood. Just hearing stories from other people about rows at football gives me a buzz.

DESCRIBE SOME OF THE METHODS AND TACTICS USED BY THE POLICE AND AUTHORITIES TO STOP FOOTBALL VIOLENCE, AND DO YOU THINK THEY WORK?

That's got to be when we played Feyenoord in the Champion's League. We'd all met early in the Grasshopper bar in Amsterdam and the plan was to get into Rotterdam well before the game. Five hundred of us got on to a train and an announcement in Dutch was broadcast. The locals got up and got off. The doors shut and we pulled off, but a journey that should have taken less than an hour, took three. It was the slowest train I've ever been on. We pulled into the station outside the stadium half an hour after kick-off.

To this day Feyenoord say we never showed, but how can you put a show on when you can't move for Old Bill? Forty of us did get into the seats above their paddock and they had the right hump about that. That was the best tactic I've ever seen.

HAVE YOU EVER BEEN SICKENED BY SOMETHING YOU'VE WITNESSED AT A GAME?

I was out in Holland with a mate of mine going to watch Feyenoord play. Just outside Amsterdam we were driving along in a convoy of cars when we pulled over. I thought it was for a piss, so everyone got out and through the mist and the drizzle came 300 Ajax fans. It was like *Braveheart* as the two sets of boys tore into one another with axes, baseball bats, knives and machetes. It was unreal. I was a guest so I didn't get involved. It went toe to toe for a few minutes and the bulk of the Ajax retreated, but a handful of them stood and were taking a serious battering.

A man later died from his injuries and people were climbing back into the cars, parked on the motorway, covered in mud and blood. We carried on to the game and it came on the radio that a man had been killed, and people still went into the ground. I didn't go in and sat in a bar mulling over in my mind the day's events. After the game they let the Feyenoord fans out one at a time and anyone with blood or mud on them were taken away. It was the sickest thing I've ever seen. People were butchered. Since then a well-known prick who writes books has cast his thoughts and views on what happened that day. A word of advice – you know fuck all, so keep that big mouth shut. Thank you. You've spoken to clowns like yourself who know nothing.

WHAT'S YOUR FAVOURITE FOOTBALL SONG OR CHANT AND WHICH IS THE WORST YOU CAN RECALL HEARING FROM ANOTHER TEAM?

'Thank you very much for the North Bank Highbury' is a favourite. We sang that to disgruntled Gooners after we'd chased them out of their end one year. I also loved singing 'We've the North Stand, We've the North Stand, We've the North Stand, Stamford Bridge', as I chased rival fans.

The sickest one I've heard has got to be the Millwall song, which goes to the tune of 'Robin Hood': 'Bobby Moore, Bobby Moore, playing at the Den, Bobby Moore, Bobby Moore, He had sex with men, Gay as you come, He takes it up the bum, Bobby Moore, Bobby Moore, Bobby Moore.'

WHAT WAS YOUR FAVOURITE BAND/RECORD DURING YOUR FOOTBALL DAYS?

'Change of Heart' by Change. 'Two Tribes' by Frankie Goes to Hollywood was probably my all-time favourite.

WHO WAS YOUR ALL-TIME FAVOURITE PLAYER?

Zola, a gentleman on and off the pitch. He's a genius, a real class act. Peter Osgood's another. I was also an admirer of Arsenal's Liam Brady, who was another class player. He once scored a hat trick against us and he was different gear.

WHERE DO YOU THINK THE NEW ENGLISH NATIONAL STADIUM SHOULD BE BUILT AND WHAT ARE YOUR THOUGHTS REGARDING THE WEMBLEY FIASCO?

I think it's a marvellous idea to move the international games around the country. The Germans do it. But I do think we should have a national stadium in London, as it's the capital city. I think moving it around the country gives everyone a fair chance to have a fight, but that's because I'm a mischief-maker. We should even let Millwall host a game. Give everyone a chance – it's good to share it around. When the internationals were at Wembley there was never any trouble, and the same when we used to play Scotland down here and the Jocks used to overrun the place. That would have never happened at somewhere like Newcastle – the Geordies wouldn't let it happen. Leeds or Boro would be the same. The boys from the teams in London hated one another, so we never got our act together.

MARTIN KING MEETS

IRVINE WELSH
CLUB: HIBERNIAN

IRVINE WELSH

THE MEET

I've known Irvine for many years and met him through John King, author of *The Football Factory*. Irvine's a top bloke who loves his football. Here he describes his football-going days.

BACKGROUND

My friends where I grew up followed Hibs but most of my extended family were of the other persuasion. I started supporting Hibs properly in the '70s as my father and most of those who went to away matches were dubbed 'football hooligans'. It was as simple as that. Kids started going away at about fifteen or sixteen and it was a risky thing to do, as you were always liable to harassment from rival supporters. You went on the excursion buses, which left St Andrew's Square. Because you were usually too young to drink in pubs you hung around the streets in numbers, as you'd be done over if you were in small groups. Despite all the bravado, I think that was really how a lot of the football mobs got started in the '70s. There was no real planning – just young, nervous kids hanging around with nowhere to go before the game.

WHAT'S YOUR FAVOURITE TERRACE FASHION?

Back then it was the daft 'Christmas tree' style dress with scarves hanging from the wrists, belts, the ubiquitous Levi's, Ben Sherman shirts and Doc Martens. It did get better as the '70s progressed and most boys had the savvy to tone it down – a bomber or Harrington with a club badge would suffice.

WHAT'S THE WORST FASHION YOU'VE EVER SEEN ON THE TERRACES?

The early '70s stuff I've just described, without a doubt. The crimes committed against fashion were horrendous enough in the '70s anyway. Mind you, even in the more fashion-conscious '80s, there were some major style lapses. I saw boys with Yasser Arafat headgear and then there was that weird deerstalker thing that appeared briefly, but thankfully never caught on. I think the Bay City Rollers-style V-neck jerseys favoured by Glaswegian fans from 1972 to, well, the present day really take the biscuit though.

DESCRIBE YOUR WORST FEELING AT A GAME.

I think the great thing about football is that as you get older you get over defeats more quickly. You learn to celebrate the victories and ignore the defeats. I think the younger you are, the more it hurts. I went to a Hibs v Celtic Scottish Cup Final in 1972 convinced that we would win. But we fell apart defensively and were thrashed 6–1.

HAVE YOU EVER INCURRED ANY SERIOUS INJURIES OR BEEN BADLY BEATEN UP AT A MATCH?

I think that if you get injured seriously you've either put yourself in the position of doing so, or you're just pretty unlucky. There are a lot of myths about football violence. Like most people from my era, it was all about mobbing up, charging the other crew, them regrouping and charging you. Everybody and every mob has ran at one time – it's nonsense to suggest otherwise. Even in huge mobs it's still usually only around fifty-a-side front liners (the same ones every time) who are seriously going at it. I remember at Motherwell one time, a barrier collapsed and all those bodies were on top of me, crushing me, and in my panic I was punching this poor cunt in the face who couldn't move his arms. I think if there had been perimeter fencing, several people might have been very seriously injured, Hillsborough style.

In the '70s the worst things were flying bottles. You could take drink into the game in those days and I remember just being bombarded with bottles and cans at Hampden, in a Cup semi-final with Rangers, and going home with my head covered in lumps. Once I'd got to my early twenties I was seldom involved as I stopped going to away games regularly, except for the big ones. Most of my friends stopped as well. I think that if you go with some characters and they drift out, you often do as well, or you get more into other things – in my case, music. It was a sort of gradual thing but I recall two pals were given custodial sentences for organising a riot at Perth.

A newer, harder, better organised Hibs crew had emerged in the mid-'80s as part of the casual movement, by which time I'd moved to London. It was more a generational thing. By the time they emerged there was really no serious hooligan element. I experienced some of the hooliganism south of the border. I got whacked with a pool cue by an Arsenal boy in a pub near Highbury one time, and was called 'Chelsea scum' when I wasn't even intending to go to the game – I was just meeting a couple of pals who were Chelsea. Talk about adding insult to injury!

HAS YOUR OWN SIDE EVER BEEN INVOLVED IN A FULL-SCALE RIOT?

In the '70s the number involved were big, so many games involving Hearts or Rangers especially were reported as full-scale riots, even if they were just the old pattern of charge, run, regroup, charge. If they took place in a busy shopping area the public panicked and the police would steam in, and some shop windows would get put in. I'm wary about terms like 'full-scale riot', though. One man's riot is another man's group punch-up.

I remember going to Hearts v Queen of the South at Dumfries with some Hearts relatives, and that was the first time I saw helicopters at a football match. In the late '70s and early '80s Hearts had the main Edinburgh mob, no doubt about it. After we beat them 7–0 at Tynecastle, it became a scary place to go to if you were Hibs. This changed again in the '80s with the emergence of the Hibs casuals (CCS). There were a few rows with Rangers at Ibrox and with Aberdeen, which developed into serious affrays. A lot of my generation who condemned the casuals did it, I think, out of jealousy. It made me laugh when I saw some '70s faces moaning about the CCS. I used to think, you've got a short memory. I think there was a big difference between a lot of the boys from the '70s and '80s at Hibs. The '70s-led hoolies tended to be more second-string types, looking to prove themselves, while the established top boys in the city were more involved in street gangs and would only mob for big games. I think the '80s casuals were probably Edinburgh's first city-wide gang, so they contained more of the top boys from all areas of town. Now it seems to have swung back to street gangs again, though there are signs that might be changing. These things tend to be cyclical.

DESCRIBE THE BEST TAKING OF AN END YOU'VE EVER WITNESSED.

In the early '70s I saw Hibs take the Hearts part of the ground's covered terracing. On that occasion a group of YLT (Leith boys) had got in early and routed Hearts before they could assemble properly. It was great fun and a fantastic source of pride for squeaky-bollocked little runts like us to witness. For most Scottish fans, due to the total lack of facilities, the ends were not covered. Hearts stood along the middle, opposite the main stand, like Man. City's Kippax. Usually, though, I have to admit that throughout the '70s Hibs were often lucky to get out off that place in one piece.

WHICH WAS YOUR OWN TEAM'S POPULAR END?

When I started going it was the Cave, behind the goal. The pitch was sloped and Hibs shot downhill into the Cave – it was brilliant. Then the club decided that there was too much bother there, and they enclosed it off and put seats in it. Even when you didn't have the likes of Rangers trying to take it, you had internal rows between, say, Leith or Niddrie or Tolcross. Shutting down the Cave killed the atmosphere in the ground for years, and it only picked up when they covered the main terracing. What a bleak place to attend football it was before that, especially on rainy nights.

WHERE DID YOU STAND OR SIT IN THE GROUND?

When the Cave shut we moved to the enclosure under the stand, then to the new covered main terracing, which was great. It still is, even though they've put seats in it and renamed it the East Terracing. It gets called the 'Cowshed' or the 'Scabby' and stands out like a sore thumb from the other three new stands. It generates the best atmosphere of any ground in Scotland. Although it's seated, nobody bothers at the big games. When they demolish it, I'll stop going – it won't be football as I knew it any more.

CAN YOU RECALL A BATTLE YOU HAVE BEEN INVOLVED IN, EITHER INSIDE OR OUTSIDE A GROUND?

At Dundee, trying to get down that fucking hill to the station. It was always a trouble spot but on one occasion it seemed like there were offs taking place everywhere. A few of us turned the corner and ran into their main mob. A couple of lads took a pretty bad beating. I was okay but took a severe crack to the jaw from something.

CAN YOU RECALL THE BEST EVER MOB YOUR TEAM HAS PUT TOGETHER?

It's difficult to compare the '70s with the '80s and now. Back in the '70s Hibs could put a healthy mob together for big games (Rangers, Hearts, and so on) especially at Easter Road. Then you could go somewhere like Montrose on a Wednesday night in the League Cup and get turned over by a bunch of farmers. It really all depended on who showed up. As I've mentioned, there was a lot of factionalism due to the rivalry between the various Edinburgh street gangs back then, and sometimes you were more likely to get it from somebody from a rival district than from a rival supporter. I remember a mate getting bottled at Tynecastle by another Hibs supporter who took the opportunity to settle an old grievance against him in the general atmosphere of pandemonium and mayhem. But the '70s was more disorganised. It was a free-for-all rammy [brawl] really, which could involve thousands.

The Hibs casuals who came through in the '80s were something else again. They were dedicated (they went to almost all the games), they had a big mob and could pull out the numbers for places like Ibrox, where Hibs seldom had any real presence before. I was surprised to come up from London and attend a Rangers v Hibs game around 1987 or 1988. Hibs only had an allocation of 1,500 tickets, but it seemed that almost everybody there was CCS!

WHO'S THE BEST RIVAL FIRM YOU'VE EVER SEEN?

Celtic and Rangers would come through to Edinburgh and swamp us in the '70s. They weren't all dedicated hoolies, though it seemed that way at the time! For hard-core hooligan numbers, probably Aberdeen in the '80s. In general, though, some of the firms I saw in London, for numbers and organisation, were very impressive. Now I think that Cardiff City and Manchester United seem to have the biggest and best mobs. You couldn't really compare Scottish firms (or most English ones) in size, but Aberdeen I would say (and this is largely anecdotal) have the most dedicated hoolies at present.

WHO ARE YOUR BIGGEST RIVALS TEAM-WISE?
Hearts, though we both now probably hate Rangers and Celtic more as they have so much cash, but we still always like to beat each other.

WHO ARE YOUR BIGGEST RIVALS FAN-WISE?
Hibs and Rangers have always had a rivalry, but the worst rows are probably still before, during and after the first Edinburgh derbies of the season.

HAVE YOU EVER JOINED UP WITH ANOTHER TEAM'S FIRM?
That thing never really happened in my day. The tourist thug is a modern phenomenon and I can't really understand it. There have been lots of alliances but they usually just come about through boys meeting each other on holiday or in clubs and becoming mates. I'm sure you'll get more of it as we become more globalised. I was given an honorary membership of the CSKA Sofia thugs by their top boys. Nice of them, but I don't really get it.

DID YOU EVER FOLLOW SCOTLAND, AND WOULD YOU PUT SCOTLAND BEFORE YOUR CLUB?
Watching the Scottish national side never really lit my fire. It was always more of a Glaswegian thing – the one time of the year Celtic and Rangers mobs would wrap in tartan and put aside their differences. Then sectarianism kicked it – Celtic fans decided that they'd follow Ireland. Rangers went tit for tat and began orientating towards England. It's perverse watching all those people trying to be what they can never be, but that's weedgies [Glaswegians] for you.

I went to Wembley in '77 and '79 (and got arrested for throwing bottles at my mate in a Trafalgar Square fountain) but I've always inclined more towards club football, basically because my mates have.

WHICH WAS THE BEST SCOTLAND ROW?
Probably v England in 1977 at Wembley, or v Wales at Anfield in a World Cup qualifier round about the same time. I'm crap on dates and seasons.

HAVE YOU EVER SUPPORTED OR LOOKED OUT FOR ANOTHER TEAM'S RESULTS?

I've a soft spot for Sheffield United and I always like to see them do well. When I lived in London I watched West Ham, Chelsea and Millwall at various times. That wasn't for the thuggery, it was just that those grounds had the best atmosphere in the '80s. Now that I'm involved in a film on the Soul Crew, I've started taking more of an interest in Cardiff. Obviously, I look out for the Hearts results hoping they do badly. I have to admit that I was a bit chuffed when they beat Celtic at Tynecastle recently to cost them the League – the arrogance of the Glasgow clubs with their dosh is too much, and I love to see them get turned over.

NAME YOUR TOP FIVE FIRMS, IN ANY ORDER.

Impossible to say as it changes all the time. I've got to put CCS top or I won't be able to set foot back in Edinburgh. Cardiff boys have shown me a lot of footage and they are very impressive in terms of numbers and commitment. The BBC in Sheffield have a good reputation for always following the hoolie code of no weapons, no bullying stragglers, replica tops, and so on, which I respect. The London mobs will always do well. They get the media publicity so they'll always be able to recruit from time to time.

WHICH IS THE WORST GROUND YOU'VE EVER BEEN TO AND WHY?

Tynecastle – for obvious reasons.

WHICH IS THE BEST STADIUM YOU'VE BEEN TO?

Easter Road – ditto.

WHO ARE THE FAIREST COPPERS YOU'VE COME ACROSS AT A MATCH?

I think that the London police give you a lot of leeway. I've seen people behave in ways that would get them instantly arrested in Scotland (threatening behaviour, drunk and disorderly) and the coppers have turned a blind eye. It's an old complaint by fans, though, the inconsistency of policing.

AND THE WORST OLD BILL?

Strathclyde (Glasgow). I was arrested by them a few years ago and they even managed to get my age wrong! You especially see it at big games around Hampden – you get crammed into pubs and if it's a nice day you can't even sit and drink a beer in the park without harassment. They seem to give Edinburgh and Aberdeen people a particularly hard time. The worst I saw was at the Hibs v Livingston Cup Semi-final of a few years back. There was never going to be any trouble there, but the way the police were acting, you'd have thought that revolution was in the air.

WHAT WOULD HAVE STOPPED YOU GETTING INVOLVED WITH THE BOYS AT MATCHES?

I only got involved initially through fear. It was a safety in numbers thing – I just didn't want to get battered when I went to away games. After that, of course, the buzz takes over, then the camaraderie and the sense of adventure. But I was never much of a fighter, so in the early days if I could have stood somewhere atmospheric and watched the game, I'd probably not have bothered. As I've said, I've known a lot of boys who were hoolies or who ran with different mobs. Many of those lads in quieter moments will admit to never throwing more than a few punches in anger, some not at all. A lot of posturing went on back then but the streets are only so wide and it's the same fifty-a-side in every mob who really go at it. People might look frightening to TV viewers when they're charging forward or snarling across police lines, but most are just there for the (safe) buzz. It's different for the dedicated top boys – they need the real combat to make their day.

DESCRIBE SOME OF THE METHODS AND TACTICS USED BY THE POLICE AND AUTHORITIES TO STOP FOOTBALL VIOLENCE, AND DO YOU THINK THEY WORK?

I don't think you can really stop it. It just ebbs and flows and it's part of social life in this country. We have to remember that the violence pre-dates the football. In fact, many clubs were formed to give people an outlet for partisan and violent behaviour. It's not the so-called thugs who have infiltrated the game – they've always been there. It's big business and television. I think they can ruin a mob with surveillance and stiff sentences, because everybody gets paranoid about grasses. It's crazy some of the sentences being handed out for football-related rowing.

HAVE YOU EVER BEEN SICKENED BY SOMETHING YOU'VE WITNESSED AT A GAME?

I've always been sickened when I've seen the bullying or beating up of stragglers or non-rowing fans by psychos in mobs. This is quite rare as most boys know the score and will just leave it at a slap or a kick up the arse, but there are always some cunts who take liberties. That's why it's all too rich for my blood nowadays. It's getting so you have fifty kung-fu experts on either side, and all this mobile phone and threat stuff is nauseating. Football thuggery seems to have moved into a kind of professionalism. There's not so much room for the healthy 'boy's own' spirit of fun, amateurism and camaraderie. But that's the way life is going in general.

WHAT'S YOUR FAVOURITE FOOTBALL SONG OR CHANT AND WHICH IS THE WORST YOU CAN RECALL HEARING FROM ANOTHER TEAM?

Best is 'Let's All Do the Hibees Bounce'. The worst are the drab sectarian songs sung by Glasgow fans. I mean, how the fuck can anybody in Scotland get excited about Irish politics when even people in Ireland aren't that bothered any more?

WHAT WAS YOUR FAVOURITE BAND/RECORD DURING YOUR FOOTBALL DAYS?

Band? I think The Jam probably. Record-wise, I remember being in a pub in Motherwell, using a table as a shield as we were being bombarded with glasses. Appropriately, the song on the jukebox was Abba's 'SOS'. It really went with the occasion.

WHO WAS YOUR ALL-TIME FAVOURITE PLAYER?

Pat Stanton.

WHERE DO YOU THINK THE NEW ENGLISH NATIONAL STADIUM SHOULD BE BUILT AND WHAT ARE YOUR THOUGHTS REGARDING THE WEMBLEY FIASCO?

I don't really care where England build their national stadium, or even if they do, but somewhere in the Midlands would be the best bet. Wembley is so difficult to get to. Hampden is a shithole, which should be demolished and made into something socially useful, like a hotel or supermarket. It has no atmosphere, and is miles away from anywhere. Scotland should have Murrayfield as the national football stadium.

CONCLUSION

Men among men. Top boys. Men with a huge passion and a pride that, I can tell you now, could put to shame many of today's professional players proclaiming allegiance to that treasured club badge. I wanted to go back to the days when a football club was its fans. For among these fans was an elite who had become the respected among the respected by those of us who still remember the terraces with all the camaraderie, the bonding, the thrill and the buzz. This elite were men of another time – another era perhaps – but nevertheless men with a certain aura about them. Huge, colourful characters recognised by all those in the know. These are the lads that, if we, the authors, could get close enough to look them straight in the eyes, we would know in an instant that these were the men we sought.

So we crossed that divide of friend and foe, that magic code, but fair play to each and every one of them, as they didn't have to feature in this book. We can take the trust given as a compliment and it is that mutual respect that we felt warranted this publication. We wanted to reveal first-hand knowledge, by way of a questionnaire, of what this football business meant to each of our interviewees.

Perhaps those of you with your own experiences, depending on your level of involvement, can have a go at the questionnaire yourselves, and hopefully have fun doing so. We also thought you might be interested to see the general conclusions to some of the most popular questions, so below we've highlighted the top ten questions and their responses.

1. WHAT'S YOUR FAVOURITE TERRACE FASHION?

As much as they felt they were individual in their selection of clothes, the choices of those interviewed fell between two categories: that of the uniform look of the original early '70s skinhead/bootboy generation, or the classic designer-wear look of the '80s casual dresser. What was equally interesting was that today's stereotypical image of the Stone Island, Burberry-wearing individual was frowned upon as being outdated, lacking in any anonymity and, worse, truly wannabe. Shame, as it was nice clobber for a while.

2. DESCRIBE YOUR WORST FEELING AT A GAME.

The popular call here was incidents of it coming on top (ie being rumbled) or getting caught out by another rival hooligan gang. Others stated the obvious bad experience of being arrested. But, of those that gave a genuine football reason, nearly all cited end-of-season play-off matches in which their team lost. The gut-wrenching feelings generated remain with those individuals to this very day. The term 'sick as a parrot' comes to mind.

3. HAVE YOU EVER INCURRED ANY SERIOUS INJURIES OR BEEN BADLY BEATEN UP AT A MATCH?

The experience of many was that this was an occupational hazard ever likely to occur. What can be noted is that, whenever the individual did come unstuck, it rarely occurred on the guy's home territory. As for serious injuries, it seems surprising the number that went through their time relatively unscathed – especially if you take into account most of those interviewed had achieved notoriety of some kind.

4. DESCRIBE THE BEST TAKING OF AN END YOU'VE EVER WITNESSED.

The taking of a rival's popular end was not as frequent as you were led to believe. The obstacles involved in getting significant numbers undetected into your opponent's end had some of those interviewed citing another club's fans' efforts as their best recollection of end taking.

5. WHO'S THE BEST RIVAL FIRM YOU'VE EVER SEEN?

Many of those interviewed voted in favour of the clubs with the real tight-knit and organised firms with plenty of lads, all well up for it. The impression that gave could easily be one of shock and awe. Chelsea, Millwall and West Ham were top with equal nominations from our terrace legends.

6. DID YOU EVER FOLLOW ENGLAND AND WOULD YOU PUT ENGLAND BEFORE YOUR CLUB?

It was interesting to see quite a few got involved on the England scene. Many were clearly patriotic, including those who said they didn't go. But, that said, it was strongly emphasised they would never put England before the support of their club.

7. NAME YOUR TOP FIVE FIRMS, IN ANY ORDER.

Not the easiest of questions as each person's experience differed, as did the period of time they were each active, so the best thing is to look for any consistency in their decision-making, and the general consensus was that Millwall and West Ham shared top vote. The next three places again went equally to Cardiff, Chelsea and Man. United. Missing out by one was Pompey. That's the book's top five. You'll have your own arguments deciding yours, but just think of some of the mobs mentioned here. Sobering thought, isn't it, gentlemen?

8. WORST OLD BILL?

For treating football fans without any respect, showing zero tolerance or for pure liberties taken, there can be no doubt the West Midlands Old Bill took the biscuit. Way behind, but not without complaint, came Yorkshire, Liverpool, Bolton and Manchester's Old Bill. And we had it all from Sunderland moaning their Old Bill are Newcastle fans. Yorkshire stood accused of seeking retribution for the miners' strike (how many years ago?), Bolton were criticised for zero-tolerance tactics, and Manchester were called Robocops. But the West Midland Police force just don't know what planet they're on.

9. DESCRIBE SOME OF THE METHODS AND TACTICS USED BY THE POLICE AND AUTHORITIES TO STOP FOOTBALL VIOLENCE, AND DO YOU THINK THEY WORK?

To put this question to guys that had spent their lifetime getting around every move the police and authorities had tried to stop them was interesting. But it can come as no surprise that they all say the most effective deterrent today is CCTV, although we had some remembering the heydays of the '70s when they cited taking the laces out of your bovver boots as being far more cost-effective. I think everyone had a pair of Dr Martens on when you went to football, but those high-legged boots were no good in the Shed end without your laces, confiscated by PC Plod. Ingenius thinking by our nation's constabulary, folks!

10. WHERE DO YOU THINK THE NEW ENGLISH NATIONAL STADIUM SHOULD BE BUILT AND WHAT ARE YOUR THOUGHTS REGARDING THE WEMBLEY FIASCO?

It's quite clear that, from all the questions put, this one provoked the strongest feelings of real outrage on how the whole thing's been handled. The general consensus was Wembley, as the home of England's national football team, is sacramental.

Cass Pennant